PLUTOCRATS

PLUTOCRATS

THE RISE *of the* NEW GLOBAL SUPER-RICH
and the FALL OF EVERYONE ELSE

———◆———

Chrystia Freeland

THE PENGUIN PRESS
New York
2012

THE PENGUIN PRESS
Published by the Penguin Group
Penguin Group (USA) Inc., 375 Hudson Street, New York, New York 10014, USA •
Penguin Group (Canada), 90 Eglinton Avenue East, Suite 700, Toronto, Ontario, Canada M4P 2Y3
(a division of Pearson Penguin Canada Inc.) • Penguin Books Ltd, 80 Strand, London WC2R 0RL, England •
Penguin Ireland, 25 St. Stephen's Green, Dublin 2, Ireland (a division of Penguin Books Ltd) •
Penguin Books Australia Ltd, 250 Camberwell Road, Camberwell, Victoria 3124, Australia
(a division of Pearson Australia Group Pty Ltd) • Penguin Books India Pvt Ltd, 11 Community Centre,
Panchsheel Park, New Delhi – 110 017, India • Penguin Group (NZ), 67 Apollo Drive, Rosedale,
Auckland 0632, New Zealand (a division of Pearson New Zealand Ltd) • Penguin Books,
Rosebank Office Park, 181 Jan Smuts Avenue, Parktown North 2193, South Africa •
Penguin China, B7 Jaiming Center, 27 East Third Ring Road North,
Chaoyang District, Beijing 100020, China

Penguin Books Ltd, Registered Offices: 80 Strand, London WC2R 0RL, England

First published in 2012 by The Penguin Press,
a member of Penguin Group (USA) Inc.

LIBRARY OF CONGRESS CATALOGING-IN-PUBLICATION DATA
Freeland, Chrystia, date.
Plutocrats : the rise of the new global super-rich and the fall of everyone else / Chrystia Freeland.
p.   cm.
Includes index.
ISBN 978-1-59420-409-8
1. Rich people—Conduct of life.   2. Poor.   I. Title.
HB251.F74 2012
305.5'234—dc23

Printed in the United States of America
3   5   7   9   10   8   6   4

DESIGNED BY AMANDA DEWEY

In memory of
my mother,
Halyna Chomiak Freeland

CONTENTS

INTRODUCTION

The poor enjoy what the rich could not before afford. What were the luxuries have become the necessaries of life. The laborer has now more comforts than the farmer had a few generations ago. The farmer has more luxuries than the landlord had, and is more richly clad and better housed. The landlord has books and pictures rarer and appointments more artistic than the king could then obtain.

—*Andrew Carnegie*

Branko Milanovic is an economist at the World Bank. He first became interested in income inequality studying for his PhD in the 1980s in his native Yugoslavia, where he discovered it was officially viewed as a "sensitive" subject—which meant one the ruling regime didn't want its scholars to look at too closely. That wasn't a huge surprise; after all, the central ideological promise of socialism was to deliver a classless society.

But when Milanovic moved to Washington, he discovered a curious thing. Americans were happy to celebrate their super-rich and, at least sometimes, worry about their poor. But putting those two conversations together and talking about economic inequality was pretty much taboo.

"I was once told by the head of a prestigious think tank in Washington, D.C., that the think tank's board was very unlikely to fund any work that had *income* or *wealth inequality* in its title," Milanovic, who wears a beard and has a receding hairline and teddy bear build, explained in a recent book. "Yes, they would finance anything to do with poverty alleviation, but inequality was an altogether different matter."

"Why?" he asked. "Because 'my' concern with the poverty of some people actually projects me in a very nice, warm glow: I am ready to use my money to help them. Charity is a good thing; a lot of egos are boosted by it and many ethical points earned even when only tiny amounts are given to the poor. But inequality is different: Every mention of it raises in fact the issue of the appropriateness or legitimacy of my income."

The point isn't that the super-elite are reluctant to display their wealth—that is, after all, at least part of the purpose of yachts, couture, vast homes, and high-profile big-buck philanthropy. But when the discussion shifts from celebratory to analytical, the super-elite get nervous. One Wall Street Democrat, who has held big jobs in Washington and at some of America's top financial institutions, told me President Barack Obama had alienated the business community by speaking about "the rich." It would be best not to refer to income differences at all, the banker said, but if the president couldn't avoid singling out the country's top earners, he should call them "affluent." Naming them as "rich," he told me, sounded divisive—something the rich don't want to be. Striking a similar tone, Bill Clinton, in his 2011 book, *Back to Work*, faulted Barack Obama for how he talks about those at the top. "I didn't attack them for their success," President Clinton wrote, attributing to that softer touch his greater success in getting those at the top to accept higher taxes.

Robert Kenny, a Boston psychologist who specializes in counseling the super-elite, agrees. He told an interviewer that "often the word 'rich' becomes a pejorative. It rhymes with 'bitch.' I've been in rooms and seen people stand up and say, 'I'm Bob Kenny and I'm rich.' And then they burst into tears."

It is not just the super-rich who don't like to talk about rising income inequality. It can be an ideologically uncomfortable conversation for many of the rest of us, too. That's because even—or perhaps particularly—in the view of its most ardent supporters, global capitalism wasn't supposed to work quite this way.

Until the past few decades, the received wisdom among economists was that income inequality would be fairly low in the preindustrial era—overall wealth and productivity were fairly small, so there wasn't that much for an elite to capture—then spike during industrialization, as the industrialists and industrial workers outstripped farmers (think of China today). Finally, in fully industrialized or postindustrial societies, income inequality would again decrease as education became more widespread and the state played a bigger, more redistributive role.

This view of the relationship between economic development and income inequality was first and most clearly articulated by Simon Kuznets, a Belarusian-born immigrant to the United States. Kuznets illustrated his theory with one of the most famous graphs in economics—the Kuznets curve, an upside-down U that traces the movement of society as its economy becomes more sophisticated and productive, from low inequality, to high inequality, and back down to low inequality.

Writing in the early years of the industrial revolution, and without the benefit of Kuznets's data and statistical analysis, Alexis de Tocqueville came up with a similar prediction: "If one looks closely at what has happened to the world since the beginning of society, it is easy to see that equality is prevalent only at the historical poles of civilization. Savages are equal because they are equally weak and ignorant. Very civilized men can all become equal because they all have at their disposal similar means of attaining comfort and happiness. Between these two extremes is found inequality of condition, wealth, knowledge—the power of the few, the poverty, ignorance, and weakness of the rest."

If you believe in capitalism—and nowadays pretty much the whole world does—the Kuznets curve was a wonderful theory. Economic progress might be brutal and bumpy and create losers along the way. But once we reached that Tocquevillian plateau of all being "very civilized men" (yes, men!), we would all share in the gains. Until the late 1970s, the United States, the world's poster child of capitalism, was also an embodiment of the Kuznets curve. The great postwar expansion was also the period of what economists have dubbed the Great Compression, when inequality shrank and most Americans came to think of themselves as middle class. This was the era when, in the words of Harvard economist Larry Katz, "Americans grew together." That seemed to be the natural shape of industrial capitalism. Even the Reagan Revolution rode on the coattails of this paradigm—trickle-down economics, after all, emphasizes the trickle.

But in the late 1970s, things started to change. The income of the middle class started to stagnate and those at the top began to pull away from everyone else. This shift was most pronounced in the United States, but by the twenty-first century, surging income inequality had become a worldwide phenomenon, visible in most of the developed Western economies as well as in the rising emerging markets.

The switch from the America of the Great Compression to the America of the 1 percent is still so recent that our intuitive beliefs about how capitalism works haven't caught up with the reality. In fact, surging income inequality is such a strong violation of our expectations that most of us don't realize it is happening.

That is what Duke University behavioral economist Dan Ariely discovered in a 2011 experiment with Michael Norton of Harvard Business School. Ariely showed people the wealth distribution in the United States, where the top 20 percent own 84 percent of the total wealth, and in Sweden, where the share of the top 20 percent is just 36 percent. Ninety-two percent of respondents said they preferred the wealth distribution of Sweden to that of the United States today. Ariely then asked his subjects to give their ideal distribution of wealth for the United States. Respondents preferred that the top 20 percent own just 32 percent of total wealth, an even more equitable distribution than Sweden's. When it comes to wealth inequality, Americans would prefer to live in Sweden—or in the late 1950s compared to the United States today. And they would like kibbutz-style egalitarianism best of all.

But the gap between the data and our intuition is not a good reason to ignore what is going on. And to understand how American capitalism—and capitalism around the world—is changing, you have to look at what is happening at the very top. That focus isn't class war; it's arithmetic.

Larry Summers, the Harvard economist and former secretary of the Treasury, is hardly a radical. Yet he points out that America's economic growth over the past decade has been so unevenly shared that, for the middle class, "for the first time since the Great Depression, focusing on redistribution makes more sense than focusing on growth."

The skew toward the very top is so pronounced that you can't understand overall economic growth figures without taking it into account. As in a school whose improved test scores are due largely to the stellar performance of a few students, the surging fortunes at the very top can mask stagnation lower down the income distribution. Consider America's economic recovery in 2009–2010. Overall incomes in that period grew by 2.3 percent—tepid growth, to be sure, but a lot stronger than you might have guessed from the general gloom of that period.

Look more closely at the data, though, as economist Emmanuel Saez did, and it turns out that average Americans were right to doubt the economic comeback. That's because for 99 percent of Americans, incomes increased by a mere 0.2 percent. Meanwhile, the incomes of the top 1 percent jumped by 11.6 percent. It was definitely a recovery—for the 1 percent.

There's a similar story behind the boom in the emerging markets. The "India Shining" of the urban middle class has left untouched hundreds of millions of peasants living at subsistence levels, as the Bharatiya Janata Party discovered to its dismay when it sought reelection on the strength of that slogan; likewise, China's booming coastal elite is a world apart from the roughly half of the population who still live in villages in the country's vast hinterland.

This book is, therefore, an attempt to understand the changing shape of the world economy by looking at those at the very top: who they are, how they made their money, how they think, and how they relate to the rest of us. This isn't *Lifestyles of the Rich and Famous*, but it also isn't a remake of *Who Is to Blame?*, the influential nineteenth-century novel by Alexander Herzen, the father of Russian socialism.

This book takes as its starting point the conviction that we need capitalists, because we need capitalism—it being, like democracy, the best system we've figured out so far. But it also argues that outcomes matter, too, and that the pulling away of the plutocrats from everyone else is both an important consequence of the way that capitalism is working today and a new reality that will shape the future.

Other accounts of the top 1 percent have tended to focus either on politics or on economics. The choice can have ideological implications. If you are a fan of the plutocrats, you tend to prefer economic arguments, because that makes their rise seem inevitable, or at least inevitable in a market economy. Critics of the plutocrats often lean toward political explanations, because those show the dominance of the 1 percent to be the work of the fallible Beltway, rather than of Adam Smith.

This book is about both economics and politics. Political decisions helped to create the super-elite in the first place, and as the economic might of the super-elite class grows, so does its political muscle. The feedback loop between money, politics, and ideas is both cause and consequence of the rise of the super-elite. But economic forces matter, too. Globalization and the technology revolution—and the worldwide economic growth they are creating—are fundamental drivers of the rise of the plutocrats. Even rent-seeking plutocrats—those who owe their fortunes chiefly to favorable government decisions—have also been enriched partly by this growing global economic pie.

America still dominates the world economy, and Americans still dominate the super-elite. But this book also tries to put U.S. plutocrats into a global context. The rise of the 1 percent is a global phenomenon, and in a globalized world economy, the plutocrats are the most international of all, both in how they live their lives and in how they earn their fortunes.

———

Henry George, the nineteenth-century American economist and politician, was an ardent free trader and such a firm believer in free enterprise that he opposed income tax. For him, the emergence of his era's plutocrats, the robber barons, was "the Great Sphinx." "This association of poverty with progress," he wrote, "is the great enigma of our times. . . . So long as all the increased wealth which modern progress brings goes but to build up great fortunes, to increase luxury and make sharper the contrast between the House of Have and the House of Want, progress is not real and cannot be permanent."

A century and a half later, that Great Sphinx has returned. This book is an attempt to unravel part of that enigma by opening the door to the House of Have and studying its residents.

PLUTOCRATS

———◆———

ONE

HISTORY AND WHY IT MATTERS

1,000,000 people overseas can do your job. What makes you so special?

—A 2009 billboard above Highway 101, the road that connects Silicon Valley with San Francisco

THE SECOND GILDED AGE

If you are looking for the date when America's plutocracy had its coming-out party, you could do worse than choose June 21, 2007. On that day, the private equity behemoth Blackstone priced the largest American IPO since 2002, raising $4 billion and creating a publicly held company worth $31 billion at the time of the offering. Steve Schwarzman, one of the firm's two cofounders, came away with a personal stake worth almost $8 billion at that time, along with $677 million in cash; the other, Pete Peterson, cashed a check for $1.88 billion and retired.

In the sort of coincidence that delights historians, conspiracy theorists, and book publishers, June 21 also happened to be the day when Peterson threw a party—at Manhattan's Four Seasons restaurant, of course—to launch his daughter Holly's debut novel, *The Manny*, which lightly satirized the lives and loves of financiers and their wives on the Upper East Side. The book fits neatly into the genre of modern "mommy lit"—*USA Today* advised its readers to take it to the beach—but the author told me that she was inspired to write it in part by her belief that "people have no clue about how much money there is in this town."

Holly is slender, with the Mediterranean looks she inherited from her Greek grandparents—strong features, dark eyes and eyebrows, thick brown hair. Over a series of conversations Ms. Peterson and I had after that book party, she explained to me how the super-affluence of recent years has changed the meaning of wealth.

"There's so much money on the Upper East Side right now," she said. "A lot of people under forty years old are making, like, $20 million or $30 million a year in these hedge funds, and they don't know what to do with it." As an example, she described a conversation at a dinner party: "They started saying, if you're going to buy all this stuff, life starts getting really expensive. If you're going to do the NetJets thing"—this is a service offering "fractional aircraft ownership" for those who do not wish to buy outright—"and if you're going to have four houses, and you're going to run the four houses, it's like you start spending some money."

The clincher, Peterson said, came from one of her dinner companions. "She turns to me and she goes, 'You know, the thing about twenty is'"—by this she means $20 million per year—"'twenty is only ten [after taxes].' And everyone at the table is nodding."

Peterson is no wide-eyed provincial naïf, nor can she be accused of succumbing to the politics of envy. But even from her gilded perch, it is obvious that something striking is happening at the apex of the economic pyramid.

"If you look at the original movie *Wall Street*, it was a phenomenon where there were men in their thirties and forties making two and three million a year, and that was disgusting. But then you had the Internet age, and then globalization, and money got truly crazy," she told me.

"You had people in their thirties, through hedge funds and Goldman Sachs partner jobs, people who were making twenty, thirty, forty million a year. And there were a lot of them doing it. They started hanging out with each other. They became a pack. They started roaming the globe together as global high rollers and the differences between them and the rest of the world became exponential. It was no longer just Gordon Gekko. It developed into a totally different stratosphere."

Ms. Peterson's dinner party observations are borne out by the data. In America, the gap between the top 1 percent and everyone else has indeed developed into "a totally different stratosphere." In the 1970s, the top 1 percent of earners captured about 10 percent of the national income. Thirty-five years later, their share had risen to nearly a third of the national income, as high as it had been during the Gilded Age, the previous historical peak. Robert Reich, the labor secretary under Bill Clinton, has illustrated the disparity with a vivid example: In 2005, Bill Gates was worth $46.5 billion and Warren Buffett $44 billion. That year, the combined wealth of the 120 million people who made up the bottom 40 percent of the U.S. population was around $95 billion—barely more than the sum of the fortunes of these two men.

These are American billionaires, and this is U.S. data. But an important characteristic of today's rising plutocracy is that, as Ms. Peterson put it, today's super-rich are "global high rollers." A 2011 OECD report showed that, over the past three decades, in Sweden, Finland, Germany, Israel, and New Zealand—all countries that have chosen a version of capitalism less red in tooth and claw than the American model—inequality has grown as fast as or faster than in the United States. France, proud, as usual, of its exceptionalism, seemed to be the one major Western outlier, but recent studies have shown that over the past decade it, too, has fallen into line.

The 1 percent is outpacing everyone else in the emerging economies as well. Income inequality in communist China is now higher than it is in the United States, and it has also surged in India and Russia. The gap hasn't grown in the fourth BRIC, Brazil, but that is probably because income inequality was so high there in the first place. Even today, Brazil is the most unequal of the major emerging economies.

To get a sense of the money currently sloshing around what we used to call the developing world, consider a conversation I recently had with Naguib Sawiris, an Egyptian telecom billionaire whose empire has expanded from his native country to Italy and Canada. Sawiris, who supported the rebels on Tahrir Square, was sharing with me (and a dinner audience at Toronto's Four Seasons hotel) his mystification at the rapacious ways of autocrats: "I've never understood in my life why all these dictators, when they stole, why didn't they just steal a billion and spend the rest on the people."

What was interesting to me was his choice of $1 billion as the appropriate cap on dictatorial looting. In his world, I wondered, was $1 billion the size of fortune to aim for?

"Yes, to cover the fringe benefits, the plane, the boat, it takes a billion," Sawiris told me. "I mean, that's my number for the minimum I want to go down—if I go down."

Meanwhile, the vast majority of American workers, who may be superbly skilled at their jobs and work at them doggedly, have not only missed these windfalls—many have found their professions, companies, and life savings destroyed by the same forces that have enriched and empowered the plutocrats. Both globalization and technology have led to the rapid obsolescence of many jobs in the West; they've put Western workers in direct competition with low-paid workers in poorer countries; and they've generally had a punishing impact on those without the intellect, education, luck, or chutzpah to profit from them: median wages have stagnated, as machines and developing world workers have pushed down the value of middle-class labor in the West.

Through my work as a business journalist, I've spent more than two decades shadowing the new global super-rich: attending the same exclusive conferences in Europe, conducting interviews over cappuccinos on Martha's Vineyard or in Silicon Valley meeting rooms, observing high-powered dinner parties in Manhattan. Some of what I've learned is entirely predictable: the rich are, as F. Scott Fitzgerald put it, different from you and me.

What is more relevant to our times, though, is that the rich of today are also different from the rich of yesterday. Our light-speed, globally connected economy has led to the rise of a new super-elite that consists, to a notable degree, of first- and second-generation wealth. Its members are hardworking, highly educated, jet-setting meritocrats who feel they are the deserving winners of a tough, worldwide economic competition—and, as a result, have an ambivalent attitude toward those of us who haven't succeeded quite so spectacularly. They tend to believe in the institutions that permit social mobility, but are less enthusiastic about the economic redistribution—i.e., taxes—it takes to pay for those institutions. Perhaps most strikingly, they are becoming a transglobal community of peers who have more in common with one another than with their countrymen back home. Whether they maintain primary residences in New York or Hong Kong, Moscow or Mumbai, today's super-rich are increasingly a nation unto themselves.

The emergence of this new virtual nation of mammon is so striking that an elite team of strategists at Citigroup has advised the bank's clients to design their portfolios around the rising power of the global super-rich. In a 2005 memo they observed that "the World is dividing into two blocs—the Plutonomy and the rest": "In a plutonomy there is no such animal as 'the U.S. consumer' or 'the UK consumer' or indeed 'the Russian consumer.' There are rich consumers, few in number but disproportionate in the gigantic slice of income and consumption they take. There are the rest, the non-rich, the multitudinous many, but only accounting for surprisingly small bites of the national pie."

Within the investing class, this bifurcation of the world into the rich and the rest has become conventional wisdom. Bob Doll, chief equity strategist at BlackRock, the world's largest fund manager, told a reporter in 2011, "The U.S. stock markets and the U.S. economy are increasingly different animals," as the prior surged, while the later stagnated.

Even Alan Greenspan, the high priest of free markets, is struck by the growing divide. In a recent TV interview, he asserted that the U.S. economy had become "very distorted." In the wake of the recession, he said, there had been a "significant recovery . . . amongst high-income individuals," "large banks," and "large corporations"; the rest of the economy, by contrast, including small businesses and "a very significant amount of the labor force," was stuck and still struggling. What we were seeing, Greenspan worried, was not a single economy at all, but rather "fundamentally two separate types of economy," increasingly distinct and divergent.

Citigroup more recently devised a variation on the theme, a thesis it calls the "consumer hourglass theory." This is the notion that, as a consequence of the division of society into the rich and the rest, a smart investment play is to buy the shares of super-luxury goods producers—the companies that sell to the plutocrats—and of deep discounters, who sell to everyone else. (As the middle class is being hollowed out, this hypothesis has it, so will be the companies that cater to it.)

So far, it's working. Citigroup's Hourglass Index, which includes stocks like Saks at the top end and Family Dollar at the bottom, rose by 56.5 percent between December 10, 2009, when it was launched, and September 1, 2011. By contrast, the Dow Jones Industrial Average went up just 11 percent during that period.

The First Gilded Age

On February 10, 1897, seven hundred members of America's super-elite gathered at the Waldorf Hotel for a costume ball hosted by Bradley Martin, a New York lawyer, and his wife, Cornelia. The *New York Times* reported that the most popular costume for women was Marie Antoinette—the choice of fifty ladies. Cornelia, a plump matron with blue eyes, a bow mouth, a generous bosom, and incipient jowls, dressed as Mary Stuart, but bested them all by wearing a necklace once owned by the French queen. Bradley came as Louis XIV—the Sun King himself. John Jacob Astor was Henry of Navarre. His mother, Caroline, was one of the Marie Antoinettes, in a gown adorned with $250,000 worth of jewels. J. P. Morgan dressed as Molière; his niece, Miss Pierpont Morgan, came as Queen Louise of Prussia.

Mark Twain had coined the term "the Gilded Age" in a novel of that name published twenty-four years earlier, but the Martin ball represented a new level of visible super-wealth even in a country that was growing used to it. According to the *New York Times*, the event was the "most elaborate private entertainment that has ever taken place in the metropolis." The *New York World* said the Martins' guests included eighty-six people whose total wealth was "more than most men can grasp." According to the tabloid, a dozen guests were worth more than $10 million. Another two dozen had fortunes of $5 million. Only a handful weren't millionaires.

The country was mesmerized by this display of money. "There is a great stir today in fashionable circles and even in public circles," the *Commercial Advertiser* reported. "The cause of it all is the Bradley Martin ball, beside which the arbitration treaty, the Cuban question and the Lexow investigation seem to have become secondary matters of public interest." Then as now, America tended to celebrate its tycoons and the economic system that created them. But even in a country that embraced capitalism, the Martin ball turned out to be a miscalculation.

It was held at a time of mass economic anxiety—in 1897, the Long Depression, which had begun in 1873 and was the most severe economic downturn the United States experienced in the nineteenth century, was just gasping to an end.

Mrs. Martin offered a trickle-down justification for her party: she announced it just three weeks beforehand, on the grounds that such a short time to prepare would compel her guests to buy their lavish outfits in New York, rather than in Paris, thus stimulating the local economy. The city's musicians' union agreed, arguing that spending by the plutocrats was an important source of employment for everyone else.

But public opinion more generally was unconvinced. The opprobrium—and, on the crest of the wider public anger toward the plutocracy the Martins had come to epitomize, the imposition of an income tax on the super-rich—the Martins faced as a result of the ball prompted them to flee to Great Britain, where they already owned a house in England and rented a 65,000-acre estate in Scotland.

The Bradley Martin ball was a glittering manifestation of the profound economic transformation that had been roiling the Western world over the previous hundred years. We've now been living with the industrial revolution for nearly two centuries. That makes it easy to lose sight of what a radical break the first gilded age was from the rest of human history. In the two hundred years following 1800, the world's average per capita income increased more than ten times over, while the world's population grew more than six times. This was something entirely new—as important a shift in how societies worked as the domestication of plants and animals.

If you lived through the first gilded age, you didn't need to be an economist to understand you were alive on one of history's hinges. In 1897, the year, as it happens, of the Bradley Martin ball, Mark Twain visited London. His trip coincided with Queen Victoria's Diamond Jubilee, the sixtieth anniversary of her coronation.

"British history is two thousand years old," Twain observed, "and yet in a good many ways the world has moved farther ahead since the Queen was born than it moved in all the rest of the two thousand put together."

Angus Maddison, who died in 2010, was an economic historian and self-confessed "chiffrephile"—a lover of the numbers he believed were crucial to understanding the world. He devoted his six-decade-long career to compiling data about the transformation of the global economy over the past two thousand years—everything from ship crossings to tobacco sales. He had a genius for crunching all those numbers together to reveal big global trends.

One of his most compelling charts shows just how dramatically the world, especially western Europe and what he called "the Western offshoots"—the United States, Canada, Australia, and New Zealand—changed in the nineteenth century: in the period between AD 1 and 1000, the GDP of western Europe on average actually shrank at an annual compounded rate of 0.01 percent. People in 1000 were, on average, a little poorer than they had been a thousand years before. In the Western offshoots the economy grew by 0.05 percent. Between 1000 and 1820—more than eight centuries—the average annual compounded growth was 0.34 percent in western Europe and 0.35 percent in the Western offshoots.

Then the world changed utterly. The economy took off—between 1820 and 1998 in western Europe it grew at an average annual rate of 2.13 percent, and in the Western offshoots it surged at an average annual rate of 3.68 percent.

That historically unprecedented surge in economic prosperity was the result of the industrial revolution. Eventually, it made all of us richer than humans had ever been before—and opened up the gap between the industrialized world and the rest, which only now, with the rise of the emerging market economies two hundred years later, can we start to imagine might ever be closed.

But wealth came at a tremendous social cost. The shift from an agrarian economy to an industrial one was wrenching, breaking up communities and making hard-learned trades redundant. The apotheosis of the Bradley Martins and their friends was part of a broader economic boom, but it also coincided with the displacement and impoverishment of a significant part of the population—the ball, after all, took place during the Long Depression, an economic downturn in the United States and Europe that endured longer than the Great Depression two generations later. The industrial revolution created the plutocrats—we called them the robber barons—and the gap between them and everyone else.

The architects of the industrial revolution understood this division of society into the winners and everyone else as an inevitable consequence of the economic transformation of their age. Here is Andrew Carnegie, the Pittsburgh steel tycoon and one of the original robber barons, on the rise of his century's 1 percent: "It is here; we cannot evade it; no substitutes for it have been found; and while the law may be sometimes hard for the individual, it is best for the race, because it insures the survival of the fittest in every department. We accept and welcome, therefore, as conditions to which we must accommodate ourselves, great inequality of environment; the concentration of business, industrial and commercial, in the hands of a few; and the law of competition between these, as being not only beneficial, but essential to the future progress of the race."

Carnegie was, of course, supremely confident that the benefits of industrial capitalism outweighed its shortcomings, even if the words he used to express its advantages—"it is best for the race"—make us squirm today. But he could also see that "the price we pay . . . is great"; in particular, he identified the vast gap between rich and poor as "the problem of our age."

Living as he did during the first gilded age, Carnegie intuitively understood better than most of us today how remarkable that chasm was, compared to the way people had lived in previous centuries. "The conditions of human life," he wrote, "have not only been changed, but revolutionized, within the past few hundred years. In former days there was little difference between the dwelling, dress, food, and environment of the chief and those of his retainers. The Indians are to-day where civilized man then was. When visiting the Sioux, I was led to the wigwam of the chief. It was like the others in external appearance, and even within the difference was trifling between it and those of the poorest of his braves. The contrast between the palace of the millionaire and the cottage of the laborer with us to-day measures the change which has come with civilization."

Carnegie, himself an immigrant who rose from bobbin boy to the top of America's first plutocracy, understood that the distance between palace and cottage was merely the outward sign of the gap between rich and poor—the scoreboard, if you will.

The change in power relations started in the workplace, and that is where it was most intensely felt: "Formerly, articles were manufactured at the domestic hearth, or in small shops which formed part of the household. The master and his apprentices worked side by side, the latter living with the master, and therefore subject to the same conditions. When these apprentices rose to be masters, there was little or no change in their mode of life, and they, in turn, educated succeeding apprentices in the same routine. There was, substantially, social equality, and even political equality, for those engaged in industrial pursuits had then little or no voice in the State."

Before the industrial revolution, we were all pretty equal. But that changed with the first gilded age. Today, Carnegie continued, "we assemble thousands of operatives in the factory, and in the mine, of whom the employer can know little or nothing, and to whom he is little better than a myth. All intercourse between them is at an end. Rigid castes are formed, and, as usual, mutual ignorance breeds mutual distrust. Each caste is without sympathy with the other, and ready to credit anything disparaging in regard to it."

That shift was particularly profound in America—one reason, perhaps, that even today the national mythology doesn't entirely accept the existence of those "rigid castes" of industrial society that Carnegie described a hundred years ago. The America of the national foundation story—the country as it was during the American Revolution—was one of the most egalitarian societies on the planet. That was the proud declaration of the founders. In a letter from Monticello dated September 10, 1814, to Dr. Thomas Cooper, the Anglo-American polymath (he practiced law, taught both chemistry and political economics, and was a university president), Thomas Jefferson wrote, "We have no paupers. . . . The great mass of our population is of laborers; our rich, who can live without labor, either manual or professional, being few, and of moderate wealth. Most of the laboring class possess property, cultivate their own lands, have families, and from the demand for their labor are enabled to exact from the rich and the competent such prices as enable them to be fed abundantly, clothed above mere decency, to labor moderately and raise their families. . . . The wealthy, on the other hand, and those at their ease, know nothing of what the Europeans call luxury. They have only somewhat more of the comforts and decencies of life than those who furnish them. Can any condition of society be more desirable than this?"

Jefferson contrasted this egalitarian Arcadia with an England of paupers and plutocrats: "Now, let us compute by numbers the sum of happiness of the two countries. In England, happiness is the lot of the aristocracy only; and the proportion they bear to the laborers and paupers you know better than I do. Were I to guess that they are four in every hundred, then the happiness of the nation would to its misery as one in twenty-five. In the

United States, it is as eight millions to zero or as all to none." Alexis de Tocqueville, visiting America two decades later, returned home to report that "nothing struck me more forcibly than the general equality of conditions among the people."

America, in the eyes of Jefferson and Tocqueville, was the Sweden of the late eighteenth and early nineteenth centuries. Data painstakingly assembled by economic historians Peter Lindert and Jeffrey Williamson have now confirmed that story. They found that the thirteen colonies, including the South and including slaves, were significantly more equal than the other countries that would also soon be the sites of some of the most vigorous manifestations of the industrial revolution: England and Wales and the Netherlands.

"If one includes slaves in the overall income distribution, the American colonies in 1774 were still the most equal in their distribution of income among households, though by a finer margin," Professor Lindert said.

In addition to seeing America as egalitarian, contemporary visitors and Americans believed the colonists were richer than the folks they had left back home—that was, after all, part of the point of emigrating. Lindert and Williamson have confirmed that story, too, with one important exception. Egalitarian America was richer, apart from the super-elite. When it came to the top 2 percent of the population, even the plantation owners of Charleston were pikers compared to England's landed gentry. Indeed, England's 2 percent were so rich that the country's average national income was nearly as high as that of the United States, despite the markedly greater prosperity of what today we might call the American middle class.

"The Duke of Bedford had no counterpart in America," Professor Lindert said. "Even the richest Charleston slave owner could not match the wealth of the landed aristocracy."

In egalitarian America, and even in aristocratic Europe, the industrial revolution eventually lifted all boats, but it also widened the social divide. One reason that process was traumatic was that it was pretty dreadful to be a loser—from their personal perspective, the Luddites, skilled weavers who wrecked the machines that made their trade unnecessary, had a point. But, as in all meritocratic 1 percent societies, the creative destruction of the industrial revolution was also traumatic for the many who made a good-faith effort to join the party but failed. Indeed, it was the pathos of these would-be winners that inspired Mark Twain to write the novel that gave the era its name.

As Twain and coauthor Charles Dudley Warner explained in a preface to the London edition of their novel, *The Gilded Age*: "In America nearly every man has his dream, his pet scheme, whereby he is to advance himself socially or pecuniarily. It is this all-pervading speculativeness which we tried to illustrate in *The Gilded Age*. It is a characteristic which is both bad and good, for both the individual and the nation. Good, because it allows neither to stand still, but drives both for ever on, toward some point or other which is ahead, not behind nor at one side. Bad, because the chosen point is often badly chosen, and then the individual is wrecked; the aggregations of such cases affects the nation, and so is bad for the nation. Still, it is a trait which is of course better for a people to have and sometimes suffer from than to be without."

The paradox was that even as Carnegie, America's leading capitalist, acknowledged that the country's economic transformation had ended the age of "social equality," political democracy was deepening in the United States and in much of Europe. The clash between growing political equality and growing economic inequality is, in many ways, the big story of the late nineteenth century and early twentieth century in the Western world. In the United States, this conflict gave rise to the populist and progressive movements and the trust-busting, government regulation, and income tax the disgruntled 99 percent of that age successfully demanded. A couple of decades later, the Great Depression further inflamed the American masses, who imposed further constraints on their plutocrats: the Glass-Steagall Act, which separated commercial and investment banking, FDR's New

Deal social welfare program, and ever higher taxes at the very top—by 1944 the top tax rate was 94 percent. In 1897, the year of the Bradley Martin ball, incomes taxes did not yet exist.

In Europe, whose lower social orders had never had it as good as the American colonists, the industrial revolution was so socially wrenching that it inspired the first coherent political ideology of class warfare—Marxism—and ultimately a violent revolutionary movement that would install communist regimes in Russia, eastern Europe, and China by the middle of the century. The victorious communists were influential far beyond their own borders—America's New Deal and western Europe's generous social welfare systems were created partly in response to the red threat. Better to compromise with the 99 percent than to risk being overthrown by them.

Ironically, the proletariat fared worst in the states where the Bolsheviks had imposed a dictatorship in its name—the Soviet bloc, where living standards lagged behind those in the West. But in the United States and in western Europe, the compromise between the plutocrats and everyone else worked. Economic growth soared and income inequality steadily declined. Between the 1940s and 1970s in the United States the gap between the 1 percent and everyone else shrank; the income share of the top 1 percent fell from nearly 16 percent in 1940 to under 7 percent in 1970. In 1980, the average U.S. CEO made forty-two times as much as the average worker. By 2012, that ratio had skyrocketed to 380. Taxes were high—the top marginal rate was 70 percent—but robust economic growth of an average 3.7 percent per year between 1947 and 1977 created a broadly shared sense of optimism and prosperity. This was the golden age of the American middle class, and it is no accident that our popular culture remembers it so fondly. The western Europe experience was broadly similar—strong economic growth, high taxes, and an extensive social welfare network.

Then, in the 1970s, the world economy again began to change profoundly, and with that transformation, so did the postwar social contract. Today two terrifically powerful forces are driving economic change: the technology revolution and globalization. These twin revolutions are hardly novel—the first personal computers went on sale four decades ago—and as with everything that is familiar, it can be easy to underestimate their impact. But together they constitute a dramatic gearshift comparable in its power and scale to the industrial revolution. Consider: in 2010, just two years after the biggest financial and economic crisis since the Great Depression, the global economy grew at an overall rate of more than 6 percent. That is an astonishing number when set alongside our pre-1820 averages of less than half a percentage point.

Indeed, even compared to the post–industrial revolution average rates, it is a tremendous acceleration. If the industrial revolution was about shifting the Western economies from horse speed to car speed, today's transformation is about accelerating the world economy from the pace of snail mail to the pace of e-mail.

For the West and the Western offshoots, the technology revolution and globalization haven't created a fresh surge in economic growth comparable to that of the industrial revolution (though they have helped maintain the 2 percent to 3 percent annual growth, which we now think of as our base case, but which is in fact historically exceptional).

What these twin transformations have done is trigger an industrial revolution–sized burst of growth in much of the rest of the world—China, India, and some other parts of the developing world are now going through their own gilded ages. Consider: between 1820 and 1950, nearly a century and a half, per capita income in India and China was basically flat—precisely during the period when the West was experiencing its first great economic surge. But then Asia started to catch up. Between 1950 and 1973, per capita income in India and China increased by 68 percent. Then, between 1973 and 2002, it grew by 245 percent, and continues to grow strongly, despite the global financial crisis.

To put that into global perspective: The American economy has grown significantly since 1950—real per capital GDP has tripled. In China, it has increased twelvefold. Before the industrial revolution, the West was a little richer than what we now call the emerging markets, but the lives of ordinary people around the world were mutually recognizable. Milanovic, the World Bank economist, surveyed the economic history literature on international earnings in the nineteenth century. He found that between 1800 and 1849 the wage of an unskilled daily laborer in India, one of the poorest countries at the time, was 30 percent that of the wage of an equivalent worker in England, one of the richest. Here's another data point: in the 1820s, real wages in the Netherlands were just 70 percent higher than those in China's Yangtze Valley. Those differences may seem large, but they are trivial compared to today's. UBS, the Swiss bank, compiles a widely cited global prices and earnings report. In 2009 (the most recent year in which UBS did the full report), the nominal after-tax wage for a building laborer in New York was $16.60 an hour, compared to $0.80 in Beijing, $0.50 in Delhi, and $0.60 in Nairobi, a gap orders of magnitude greater than the one in the nineteenth century. The industrial revolution created a plutocracy—but it also enriched the Western middle class and opened up a wide gap between Western workers and those in the rest of the world. That gap is closing as the developing world embraces free market economics and is experiencing its own gilded age.

Professor Lindert worked closely with Angus Maddison and is a fellow leader of the "deep history" school, a movement devoted to thinking about the world economy over the long term—that is to say, in the context of the entire sweep of human civilization. He believes that the global economic change we are living through today is unprecedented in its scale and impact. "Britain's classic industrial revolution is far less impressive than what has been going on in the past thirty years," he told me. The current productivity gains are larger, he explained, and the waves of disruptive innovation much, much faster.

Joel Mokyr, an economist at Northwestern University and an expert on the history of technological innovation and on the industrial revolution, agrees.

"The rate of technological change is faster than it has ever been and it is moving from sector to sector," Mokyr told me. "It is likely that it will keep on expanding at an exponential rate. As individuals, we aren't getting smarter, but society as a whole is accumulating more and more knowledge. Our access to information and technological assistance in going through the mountains of chaff to get to the wheat—no society has ever had that. That is huge."

This double-barreled economic shift has coincided with an equally consequential social and political one. MIT researchers Frank Levy and Peter Temin describe the transformation as a move from "The Treaty of Detroit" to the "Washington Consensus." The Treaty of Detroit was the five-year contract agreed to in 1950 by the United Auto Workers and the big three manufacturers. That deal protected the carmakers from annual strikes; in exchange, it gave the workers generous health care coverage and pensions. Levy and Temin use "The Treaty of Detroit" as a shorthand to describe the broader set of political, social, and economic institutions that were established in the United States during the postwar era: strong unions, high taxes, and a high minimum wage. The Treaty of Detroit era was a golden age for the middle class, and a time when the gap between the 1 percent and everyone else shrank.

But in the late 1970s and early 1980s, the Treaty of Detroit began to break down. This was the decade of Ronald Reagan and Margaret Thatcher. They both sharply cut taxes at the top—Reagan slashed the highest marginal tax rate from 70 percent to 28 percent and reduced the maximum capital gains tax to 20 percent—reined in trade unions, cut social welfare spending, and deregulated the economy.

This Washington Consensus was exported abroad, too. Its greatest impact, and its greatest validation, was in communist regimes. The collapse of communism in the Soviet bloc and the adoption of market economics in communist China ended that ideology's seventy-year-long intellectual and political challenge to capitalism, leaving the market economy as the only system anyone has come up with that works. That red threat was one reason the plutocrats accepted the Treaty of Detroit, and its even more generous European equivalents. The red surrender emboldened the advocates of the

Washington Consensus and helped them to create the international institutions needed to underpin a globalized economy.

These three transformations—the technology revolution, globalization, and the rise of the Washington Consensus—have coincided with an age of strong global economic growth, and also with the reemergence of the plutocrats, this time on a global scale. Among students of income inequality, there is a fierce debate about which of the three is the most important driver of the rise of the 1 percent. Ideology helps to shape the argument. If you are a true-faith believer in the Washington Consensus, you tend to believe rising income inequality is the product of impersonal—and largely benign—economic forces, like the technology revolution and globalization. If you are a liberal and regret the passing of the Treaty of Detroit, you tend to attribute the changed income distribution chiefly to politics—a process Jacob Hacker and Paul Pierson have powerfully described in *Winner-Take-All Politics*.

This is an important argument, with real political implications. But, viewed from the summit of the plutocracy, both sides are right. Globalization and the technology revolution have allowed the 1 percent to prosper; but as the plutocrats have been getting richer and more powerful, the collapse of the Treaty of Detroit has meant we have taxed and regulated them less. It is a return to the first gilded age not only because we are living through an economic revolution, but also because the rules of the game again favor those who are winning it.

"The bottom line: we may not be able to reverse the trend, but don't make it worse," Peter Orszag, President Barack Obama's former budget chief, told me. "Most of this is coming from globalization and technological change, not from government policy. But instead of leaning against the wind, we have been putting a little more wind in the sails of rising inequality."

THE TWIN GILDED AGES—ENTER THE BRICS

On a bitter evening in mid-January 2012, a group of bankers and book publishers gathered on the forty-second floor of Goldman Sachs's global headquarters at the southern tip of Manhattan. The setting could not have been more American—the most eye-catching view was of the skyscrapers of midtown twinkling to the north, and a jazz ensemble played softly in one corner.

But the appetizers were an international mishmash—thumb-sized potato pancakes with sour cream and caviar, steaming Chinese dumplings, Indian samosas, Turkish kebabs. That's because the party was in honor of the Goldman thinker who served notice to the Western investment community a decade ago that the Internet revolution wasn't the only economic game in town. The world was also being dramatically transformed by the rise of the emerging markets, in particular the four behemoths that Jim O'Neill, then chief economist at Goldman Sachs, dubbed the BRICs: Brazil, Russia, India, China.

In the book Mr. O'Neill launched at his January party, *The Growth Map: Economic Opportunity in the BRICs and Beyond*, he argues that the BRIC concept "has become the dominant story of our generation" and introduces readers to "the next eleven" emerging markets, which are joining the BRICs in transforming the world.

The group of Goldman executives who toasted Mr. O'Neill in New York are in the vanguard of one of the consequences of the powerful economic forces he describes—the rise, in the developed Western economies, of the 1 percent and the creation of what many are now calling a new gilded age. In the nineteenth century, the industrial revolution and the opening of the American frontier created the Gilded Age and the robber barons who ruled it; today, as the world economy is being reshaped by the technology revolution and globalization, the resulting economic transformation is creating a new gilded age and a new plutocracy.

But this time around, it really is different: we aren't just living through a replay of the Gilded Age—we are living through two, slightly different gilded ages that are unfolding simultaneously. The industrialized West is experiencing a second gilded age; as Mr. O'Neill has documented, the emerging markets are experiencing their first gilded age.

The resulting economic transformation is even more dramatic than the first gilded age in the West—this time billions of people are taking part, not just the inhabitants of western Europe and North America. Together, these twin gilded ages are transforming the world economy at a speed and a scale we have never experienced before.

"It is structurally much more extreme now in multiple dimensions," said Michael Spence, a Nobel Prize–winning economist, adviser to the Chinese government's twelfth five-year plan, and author of *The Next Convergence: The Future of Economic Growth in a Multispeed World*, a book exploring the interaction of these twin gilded ages. "Now that the emerging economies are pretty big, this is just a harder problem. It is so different from previous economic change that I think these are issues that we have never wrestled with before.

"In the two hundred years from the British industrial revolution to World War Two there were asymmetries in the world economy, but the entire world wasn't industrializing and it wasn't interacting in the same way," Professor Spence told me. "These are complex phenomena and we should approach them with humility."

THE TWIN GILDED AGES

The gilded age of the emerging markets is the easiest to understand. Many countries in Asia, Latin America, and Africa are industrializing and urbanizing, just as the West did in the nineteenth century, and with the added oomph of the technology revolution and a globalized economy. The countries of the former Soviet Union aren't industrializing—Stalin accomplished that—but they have been replacing the failed central planning regime that coordinated their creaky industrial economy with a market system, and many are enjoying a surge in their standard of living as a result. The people at the very top of all of the emerging economies are benefiting most, but the transition is also pulling tens of millions of people into the middle class and lifting hundreds of millions out of absolute poverty.

Going through your first gilded age while the West goes through its second one makes things both harder and easier. One reason it is easier is that we've seen this story before, and we know that, for all the wrenching convulsions along the way, it has a happy ending: the industrial revolution hugely improved the lives of everyone in the West, even though it opened the vast gap in standard of living between East and West that we still see today.

We didn't know that for sure during the first gilded age—remember that it was the dark, satanic mills of the industrial revolution that eventually inspired the leftist revolt against capitalism and the bloody construction, by those revolutionaries who succeeded, of an economic and political alternative. But today, the evidence that capitalism works is clear, and not only in the wreckage of the communist experiment.

The collapse of communism is more than a footnote to today's double gilded age. Economic historians are still debating the connection between the rise of Western democracy and the first gilded age. But there can be no question that today's twin gilded ages are as much the product of a political revolution—the collapse of communism and the triumph of the liberal idea around the world—as they are of new technology.

The combined power of globalization and the technology revolution has also turbocharged the economic transformation of the emerging markets, which is why Mr. O'Neill's BRICs thesis has been so powerfully borne out.

"We are seeing much more rapid growth in developing countries, especially China and India, because the policies and technologies in the West have allowed a lot of medium-skilled jobs to be done there," said Daron Acemoglu, professor of economics at the Massachusetts Institute of Technology and a native of one of O'Neill's "Next 11," Turkey. "They are able to punch above their weight because technology allows us to better arbitrage differences in the world economy."

This means, Professor Acemoglu argues, that the first gilded age of the developing world is proceeding much faster than it did in the West in the nineteenth century.

"In the 1950s, labor was cheap in India, but no one could use that labor effectively in the rest of the world," Professor Acemoglu said. "So they could only grow going through the same stages the West had done. Now the situation is different. China can grow much faster because Chinese workers are much better integrated into the world economy."

Yet the successes of this economic revolution can also make living through your own first gilded age in the twenty-first century harder to endure. Once television, the Internet, and perhaps a guest-worker relative reveal to you in vivid real time the economic gap between you and your Western peers, growth of even 4 or 5 percent might feel too slow. That will be especially true when you see your own robber barons living a life of twenty-first-century plutocratic splendor, many of whose perks (a private jet, for instance, or heart bypass surgery) would have dazzled even a Rockefeller or a Carnegie.

Meanwhile, as emerging economies go through their first gilded age, the West is experiencing its second one. Part of what is happening is a new version of the industrial revolution. Just as the machine age transformed an economy of farm laborers and artisans into one of combine harvesters and assembly lines, so the technology revolution is replacing blue-collar factory workers with robots and white-collar clerks with computers.

At the same time, the West is also benefiting from the first gilded age of the emerging economies. If you own a company in Dallas or Düsseldorf, the urbanizing peasants of the emerging markets probably work for you. That is good news for the plutocrats in the West, who can reap the benefits of simultaneously being nineteenth-century robber barons and twenty-first-century technology tycoons. But it makes the transition even harsher for the Western middle class, which is being buffeted by two gilded ages at the same time.

A survey of nearly ten thousand Harvard Business School alumni released in January 2012 illustrated this gap. The respondents were very worried about U.S. competitiveness in the world economy—71 percent expect it to decline over the next three years. But this broad concern looks very different when you separate the fate of American companies from the fate of American workers: nearly two-thirds of the Harvard Business School grads thought workers' wages and benefits would be in jeopardy, but less than half worried that firms themselves would be in trouble.

"When a company is stressed and has issues, it has a much greater set of options than a U.S. worker does," said Michael Porter, the professor who led the study. "Companies perceive that they can do fine and they can do fine by being one of the 84 percent that moved offshore, and they can also do fine by cutting wages."

"Although the overall pie is getting bigger, there are plenty of people who will get a smaller slice," said John Van Reenen, head of the Center for Economic Performance at the London School of Economics. "It is easy to say, 'Get more education,' but if you are forty or fifty, it is hard to do. In the last fifteen years, it is the middle classes who have suffered."

THE CHINA SYNDROME

"The China Syndrome," a 2011 paper on the impact of trade with China by a powerful troika of economists—David Autor, David Dorn, and Gordon Hanson—underscored what is going on. The empirical study is particularly significant because it marks a shift in consensus thinking in the academy. In the debate about the causes of growing income inequality, American economists have tended to opt for technology as the driving force. But, drawing on detailed data from local labor markets in the United States, the authors of "The China Syndrome" argue that globalization, and in particular trade with the mighty Middle Kingdom, are today also having a huge impact on American blue-collar workers: "Conservatively, it explains one-quarter of the contemporaneous aggregate decline in U.S. manufacturing employment."

The deleterious effects go beyond those workers who lose their jobs. In communities hit by the China Syndrome, wages fall—particularly, it turns out, outside the manufacturing sector—and some people stop looking for work. The result is "a steep drop in the average earnings of households." Uncle Sam gets hit, too, especially in the form of increased disability payments.

Messrs. Autor, Dorn, and Hanson are no protectionists. But, in a challenge to the "one nation under God" view of the world, they offer a sharp reminder that the costs and benefits of trade are unevenly shared. As they put it, their finding does not "contradict the logic" of arguments favoring free trade; it just "highlights trade's distributional consequences."

That distributional impact is, in the term of art used by economists, to polarize the labor market: there are better and more highly paid jobs at the top, not much change for the low-skill, low-income jobs at the bottom, but a hollowing out of the jobs in the middle, which used to provide the paychecks for the American middle class. Maarten Goos and Alan Manning, writing about the same phenomenon in the UK, call it the division into "lousy and lovely" jobs.

A recent investigation of the direct employment impact of the iPod is a case study in these lousy and lovely jobs—and shows where some of what used to be the jobs in the middle have gone. The research is the work of Greg Linden, Jason Dedrick, and Kenneth Kraemer, a troika of scholars who in a pair of recent papers have examined how the iPod has created jobs and profits around the world. One of their findings is that in 2006 the iPod employed nearly twice as many people outside the United States as it did in the country where it was invented—13,920 in the United States and 27,250 abroad.

You probably aren't surprised by that figure, but if you are American, you should be a little worried. That is because Apple is the quintessential example of the Yankee magic everyone from Barack Obama to Rick Santorum insists will pull this country out of its jobs crisis, evidence of America's remarkable ability to produce innovators and entrepreneurs. But today those thinkers and tinkerers turn out to be more effective drivers of job growth outside the United States than they are at home.

You don't need to read the iPod study to know that a lot of those overseas workers are in China. But given how large that Asian behemoth currently looms in the U.S. psyche, it is worth noting that less than half of the foreign iPod jobs—12,270—are in the Middle Kingdom. Another 4,750 are in the Philippines, which, with a population of just 92 million compared to China's 1.3 billion, has in relative terms been a much bigger beneficiary of Steve Jobs's genius. This is a point worth underscoring, because some American pundits and politicians like to blame their country's economic woes on China's undervalued currency and its strategy of export-led growth. In the case of the Apple economy, that is less than half the story.

Now come what might be the surprises. The first is that even though most of the iPod jobs are outside the United States, the lion's share of the iPod salaries are in the United States. Those 13,920 American workers earned nearly $750 million. By contrast, the 27,250 non-American Apple employees took home less than $320 million.

That disparity is even more significant when you look at the composition of America's iPod workforce. More than half the U.S. jobs—7,789—went to retail and other nonprofessional workers (office support staff, freight and distribution workers, etc.). Those workers earned just $220 million.

The big winners from Apple's innovation were the 6,101 engineers and other professional workers in the United States who made more than $525 million. That's more than double what the nonprofessionals in the United States made, and significantly more than the total earnings of all of Apple's foreign employees. The other jobs are lousy; these are the highly paid lovely ones.

Here in microcosm is why America is so ambivalent about globalization and the technology revolution. The populist fear that even America's most brilliant innovations are creating more jobs abroad than they are at home is clearly true. In fact, the reality may be even grimmer than populist critics realize, since more than half of the American iPod jobs are relatively poorly paid and low skilled.

But America has winners, too: the engineers and other American professionals who work for Apple, whose healthy paychecks are partly due to the bottom-line benefit the company gains from cheap foreign labor. Apple's shareholders have done even better. In the first of their pair of iPod papers, published in 2007, Linden, Dedrick, and Kraemer found that the largest share of financial value created by the iPod went to Apple. Even though the devices are made in China, the financial value added there is "very low."

Rich countries can hold on to some manufacturing jobs, of course, but doing so often means making those jobs a little lousier. Consider, for example, the argument Caterpillar used in a 2012 labor dispute with workers at a locomotive assembly plant in London, Canada. Workers at a Caterpillar plant south of the border in La Grange, Illinois, where they produce rail equipment, earn less than half of what their Canadian brethren make in wages and benefits. You could call that a victory for Canadian unions, and a sign that the country's political culture has done a better job of protecting its workers. But Caterpillar's response to that success has been to lock out its better-paid Canadian workforce and move some of the production to a newly opened plant in Muncie, Indiana. There is a similar story behind GE's much ballyhooed return of some manufacturing jobs to the United States. Workers at the North Carolina factory GE opened in 2011 earned an average hourly wage of eighteen dollars, barely half of what unionized workers in older GE plants make.

This is the downside of the triumph of Western workers over the past century and a half that Milanovic documented. In his paper, Milanovic predicted the gap between Western workers and those in developing countries would mean huge migratory pressure as people moved to higher-wage countries. But in an age when goods and capital flow more freely around the world than people, the more likely outcome may be the jobs moving to them.

This tension of our second gilded age was familiar to Andrew Carnegie during the first one, and plays into the division of society into the rich and the rest, which he, too, perceived: "Under the law of competition, the employer of thousands is forced into the strictest economies, among which the rates paid to labor figure prominently, and often there is friction between the employer and the employed, between capital and labor, between rich and poor. Human society loses homogeneity." Capitalism, Carnegie believed, required employers to drive the hardest possible bargain with their workers.

When I raised the issue with Joe Stiglitz, the Nobel Prize–winning economist and longtime Cassandra about the downsides of globalization, he practically crowed with vindication. "The economic theory is very clear," he said. "What happens when you bring together countries which are very different, like the United States and China—what happens is that the wages in the high-wage country get depressed down. This was predictable. Full globalization would in fact mean the wages in the United States would be the same as the wages in China. That's what you mean by a perfect market. We don't like that."

The truth is we are no longer living in "one nation under God"; we are living in one world under God. Globalization is working—the world overall is getting richer. But a lot of the costs of that transition are being borne by specific groups of workers in the developed West.

We are accustomed to thinking of the left as having an internationalist perspective. Liberals are the sort of people who worry about poverty in Africa or the education of girls in India. The irony today is that the real internationalists are no longer the bleeding-heart liberals; they are the cutthroat titans of capital.

Here, for instance, is what Steve Miller, the chairman of insurance giant AIG and one of Detroit's legendary turnaround bosses (he wrote a bestselling memoir called *The Turnaround Kid*), had to say to me at Davos about globalization and jobs: "Well, first off, as a citizen of the world, I think everyone around the world, no matter what country they're in, should have the opportunities that we have gotten used to in the United States. Globalization is here. It's a fact of life; it's not going away. And it does mean that for different levels of skill there's going to be something of a leveling out of pay scales that go with it, particularly for jobs that are mobile, if the products can be moved, which is not everything."

No matter what passport you hold, if you run or own a global company, that is not really a big deal. But, as Autor, Dorn, and Hanson show, if you are an American worker, that "leveling out" can be painful indeed.

Professor Van Reenen said these tensions have been building for years but have been laid bare by the financial crisis. That, he believes, has sparked a wave of populist protest, ranging from the Tea Party on the right to the Occupy movement.

"These things have been going on for a couple of decades," he said. "What has happened is, with the rise of the financial crisis, all of these things are coming into sharp relief."

The twin gilded ages are speeding each other up: The industrialization of the emerging economies is creating new markets and new supply chains for the West—iPhones are produced in China, and also sold there. The new technologies of the West's second gilded age, meanwhile, have accelerated the developing world's first gilded age—it is a lot easier to build a railway or a steel mill in an age of computers and instant communication than it was in the nineteenth century—and the developed economies, too, offer a rich market for the industrializing developing world.

"India's gilded age is going to be a combination of America's first gilded age and the second gilded age," Ashutosh Varshney, a professor of political science at Brown University who was born in India and now spends half his time in Bangalore, where his wife and son live full-time, told me at a meeting of the World Economic Forum in Mumbai in November 2011. "India is going through this phenomenon in the twenty-first century. . . . The pace at which information traveled in the nineteenth century was very different. Today eight hundred million Indians are connected through mobile phones."

The two gilded ages can also get in each other's way. As good an explanation as any for the 2008 financial crisis is that it is the result of the collision between China's gilded age and the West's—the financial imbalances that are an essential part of China's export-driven growth model also played a crucial role in inflating the credit bubble that burst with such devastating consequences in 2008.

The two gilded ages have a lot in common, and they are reinforcing each other. But both transformations are creating intense political and social pressures, partly because change is always hard, and partly because the rewards of this sort of convulsive shift are so unequal.

Moreover, this time around, the whole world no longer has the escape valve that, at least for a time, released some of the pressures of the original industrial revolution—the frontiers of North and South America. When the strain of urbanization became too tough, or too unfair, Europe's huddled masses could emigrate. Even with that option, it is worth remembering, the conflicts and inequities created by industrialization and urbanization were ultimately resolved in the West only after a half century of revolution and war.

"In the long run, we are in good shape," said Professor Van Reenen. "It depends on your time horizon. After all, the Great Depression and World War II were a massive cost to humanity. Eventually, humanity will prosper. Capitalism does work, but over the medium term, thirty or forty years, there could be incredible dislocations. I am very worried about what happens over the next year or so."

Looked at from the international, Olympian perspective of the super-elite, the cost of these short-term "dislocations" pales in comparison with the transformative power of the twin gilded ages.

Mr. O'Neill concludes his book with a heartfelt rebuttal of the gloomsters, with their emphasis on rising national income inequality and the hollowing out of the Western middle class:

> This is an exciting story. It goes far beyond business and economics. We are in the early years of what is probably one of the biggest shifts of wealth and income disparity ever in history. It irritates me when I hear and read endless distorted stories of how only a few benefit and increase their wealth from the fruits of globalization, to the detriment of the marginalized masses. Globalization may widen inequality within certain national borders, but on a global basis it has been a huge force for good, narrowing inequality among people on an unprecedented

scale. Tens of millions of people from the BRICs and beyond are being taken out of poverty by the growth of their economies. While it is easy to focus on the fact that China has created so many billionaires, it should not be forgotten that in the past fifteen or so years, 300 million or more Chinese have been lifted out of poverty. . . . We at Goldman Sachs estimate that 2 billion people are going to be brought into the global middle class between now and 2030 as the BRIC and N-11 economies develop. . . . Rather than be worried by such developments, we should be both encouraged and hopeful. Vast swaths of mankind are having their chance to enjoy some of the fruits of wealth creation. This is the big story.

Mr. O'Neill's empathy for the prospering people of China and India isn't the only reason to be optimistic about the twin gilded ages. Another is that the experience of the past two centuries has taught us that, with time, the creative destruction of capitalism inevitably brings an overall improvement in everyone's standard of living.

That was what John Baranowski, the general manager of accounting and operations at Greyhound Lines, the bus company based in Dallas, Texas, argued in reply to an essay by W. Brian Arthur, a professor at the Santa Fe Institute, about the computer revolution and the rise of a second economy in which most of the work is done by machines talking to other machines, with little intervention by humans. "Wealth will be created but also spent in some form we cannot imagine," Mr. Baranowski wrote. "Past productivity eliminated millions of jobs and created millions more—and while it is highly disruptive, there is no precedent for a long-term negative impact on total jobs and no reason to expect that the future (and the second economy's impact) will be different."

Professor Arthur's counterpoint was to hope that Mr. Baranowski is right, but to caution that we have no proof that today's technology revolution really will eventually make all of us richer.

"I only hope you are right that the new prosperity will create new jobs," Professor Arthur wrote. "The idea that this always happens is called Say's law in economics, and it's now held by economists to be a tenet of faith, not true in reality. Since the second economy began, in the early and mid-1990s, we've had wave after wave of downsizing and layoffs, and now we have ongoing structural joblessness. I hope jobs will be created, and maybe they will. More likely, the system, as so many times before in history, will have to readjust radically. It needs to find new ways to distribute the new wealth."

HAPPY PEASANTS AND MISERABLE MILLIONAIRES

Both the Western critics and the Western fans of globalization tend to agree about one thing: the emerging markets, particularly their rising middle classes, are among the big winners. As far as GDP goes, that is certainly true. But, just as the West's first gilded age was not perfectly benign for everyone living through it, the developing world's age of creative destruction is bumpy.

For one thing, international studies of the correlation between income and happiness have recently uncovered a counterintuitive connection. Until a few years ago, the reigning theory about money and happiness was the Easterlin paradox, the 1974 finding by Richard Easterlin that, beyond a relatively low threshold, more money didn't make you happier. But as better international data became available, economists discovered that the Easterlin paradox applies only across generations within a single country— you are probably not happier than your parents were, even though you are probably richer. But across countries, what millions of immigrants have always known to be true really is: the people of rich countries are generally happier than the people of poor countries.

The latest contrarian finding, however, is that moving to that state of greater wealth and greater happiness is decidedly unpleasant. As Angus Deaton, in a review of the 2006 Gallup World Poll, concluded, "Surprisingly, at any given level of income, economic growth is associated with lower reported levels of life satisfaction." Eduardo Lora and Carol Graham call this the "paradox of unhappy growth." Two separate studies of China, for example, have found that peasants who move to the city are richer but more frustrated with their income than they had been back on the farm. Palagummi Sainath, an award-winning Indian journalist who made his name when he switched from covering the business titans of "India Shining" to the underclasses who were left behind, tells the same story: Indians who move from impoverished villages to urban slums have a better chance of finding work, but little social security comes with it. And Betsey Stevenson and Justin Wolfers have found that the paradox of unhappy growth is particularly true in the first stages of growth in "miracle" economies, such as South Korea or Ireland—the moment when the tigers take their first leap is also the time when their people are unhappiest.

No one has come up with a definitive explanation of the unhappy growth paradox, but the economists who study it speculate that the uncertainty and inequality of these periods of rapid economic change may be to blame. Even if our country's economy overall is growing strongly and we are doing well ourselves, we know that we are living through a period of what Joseph Schumpeter called "creative destruction." That volatility, and the painful consequences it has for the losers, makes even the winners anxious.

The tension in emerging markets isn't only psychological. As in the West, a big part of the story of the developing world's first gilded age is the "friction . . . between capital and labor, between rich and poor" that Carnegie identified more than a century earlier.

I caught a glimpse of it at a World Bank panel I moderated in Washington, D.C., in September 2011. Manish Sabharwal, the CEO of TeamLease, India's leading supplier of temporary workers, said one of India's big challenges was increasing the number of people in the formal economy (as opposed to the black-market economy) working in manufacturing. At just 12 percent of the labor force, low-wage India, astonishingly, has the same percentage of workers in manufacturing as the United States does.

Stella Li, the vice president of automaker BYD, one of China's manufacturing stars, jumped into the discussion. "I have the answer," she told Sabharwal. BYD, she said, had gone into India with high hopes. "We think India is a great place for our second-biggest manufacturing," she explained, and BYD liked the quality of the Indian labor force: "The employee labor is good—they are working hard, very smart, and quite good." The problem was political: "They have a strike . . . then they ask for money, it takes a long discussion, they have to stop manufacturing for like one month." By contrast, she noted, "In China, we have no strike. If they have a strike, the government will get involved, tell workers, 'I will help you, but go back to work.'"

At this point, I couldn't resist asking whether in the authoritarian People's Republic, harsh measures might be used to force protesters back to work. Strikers might even be sent to jail, I suggested.

"No," Ms. Li replied instantly. "It is just the government nicely talking, 'What do you need? I'm taking care of you. Don't worry. But you should go back to work.'"

BYD's response to India's more aggressive unions, Ms. Li said, was to back away from its initial plan to make the country "kind of our backyard for manufacturing . . . So, we have five thousand to six thousand employees there. Initially we wanted to grow huge, like we can be over fifty thousand jobs over there."

As in the West, moving production somewhere else is one response to bolshie unions. The other is technology. As Kiran Mazumdar-Shaw, India's richest self-made woman entrepreneur, said to her employees: "If you join the union, I'm going to automate, and you'll all be out of jobs." And here's the twist—she made this comment to a *New Yorker* journalist whose profile largely focused on Mazumdar-Shaw's philanthropic commitment to improving the lives of India's poorest people. The union didn't listen, so Mazumdar-Shaw automated their jobs away.

THE WINNERS: THE DATA

We do know one thing for certain—whether it is Indian entrepreneurs like Shaw, or Chinese executives like Li, or Western financiers like O'Neill, those at the top around the world are doing very well indeed in this era of the twin gilded ages. One of the most respected students of today's surging income inequality is Emmanuel Saez, a lanky, curly-haired forty-one-year-old Frenchman who teaches economics at UC Berkeley and won one of his profession's top prizes in 2009. Working with his colleague Thomas Piketty of the Paris School of Economics, Saez has documented the changing shape of income distribution in the United States over the past century.

From the mid-1920s to 1940, the share of income going to the top 10 percent was around 45 percent. During the Second World War it declined to around 33 percent and remained essentially flat until the late 1970s. Since then, it has been climbing dramatically. By 2006, the top 10 percent earned 50 percent of national income, even more than it did in 1928, at the height of the Roaring Twenties.

But the biggest shift in income isn't between the top 10 percent and everyone else—it is *within* the top 10 percent, Saez and Piketty found. Almost all the gains are at the very apex of the distribution: during the economic expansion of 2002 to 2006, three-quarters of all income growth in the United States went to the top 1 percent of the population. The social gap isn't just between the rich and the poor; it is between the super-rich and the merely wealthy (who may not feel quite so wealthy when they compare themselves with their super-successful peers).

Here's how that translated into U.S. average family income in 2010, according to Saez: Families in the top 0.01 percent made $23,846,950; that dropped sharply to $2,802,020 for those in the top 0.1 to 0.01 percent. Those in the top 1 percent made $1,019,089; those in the top 10 percent made $246,934. Meanwhile, the bottom 90 percent made an average $29,840.

Even among the super-super-rich—the people on the annual *Forbes* rich list—the greatest gains have been at the tip of the pyramid. A recent academic study of the *Forbes* list of the four hundred richest Americans found that between 1983 and 2000 all of the wealthy prospered, but the very richest did best of all. In the course of those years, the top 25 percent of this group became 4.3 times wealthier, while the bottom 75 percent of them got "only" 2.1 times richer.

In 2011, in its annual report on the world's rich, Credit Suisse, the international investment bank, noted that the number of super-rich—whom it delicately dubs "ultra high net worth individuals," or UHNWIs, with assets above $50 million—surged: "Although comparable data on the past are sparse, it is almost certain that the number of UHNW individuals is considerably greater than a decade ago. The general growth in asset values accounts for some of the increase, along with the appreciation of other currencies against the U.S. dollar. However, it also appears that, notwithstanding the credit crisis, the past decade has been especially conducive to the establishment of large fortunes."

Overall, Credit Suisse calculated that there were about 29.6 million millionaires—people with more than $1 million in net assets—in the world, about half a percent of the total global population. North Americans are no longer the largest group—they account for 37 percent of the world's millionaires, slightly fewer than the 37.2 percent who are European. Asia-Pacific, excluding China and India, is home to 5.7 million (19.2 percent), while there are just over 1 million in China (3.4 percent). The remaining 937,000 live in India, Africa, or Latin America.

There were 84,700 UHNWIs in the world in 2011, of whom 29,000 owned net assets worth more than $100 million, and of whom 2,700 were worth half a billion dollars—nearly enough to maintain the level of perks Naguib Sawiris deems acceptable. A total of 37,500 UHNWIs are in North America (44 percent); 23,700 (28 percent) are in Europe; and 13,000 are in Asia-Pacific excluding China and India (15 percent).

When it comes to super-wealth, the United States is unassailably at the top. America is home to 42 percent of all UHNWIs, with 35,400. China is in second place, with 5,400, or 6.4 percent of the total, followed by Germany (4,135), Switzerland (3,820), and Japan (3,400). Russia has 1,970, India 1,840, Brazil 1,520, Taiwan 1,400, Turkey 1,100, and Hong Kong 1,030.

Given the underlying economic forces that are roiling the globe, Saez said he sees no reason that this trend won't continue. The rapid emergence of the very rich from the financial crisis would seem to support that view: Saez has found that in the 2009–2010 recovery, 93 percent of the gains were captured by the top 1 percent. The plutocrats did even better than the merely affluent—37 percent of these gains went to the top 0.01 percent, the 15,000 Americans with average incomes of $23.8 million. Another example: in 2009, the country's top twenty-five hedge fund managers earned an average of more than $1 billion each—or more than they had made in 2007, the previous record year.

"Probably if you had looked at the situation in the late nineteenth century, it would have looked like today. You would have said, 'Look, those guys are also self-made,'" Saez told me when I visited him in his office in Berkeley. "The way I see it is first you have a wave of innovation that creates self-made wealth, and then that wealth is passed on to the next generation and then you have heirs. So really the big question for the new era is whether the new rich, the self-made rich, are going to pass their wealth to their heirs or whether it's going to be given to charity and to what extent. It's probably going to be both, but I think the wave of heirs should happen down the road, barring an extreme change in behavior in charitable giving."

On February 13, 2007, almost exactly 120 years after the Martin ball, a leader of a new, ascendant American plutocracy hosted another epoch-making gala, also on Park Avenue, this time at the Armory, less than a mile directly north of the grand hotel rooms where the Martins and their friends had frolicked.

The guests at Steve Schwarzman's sixtieth-birthday bash didn't come in costume, and they arrived at eight p.m., not ten thirty p.m., but in many other ways his celebration echoed New York's most famous nineteenth-century entertainment. The ladies were bejeweled, many of the guests were moguls (Mike Bloomberg, John Thain, Howard Stringer), and the entertainment was lavish—its highlight was a half-hour live performance by Rod Stewart, for which he was reportedly paid $1 million.

Schwarzman's friends evoked the same economic stimulus defense of the lavish celebration Martin's supporters had voiced a century earlier. "This is good for the entire economy," argued Julian Niccolini, a co-owner of the Four Seasons restaurant (where both Schwarzman and Peterson père keep a running tab) and a guest at Schwarzman's party. "People spend money on champagne, they spend money on flowers, they spend money on music, and that creates jobs for all of us."

As in 1897, public opinion didn't buy it. Unlike the Martin ball, Schwarzman's party took place in a generally roaring economy. But seven months later, the bubble began to burst with a freeze in the global credit markets, and within eighteen months America was suffering its worst financial and economic crisis since the Great Depression. Schwarzman didn't leave the country for good—though he did move to Paris for six months in 2011—but he did admit that had he been able to foresee the consequences of his $3 million birthday extravaganza, he would have reconsidered.

◆

TWO

CULTURE OF THE PLUTOCRATS

Somebody ought to sit down and think about this, because your
corporate types are soon going to be a stateless superclass, people
who live for deals and golf dates and care a lot more about where
you got your MBA than the country you were raised in. It's the
Middle Ages all over again, these little unaffiliated duchies and
fiefdoms, flying their own flags and ready to take in any vassal
who will pledge his life to the manor. Everybody busy patting
himself on the back because the Reds went in the dumper is
going to be wondering who won when Coca-Cola applies for a
seat in the U.N.

—*Scott Turow,* Pleading Guilty

THE MOST FAMOUS AMERICAN ECONOMIST
YOU'VE NEVER HEARD OF

Henry George is the most famous American popular economist you've
never heard of, a nineteenth-century cross between Michael Lewis, Howard Dean, and Ron Paul. *Progress and Poverty*, George's most important
book, sold three million copies and was translated into German, French,
Dutch, Swedish, Danish, Spanish, Russian, Hungarian, Hebrew, and Mandarin. During his lifetime, George was probably the third best-known
American, eclipsed only by Thomas Edison and Mark Twain. He was ad-

mired by foreign luminaries of the age, too—Leo Tolstoy, Sun Yat-sen, and Albert Einstein, who wrote that "men like Henry George are rare, unfortunately. One cannot imagine a more beautiful combination of intellectual keenness, artistic form and fervent love of justice." George Bernard Shaw described his own thinking about the political economy as a continuation of the ideas of George, whom he had once heard deliver a speech.

In 1886, the year the Statue of Liberty was erected, George came second in the New York mayoral race, attracting an official tally of 68,110 votes and beating the Republican candidate, a rambunctious young patrician named Theodore Roosevelt. George's supporters alleged that if it were not for vote rigging by the Tammany Hall machine—whose candidate, Abram Hewitt, was the winner—George would have been elected mayor. But even as runner-up, George is credited by many with ushering in the Progressive Era in American politics. Friedrich Engels called the vote "an epoch-making day" and St. Louis labor leaders predicted it would become "the battle cry for all the enslaved toilers from the Atlantic to the Pacific." George's unexpected effectiveness at creating a working-class electoral coalition both inspired progressive politicians—including the twenty-eight-year-old Roosevelt—and helped convince business elites of the prudence of compromise. Abram Hewitt, son-in-law of millionaire Peter Cooper and the successful Tammany Hall man, himself recognized "that 68,000 people have deliberately declared that they have grievances which ought to be redressed." George ran for mayor of New York again in 1897, but died four days before election day. He was given a statesman's send-off—his coffin lay in state at Grand Central Station, where more than one hundred thousand people came to pay their respects. It was the largest crowd of mourners in New York City since Abraham Lincoln's funeral in 1865. The *New York Times* quoted one George fan who said, "Not even Lincoln had a more glorious death."

George's personal journey to the public arena was typical of the hard and adventurous lives of nineteenth-century Americans. Born in Philadelphia in 1839, the second in a family of ten, he left school at fourteen and took a job as a seaman on the *Hindoo*, a full-rigged ship of 586-ton register with a crew of twenty men and a cargo of five hundred thousand feet of lumber. The ship sailed to India, where he was struck by the poverty rather than the exotica that beguiled many of his contemporaries, and to Australia, where he discovered, and eventually imported back to America, the secret ballot. When George came home, he apprenticed as a printer, then worked his way to gold rush–frenzied San Francisco on the *Shubrick*, which sailed to the West Coast by way of Cape Horn. George didn't find gold, so he supported himself and what soon grew to be a family of six by setting type, writing editorials, and—his cushiest job—working as a gas meter inspector. The family's fortunes were often precarious. Here is how George described the day his second son, who grew up to become a New York State congressman, was born: "I stopped a man [on the street]—a stranger—and told him I wanted five dollars. He asked what I wanted it for. I told him that my wife was confined and that I had nothing to give her to eat. He gave me the money. If he had not, I think I was desperate enough to have killed him."

For all his peripatetic and odd-jobbing early years, intellectually George turned out to be what Isaiah Berlin would have called a hedgehog, a thinker focused intensely on a single question. For George, that question was what he saw as the central and troubling paradox of the Gilded Age, the puzzling coexistence of, as he put it in the title of his bestseller, progress and poverty.

As he said during the 1886 mayoral campaign, the two key questions were "Why should there be such abject poverty in this city?" and "What do we propose to do about it?"

Like most Americans of his era—a time when the industrial revolution was coming into full flower and the American frontier was being settled—George thrilled to the self-evident progress of the times. "The present century has been marked by a prodigious increase in wealth-producing power," he writes in the opening of *Progress and Poverty*. "The utilization of steam and electricity, the introduction of improved processes and labor-saving machinery, the greater subdivision and grander scale of production, the wonderful facilitation of exchanges, have multiplied enormously the effectiveness of labor." George goes on to list some of the amazing transformations of his age: "the steamship taking the place of the sailing vessel, the railroad train of the wagon, the reaping machine of the scythe, the threshing machine of the flail . . . the great workshops where boots and shoes are turned out by the case with less labor than the old-fashioned cobbler could have put on a sole, the factories where, under the eye of a girl, cotton becomes cloth faster than hundreds of stalwart weavers could have turned it out with their hand looms."

Today, "the wealth-producing power" of those inventions is indisputable. Even at a time of weak economic growth, and after decades of stagnant wages, middle-class Americans enjoy a standard of living beyond the reach of the robber barons of George's day—electricity, plumbing, hot running water, cars, jet travel, and a life expectancy that has increased by nearly thirty years for white men (and much more for blacks and women). But in March 1879, when *Progress and Poverty* was published, the Long Depression, a sixty-five-month-long period of economic contraction that afflicted both the United States and Europe, was just whimpering to an end. From that perspective, the perplexing reality was that the industrial revolution wasn't delivering: "We are coming into collision with facts which there can be no mistaking. From all parts of the civilized world come complaints of industrial depression; of labor condemned to involuntary idleness; of capital massed and wasting; of pecuniary distress among businessmen; of want and suffering and anxiety among the working classes."

What George found most mysterious about the economic consequences of the industrial revolution was that its failure to deliver economic prosperity was not uniform; instead it had created a winner-take-all society. "Some get an infinitely better and easier living," he wrote, "but others find it hard to get a living at all. The 'tramp' comes with the locomotives, and almshouses and prisons are as surely the marks of 'material progress' as are costly dwellings, rich warehouses and magnificent churches. Upon streets lighted with gas and patrolled by uniformed policemen, beggars wait for the passerby, and in the shadow of college, and library, and museum, are gathering the more hideous Huns and fiercer Vandals of whom Macaulay prophesied."

George's diagnosis was beguilingly simple: the fruits of innovation weren't widely shared because they were going to the landlords. This was a very American indictment of industrial capitalism. At a time when Marx was responding to Europe's version of progress and poverty with a wholesale denunciation of private property, George was an enthusiastic supporter of industry, free trade, and a limited role for government. His culprits were the rentier rich, the landowners who profited hugely from industrialization and urbanization but did not contribute to it.

George had such tremendous popular appeal because he addressed the obvious inequity of nineteenth-century American capitalism without disavowing capitalism itself. George wasn't trying to build a communist utopia. His campaign promise was to rescue America from the clutches of the robber barons and to return it to "the democracy of Thomas Jefferson." That ideal—as much Tea Party as Occupy Wall Street—not only won support among working-class voters and their leaders, like Samuel Gompers, but also resonated with many small-business owners. Robert Ingersoll, a Republican orator, attorney, and intellectual, was a George supporter. He urged his fellow Republicans to back his man and thereby "show that their sympathies are not given to bankers, corporations and millionaires."

THE WORKING RICH

George's popularity is an example of the appeal of the rentier critique—a vision of capitalism without the cronies. That's something we can all subscribe to. It is also one reason coming to terms with today's super-elite is trickier than it was in the age of the robber barons. The crony class is, of course, still alive and well. But one of the striking characteristics of modern-day plutocrats is that, in contrast with their nineteenth-century predecessors, they are largely the working rich. Even today's rent-seeking plutocrats work for a living—Carlos Slim or the Russian oligarchs owe their fortunes to rents they captured themselves, not to estates conquered by distant ancestors.

We are mesmerized by the extravagance of the super-elite: the personal jet owned by hedge funder Ken Griffin, which is large enough to include its own nursery; or Microsoft cofounder Paul Allen's 414-foot yacht, *The Octopus*, which is home to two helicopters, a submarine, and a swimming pool. But if their excesses seem familiar, even archaic, in other ways today's plutocrats represent a new phenomenon. The wealthy of F. Scott Fitzgerald's era were shaped, he wrote, by the fact that they had been "born rich." They knew what it was to "possess and enjoy early." These were the great-grandchildren of the rentier elite John Stuart Mill had described half a century earlier: "The ordinary progress of a society which increases in wealth, is at all times tending to augment the incomes of landlords; to give them both a greater amount and a greater proportion of the wealth of the community, independently of any trouble or outlay incurred by themselves. They grow richer, as it were in their sleep, without working, risking, or economizing."

That's not the case for much of today's super-elite. "Fat cats who owe it to their grandfathers are not getting all of the gains," Peter Lindert, the economic historian, told me. "A lot of it is going to innovators this time around. There is more meritocracy in Bill Gates being at the top than the Duke of Bedford." Even Saez, the pioneering economic data jock who is deeply worried about the social and political consequences of rising income inequality, concurs that a defining quality of the current crop of plutocrats is that they are the "working rich." He has found that in 1916 the richest 1 percent of Americans received only one-fifth of their income from paid work; in 2004, that figure had risen threefold, to 60 percent. "As a consequence, top executives (the 'working rich') have replaced top capital owners (the 'rentiers') at the top of the income hierarchy during the twentieth century," Saez and Piketty write in their seminal paper on the subject.

Michael Lindsay, a professor at Rice University who has interviewed more than five hundred American leaders as part of the multiyear Platinum Study of the background and behavior of the nation's bosses, has reached the same conclusion. Speaking at a Columbia University conference on elites in the fall of 2010, Lindsay said that nowadays most of America's business, nonprofit, and academic chiefs hadn't inherited their money or come from privileged backgrounds.

An October 2011 study of income inequality in the United States by the

Congressional Budget Office, the nonpartisan government research unit, tells the same story of a shift at the top from income earned on capital—getting rich in your sleep—to income earned through wages. The contrast isn't just between today's super-elite and those of the Gilded Age; there has been a marked switch to wages since the end of the 1970s. As the gap between the top and everyone else has grown, so has the reliance of the 1 percent on wage income, rather than capital. Here's how the CBO describes the transition:

> Capital income excluding capital gains—in other words, interest, dividends and rents—has generally been a declining source of income among the highest-income households. Its share dropped from 42 percent of market income excluding capital gains in 1979 to 21 percent in 2002. . . . The changing composition of income for the highest-income households reflects a much longer trend. Over the entire twentieth century, capital income declined sharply in importance for high-income taxpayers. The labor share of income for the top income groups was higher in 2007 than before World War II, as highly compensated workers have replaced people whose income is from property or securities at the top of the income distribution.

This is true even at the very, very top. When three economists, one of whom works in the Office of Tax Analysis at the U.S. Treasury, crunched the numbers for 2005, they found that even among the top 0.01 percent—true plutocrats who earn at least $10 million a year—wages are far more important than rents. Salary income and business income accounted for 80 percent of their income excluding capital gains and 64 percent including capital gains. And, as with the 1 percent, the shift toward wages has coincided with the emergence of the winner-take-all economy. These figures were a quarter lower in 1979: 61 percent and 46 percent.

You can see that change in the life stories of today's plutocrats. Pete Peterson, for example, is the son of a Greek immigrant who arrived in America at age seventeen and worked his way up to owning a diner in Nebraska;

his Blackstone cofounder, Steve Schwarzman, is the son of a Philadelphia-area retailer. Leon Cooperman, a Goldman Sachs veteran and hedge fund billionaire who has become an outspoken critic of the White House, made a point of his own humble background in an open letter to the president that he circulated in the autumn of 2011: "While I have been richly re-warded by a life of hard work (and a great deal of luck), I was not to-the-manor-born. My father was a plumber who practiced his trade in the South Bronx after he and my mother emigrated from Poland. I was the first mem-ber of my family to earn a college degree. I benefited from both a good public education system (P.S. 75, Morris High School and Hunter College, all in the Bronx) and my parents' constant prodding."

Forbes classifies 840 of the 1,226 people on its 2012 billionaire ranking as self-made. It's true that few of today's plutocrats were born into the sort of abject poverty that can close off opportunity altogether—a strong early education is pretty much a precondition, and it is very useful to have a fa-ther who is an affluent professional—but the bulk of their wealth is gener-ally the fruit of hustle, intelligence, and a lot of luck. They are not aristocrats, by and large, but rather economic meritocrats, preoccupied not only with consuming wealth but also with creating it.

Nor is this true only in America, with its national faith in the Horatio Alger story. The global capitalist boom has allowed some people at the bot-tom of even the most traditionally stratified societies to rise to the top. Consider the small but growing community of plutocratic Dalits, the Indian caste once known as the untouchables. In some parts of rural India, Dalits are still not allowed to drink from the village well, and Dalit children are segregated in a special corner of their schoolrooms, lest their spiritual taint contaminate their higher-caste classmates. But India now has Dalit multi-millionaires, like Ashok Khade, owner of a company that builds and refur-bishes offshore drilling rigs, and subject of a recent front-page profile in the *New York Times*. As one Dalit businessman told a reporter, "We are fighting the caste system with capitalism."

Being self-made is central to the self-image of today's global pluto-crats. It is how they justify their luxuries, status, and influence. One way to eavesdrop on the way plutocrats talk to each other is to read the glossy limited-edition magazines written just for them. An example is the rather unimaginatively titled *Luxos*, which calls itself "Your local guide to global luxury" and can be found in the rooms of very fancy European hotels. One recent issue included an interview with Torsten Müller-Ötvös, the CEO of Rolls-Royce. Here is what he had to say about his buyers: "We have witnessed substantial changes over the last years. The Rolls-Royce generation of today has become much younger. Our youngest Rolls-Royce customer for example is a twenty-eight-year-old entrepreneur from India. We find that many of our customers have earned their success through their own work, and they want to reward themselves with a Rolls-Royce."

Indeed, if you are looking to define the archetypal member of the super-elite, he isn't Jane Austen's Mr. Darcy, with his gorgeous acres of Pemberley. He—and they are almost all still men—is an aggressive, intensely educated mathematician, the son of middle- or upper-middle-class parents, who made his first fortune young.

THE RISE OF THE ALPHA GEEKS

The rise of the alpha geeks is most obvious in Silicon Valley, a culture and an economic engine they created. But you can find them everywhere you find the plutocracy. The alpha geeks are the dominant tribe in Bangalore, the Indian city that invented technology outsourcing. In their incarnation as engineers, they overwhelmingly populate the Communist Party leadership in China, where political nous is a surer path to wealth than filing patents. The Russian oligarchs are a textbook example of crony capitalism, yet six of the original seven earned degrees in math, physics, or finance before becoming natural resource tycoons. Carlos Slim, who studied engineering in college and taught algebra and linear programming as an undergraduate, attributes his fortune to his facility with numbers. So does Steve Schwarzman, who told me he owed his success to his "ability to see patterns that other people don't see" in large collections of numbers.

People inside the super-elite think the rise of the data geeks is just beginning. Elliot Schrage is a member of the tech aristocracy—he was the communications director for Google when it was the hottest company in the Valley and jumped to the same role at Facebook just as it was becoming a behemoth. At a 2009 talk he gave to an internal company meeting of education and publishing executives, Schrage was asked what field we should encourage our children to study. His instant answer was statistics, because the ability to understand data would be the most powerful skill in the twenty-first century.

The rise of the alpha geeks means the 1 percent is more fiercely educated and the returns on elite education are higher than ever before. One way to understand why we are living in a golden age of the nerds is with a metaphor invented by Jan Tinbergen, joint winner of the first Nobel Prize in economics: the race between education and technology. That idea is the title of and conceptual framework for a recent book by Larry Katz and Claudia Goldin, the Harvard pair who study how the interplay between new technologies and education shapes income distribution.

In the nineteenth century, as the first gilded age was reaching its peak, technology raced ahead of education. As a result, if you were what counted as highly educated in that age—which was finishing high school (remember, bestselling author Henry George left school at fourteen)—you could command a premium compared to unskilled workers. Over the next fifty years, as America invested massively in public high schools, education caught up with technology, and the nerd premium narrowed. For Americans born from the 1870s to about 1950, every decade was accompanied by an increase of about 0.8 years of education. As Goldin and Katz write, "During that 80-year period the vast majority of parents had children whose educational attainment greatly exceeded theirs."

But about thirty years ago, that increase in education stopped while technology continued to race ahead. The result is the rise of the geeks. In one example, the wage premium earned by young college graduates compared to young high school graduates more than doubled between 1979 and 2005. Getting a college degree adds almost a full million dollars to your lifetime earnings. Economists Thomas Philippon and Ariell Reshef, who have studied the connection between deregulation and soaring incomes in finance, found that the wage premium for a college education increased from 0.382 in 1970 to 0.584 in 2005, an increase of more than 50 percent—a figure that goes a long way in explaining why income inequality has soared. As another economist, Thomas Lemieux, concluded in a 2006 study of the subject, "Most of the increase in wage inequality between 1973 and 2005 is due to a dramatic increase in the return to post-secondary education."

Moreover, broad measures of the return on education understate the rise of the super-smart in one crucial respect. Just as the winner-take-all economy rewards those at the very top much more richly than those one rung beneath them, a super-elite education has outsize rewards.

Any middle-class parent living in a city that is home to a significant community of the 0.1 percent—and that means not just the obvious centers of New York, San Francisco, and London, but also emerging metropolises like Mumbai, Moscow, and Shanghai—knows that the perceived high value of an elite education has prompted a Darwinian pedagogical struggle that begins in nursery school. That contest has prompted absurdities like the story of Jack Grubman, the Citigroup tech analyst who made positive recommendations about companies he thought were weak in exchange for support from his boss, Sandy Weill, for his twin two-year-olds' application to attend the 92nd Street Y, probably the most sought-after nursery school in Manhattan.

It is easy to dismiss these contortions as nouveau riche excess or a neurotic example of a child-centered culture run amok. But the reality is more disturbing. In a recent essay, University of Queensland economist John Quiggin calculated that the total first-year class of the Ivy League universities— around twenty-seven thousand—is just under 1 percent of the U.S. college-age population of around three million. And in our education-driven, winner-take-all economy, that 1 percent of eighteen-year-olds has a huge edge in forming the 1 percent as adults. "With those numbers in mind," Quiggin writes, "the ferocity of the admissions race for elite institutions is unsurprising. Even with the steadily increasing tuition fees, parents and students correctly judge that admission to one of the 'right' colleges is a make-or-break life event, far more than a generation ago."

To understand how hard it is to get into an elite university, the lengths students go to be admitted, and the extent to which the biggest perk of being born rich isn't inheriting a trust fund—it is being expensively educated— consider this story from inside the Harvard admissions process. When he was president of the university, Larry Summers liked to drop in on the deliberations of the admissions committee.

He was struck by one particularly difficult case. He explained: "There's a kid. You know, Harvard gets huge numbers of really strong applications. Kid comes from a good private school in a major city. Kid's got good grades— not unbelievable grades, but really strong grades. Kid's got test scores— really good test scores, but not remarkable test scores. So he looks like a kid that would do fine at Harvard. But we've got seven thousand kids like him and we've got two thousand slots. But the kid did have one thing that was really quite special. And that was this. Kid spoke Mandarin. The reason the kid spoke Mandarin was that he had done a really terrific and dedicated job working with his Mandarin tutor three days a week after school since he'd been in ninth grade. And he was serious about it and he had really worked at it and he was fluent in Mandarin. Not many people are. And he hadn't done it as part of a school program, he'd done it as an activity that he had chosen himself. But what's the right way to react to that? One way to react, which I think on balance in that particular case was probably the right one, was this really is an impressive achievement that counts for a lot. On the other hand, what fraction of families in the United States or Canada would have the wherewithal to get for their child a Mandarin tutor three days a week for four years? How do you think about that? And were we perpetuating privilege? Or were we recognizing merit?"

Getting into the "right" college is just a start. As the baby boomers aged into the commencement address generation, their standard advice to graduates was, as Steve Jobs memorably enjoined, to "have the courage to follow your heart and intuition," to "love what you do," and never to "settle." Drew Faust, in her third commencement address as president of Harvard University, urged the graduating students to adopt her "parking space theory of life": "Don't park ten blocks away from your destination because you think you'll never find a closer space. Go where you want to be. You can always circle back to where you have to be." But the winner-take-all economy turns out to be unforgiving of people who spend too long finding themselves. A 2011 study by *Ad Age*, the advertising trade magazine, found that to break into the 1 percent in your lifetime, you need to be earning an annual income of $100,000 by the time you are thirty-five.

NOT EVERYONE GETS A SECOND ACT

What's new isn't so much the pure power of getting an early start. That's both easy to intuit and well reported. One example is a 1968 study of Nobel Prize winners by social scientist Robert Merton. He found that one striking shared characteristic of the future Nobelists was being talented enough and focused enough at a young age that they were able to find their way into the labs of the most eminent scientists in their fields—"of 55 American laureates, 34 worked in some capacity as young men under a total of 46 Nobel Prize winners."

The bigger shift has been that, in a time of rapid economic change, there are fewer second chances for those who don't take off from the starting blocks at a sprint, or who run in the wrong direction for their first few laps. That was true during the industrial revolution. As Alfred Marshall, the pioneering nineteenth-century English economist, wrote, "The conditions of industry change so fast that long experience is in some trades almost a disadvantage, and in many it is of far less value than a quickness in taking hold of new ideas and adapting one's habits to new conditions. A man is likely to earn less after he is fifty years old than before he is thirty."

Marshall, who transformed economics by going out and doing field research, made that observation in 1890. A century and a quarter later and on another continent, you could hear remarkably similar comments from leaders of the Internet revolution. "A lot of professional writers apply here," Keith

Griffith, the director of editorial recruiting at Groupon, the Chicago-based Internet sales site, told a reporter in 2011, five months before the start-up's $700 million IPO. "I've had applicants from *Rolling Stone*, the *Wall Street Journal*. But it's really hard to get them to do what we're looking for. It's easier to teach people than unteach them."

This volatility makes us unhappy. Carol Graham, a researcher at the Brookings Institute, has identified what she calls the paradox of the happy peasant and the miserable millionaire—ambitious members of the middle class in fast-growing economies are actually less happy than poor people in more stable societies. One reason for the distress of the group Graham calls the "frustrated achievers," she believes, is the uncertainty of their economic position. They worry that at any moment they could lose their jobs and savings and drop back down to the bottom.

By contrast, early super-success is a useful hedge against the vagaries of an unpredictable economy. Many of today's plutocrats stumbled a decade or two into their careers, but by then they had already accomplished so much that they were poised to seize even larger opportunities.

The premium on early success means that the alpha geeks of the super-elite have been driven from a young age. The dorm room incubation of our most important technology companies is common knowledge. That's where hedge funds are starting, too. Bill Ackman, the most influential activist investor in America today, whose targets have included J.C. Penney and Target, founded his first hedge fund with a classmate right after graduating with an MBA from Harvard. Ken Griffin, the billionaire founder of Citadel, the Chicago-based hedge fund, started trading bonds out of his college dorm room.

The pattern holds for many of the emerging markets plutocrats, too. Carlos Slim, who bought his first share when he was twelve, started to make serious money straight out of college, when he was one of Los Casabolseros, or Stock Market Boys, a group of aggressive young men who traded shares on the Mexican stock market and played dominoes together after the market closed. Many of the Russian oligarchs first ventured into commerce while they were students taking advantage of Mikhail Gorbachev's tentative perestroika reforms to open businesses as diverse as window washing and computer programming.

The result is a super-elite whose members have been working to join it for most of their conscious lives—if not since nursery school, certainly since high school, when the competition for those elite college places begins in earnest. College, which boomers may fuzzily recall as a halcyon season of parties and self-discovery, has become, for the future 1 percent, a grueling time to found your start-up or to build a transcript that will earn a first job at an elite firm like Goldman Sachs or McKinsey. One sign of the shift is the illicit drug of choice among the gilded youth—Adderall. Its great virtue, one Princeton engineer told me, is that you can study for twenty-four hours without losing your concentration or needing to sleep.

ORPHANS OF CAPITAL

For those who make it, the relentless pace continues. One badge of membership in the super-elite is jet lag. Novelist Scott Turow calls this the "flying class" and describes its members as "the orphans of capital" for whom it is a "badge of status to be away from home four nights a week." The CEO of one of the most prestigious multinationals recently climbed Mount Kilimanjaro with his daughter to celebrate her graduation from college. He told a friend the two-week expedition was the longest they had ever been together.

"They make a lot of money and they work incredibly hard and the husbands never see their children," Holly Peterson said of the financiers of the Upper East Side. Their lives are driven not by culture or seasons or family tradition, but by the requirements of the latest deal or the mood of the markets. When Mark Zuckerberg rebuffed Yuri Milner's first approach, the Russian investor, who was already a multimillionaire, turned up at the Internet boy wonder's office in Palo Alto the next day, a round-trip journey of twelve thousand miles. In November 2010, the number two and heir apparent of one of the top private equity firms told me he was about to make a similar journey. I was a having a drink with him near Madison Park on a Wednesday night. He told me he needed to leave by eight p.m., because he had to fly to Seoul that evening. He planned to make the fourteen-thousand-mile round-trip for a ninety-minute meeting. His putative partners had invited him to Korea just forty-eight hours before, on the Monday of that week. It was, he told me, "a test of our commitment." When the European sovereign debt crisis came to dominate the markets in 2011, New York traders started to set their alarm clocks for two thirty a.m., in time for the opening bell in Frankfurt. Some investors in California didn't bother going to bed at all.

Wall Street e-mail in-boxes give you a flavor of the working lives of financiers, at least as they perceive them. In the spring of 2010, when the Obama administration first proposed a millionaires' tax, an anonymous screed pinged its way around trading desks and into the electronic mail of a few journalists. It begins with the declaration "We are Wall Street," and goes on to describe the intense workdays of traders: "We get up at 5 a.m. and work till 10 p.m. or later. We're used to not getting up to pee when we have a position. We don't take an hour or more for a lunch break. We don't demand a union. We don't retire at 50 with a pension. We eat what we kill."

A Machine for Destroying the Ego

Even when they are not traveling, the super-elite inhabit a volatile world. Jobs at the top are very insecure, and becoming more so. The average tenure of a Fortune 500 CEO has fallen from 9.5 years to 3.5 years over the past decade. That's true lower down the food chain, too. Thomas Philippon, the economist who documented the connection between deregulation and soaring salaries on Wall Street, also found that the jobs of financiers were very insecure. Nor does being your own boss protect you from the uncertainty of the markets. At a 2011 seminar at the Central European University in Budapest devoted to the psychology of investing, George Soros told the gathered academics that "the markets are a machine for destroying the ego." Popular culture has taught us to imagine the chiefs of Wall Street as strut-

ting masters of the universe. That's partly true. But they are also chroni-
cally exhausted men terrified that their latest trade will turn out to be a
multimillion-dollar mistake that costs them their job. Soros, secular to his
fingertips, describes investing mistakes as "sins" when he talks about them
with his team.

"If you push towards an Apple world, a Google world, that's all about
brutal efficiencies. The guys on the top are constantly updating their models. It's a brutal world, actually. You have to be really on the ball and fast,"
Eike Batista, the oil and mining magnate who is the richest man in Brazil
and one of the ten richest men in the world, told me. "A year and a half ago,
we didn't know about tablets, right? Tablet is basically killing the PC world.
So, you know, congratulations to Apple, which had the vision that it would
create a dramatic change. Everybody has to change now. Look at the brutal
change that is being used through that thing. And so, if the others don't
move, they're going to be dead tomorrow."

Batista used the Apple analogy as a way to communicate with me, a
North American, in an idiom he thought I would understand. But he was
really talking about a Darwinian struggle at the very top in Brazil, one of the
fastest-growing economies in the world: "Of the 10 percent wealthiest, you
know, 70 percent of this 10 percent wealthiest made their money in the last
ten years. Voilà. So, a massive social movement." Batista is one of those ar-
rivistes, and the old guard doesn't like him or his ilk one bit, he told me.
"You have to accept criticism—that's part of a democratic system like we
have in Brazil," he said, half triumphantly, half ruefully.

None of which is meant to make you pity the super-elite. The famous
Whitehall study of the British civil service documented something humans
have suspected for centuries: power is good for your health. The UK research, which was launched in 1967, found that the higher up in the bureau-
cracy you were, the longer you lived. That's equally true of today's super-elite.
They may be anxious and overworked. But it is still a lot better to be a trader
or a CEO earning several million dollars a year—and guaranteed a golden

parachute—than a minimum-wage cleaner working those same sixty hours a week but without the comforts of a private jet, a housekeeper, or medical insurance. Still, to understand the mind-set of the super-elite, your starting point should be the reality—and their own self-perception—that they, too, lead anxious, overworked, and uncertain lives.

SECULAR SAINTS

The money certainly helps justify those long hours. But the super-elite also bask in a culture that, at least until the 2008 financial crisis, was happy to regard them as the heroes of our age. Their virtue need not manifest itself in any of the traditional Judeo-Christian values—Steve Jobs, who currently dominates the iconostasis, was an egotistical jerk who often treated employees, family (including his daughter), and ordinary mortals who dared to e-mail him with cruelty or disdain. But we do need them to succeed in business because of their sheer superiority to everyone else—part of the appeal of the Jobs story is his second coming at Apple, when he showed up the mediocrities who had ousted him.

Most important of all, the plutocrats, and their chorus in the popular culture, are keen to believe they are not engaged on an entirely selfish mission. Carnegie asserted that knights of capitalism like himself "and the law of competition between these" were "not only beneficial, but essential to the future progress of the race." No one would talk like that today, but our champions of capital do like to describe their work in strikingly moral terms. Google's company motto is "Don't be evil," and at a recent company conference, Larry Page, Google's cofounder and now its CEO, said earnestly that one of Google's greatest accomplishments was to save lives—thanks to the search engine, for instance, people can type in their symptoms, learn immediately they are having a heart attack, and get life-saving help sooner than they would have otherwise. The self-driving car, one of Page's pet projects, would eventually, he argued, save more lives than any political, social, or humanitarian effort.

"It's not possible in tech to frame your ambitions aside from those who are making the world a better place," Eric Schmidt, former CEO of Google, told me. "I think it has a lot to do with the way Silicon Valley was formed and the university culture. The egalitarian culture. The liberal culture there. People are often surprised by that. . . . And I always try to explain to people that people actually came to Google not to get wealthy, but to change the world. And I genuinely believe that."

Another way to believe our plutocrats are heroes battling for the collective good is to think of capitalism as a liberation theology—free markets equal free people, as the editorial page of the *Wall Street Journal* asserts. One of the most convincing settings for this vision is Moscow, where in October 2010 you could hear it ringingly delivered by Pitch Johnson, one of the founders of the venture capital business in Silicon Valley, in a public lecture to business school students about capitalism and innovation.

Johnson, who was a fishing buddy of Hewlett-Packard cofounder Bill Hewlett, is a genial octogenarian with a thick white head of hair, glasses, and a Santa Claus waistline. He has made something of a project of Russia, having traveled there twenty times since 1990 (he got a particular kick out of flying his private jet into what was then still Soviet airspace). As Johnson tells it, capitalism is about more than making money for yourself—it is about liberating your country. "Those of you who practice economic freedom will also cause your country to have more political freedom," Johnson promised with great enthusiasm. "I would call you the revolutionaries of this era of your country."

Who Sold Summer?

The *Spectator* is the house newsletter of Britain's conservative establishment, the product of a literary and political hothouse whose writers are known for throwing the best parties in London and causing the occasional political scandal with their high-profile extramarital high jinks. Don't be deceived by its modest circulation of less than sixty-five thousand; three editors of the *Spectator* have gone on to serve in the cabinets of Tory prime ministers, and one, Boris Johnson, is currently the mayor of London. The phrase "young fogey" was coined on the pages of the *Spectator* in 1984, and the magazine remains proud to speak in a posh accent—you'll learn more in the Speccie, as its devotees call it, about fox hunting than you will about pop stars.

That's why the *Spectator*'s pronouncements on elite English culture should be taken seriously. And in a cover story published in June 2011, the magazine announced a sea change. "Who Sold Summer?" the headline asked, with the answer in the subhead: "On how a very English social season became the property of the international elite."

The author's point was that the hoary old fixtures of English cultural life—horse racing at Ascot or Epsom, cricket at the Oval or Lord's, opera at Covent Garden or Glyndebourne—which had once belonged to the *Spectator* community, had been taken over by the global super-elite. "For the super-rich, the world isn't divided into countries any more; just rich and poor parts. And, like swallows, their favoured rich parts in summer are now their English bolt-holes in the north," writes Harry Mount, the author of the essay, who also happens to be a second cousin of David Cameron, Britain's aristocratic Conservative prime minister, a graduate of Westminster, one of Britain's most exclusive private schools, and a former member of the Bullingdon Club, the exclusive and controversial private society at Oxford. "Britain now has a Wimbledon economy: we provide the charming venue, and foreigners come over to enjoy themselves on Centre Court. The paradox is that the recession has accelerated the globalisation of England. The English have been hard hit: with half a million jobs lost, and our rich stung—or chased abroad—by the 50p tax and the tax on bank bonuses. But the globalised elite, with their money parked offshore, have emerged almost untouched: their assets diversified, their wealth hitched to the booming East."

Mount chronicles the global super-elite's takeover of the English rituals that until very recently belonged to his class and clan. But what he has observed on the playing fields of Eton is actually a worldwide phenomenon. The plutocrats are becoming a transglobal community of peers who have more in common with one another than with their countrymen back home. Whether they maintain primary residences in New York or Hong Kong, Moscow or Mumbai, today's super-rich are increasingly a nation unto themselves.

"There's an interaction between the global elite, as you call them, and the media, as follows, which has to do with sort of the, for lack of a term, sexiness of it all," Eric Schmidt told me in his Google office in Mountain View. "Magazines are now publishing the destinations that everyone goes to. So, there's a list, okay? So let me tell you what the list is. There's Davos. There's the Oscars. There's the Cannes Film Festival. There's Sun Valley. There's the TED conference. There's Teddy Forstmann's conference. There's UN Week, Fashion Week. In London, there is Wimbledon Week, which is the last week of June.

"These have become global events, when they were local events," Schmidt explained. "They're not nearly as much fun as they were when I was reading about them in the paper. Because the pictures were much better than the reality. But because I see myself as a global citizen, I go anyway. . . . The math is that people want to be where other smart and interesting people are. . . . There's a perception you have to be there. And globalization, air travel, allows you to do this. So, the people that you're describing travel a lot. And they also have multiple homes, right? So, the rigors of travel are not so bad if you have a home in London. I don't have these things, by the way."

No one studies the super-elite more assiduously than their would-be bankers. Like its rivals, every year Credit Suisse publishes a Global Wealth Report, an address book, health checkup, and love letter to the world's money. In its 2011 edition, Credit Suisse noted the difference between the world's rising middle class, which remains rooted in and defined by nationality, and the increasingly shared and global character of people at the very top:

The base of the wealth pyramid is occupied by people from all countries of the world at various stages of their life-cycles; in contrast, HNW [high net worth, defined as people with an investable income of between $1 million and $50 million] and UHNW [ultra high net worth, defined as people with an investable income of at least $50 million] individuals are heavily concentrated in particular regions and countries, sharing a much more similar lifestyle. Even members at other locations tend to participate in the same global markets for high coupon consumption items. The wealth portfolios of individuals are also likely to be similar, dominated by financial assets and, in particular, equity holdings in public companies traded in international markets.

The UHNWIs themselves describe the same experience. As Glenn Hutchins, cofounder of the private equity firm Silver Lake, puts it, "A person in Africa who runs a big African bank and went to Harvard Business School has more in common with me than he does with his neighbors, and I have more in common with him than I do with my neighbors." The circles he moves in, Hutchins explains, are defined by "interests" rather than "geography": "Beijing can look a lot like New York. You see the same people, you eat in the same restaurants, you stay in the same hotels. We are much less place-based than we used to be."

Aditya Mittal, the CFO of ArcelorMittal and son of its billionaire founder, is one of the foreign-born plutocrats who have taken over the *Spectator*'s traditional England. Mittal was born in Indonesia, educated in the United States, holds an Indian passport, and today lives in London.

"I think, in a sad sense, these cities are so similar now because of globalization," Mittal told me over coffee in Manhattan. "I mean the difference in identity is not as significant as it used to be. For a global businessman, you can achieve almost the same set of objectives whether you're in London, New York, or a place like Singapore. You have access to talent, you have access to bankers, lawyers, you have access to good restaurants, good hotels. I mean, the main components of running a business can be found in any big city. So you can live in any of these cities and it's not such a big change anymore to move from, say, London to New York. Of course, that's a good thing in many ways, but I hope they don't lose their individual identity too much."

"There are more and more global CEO meetings in the emerging markets, especially China," Dominic Barton, managing director of McKinsey, told me over breakfast in midtown Manhattan. Barton, a Canadian who lives in London but whose secretary is based in Singapore, was due to see Steve Schwarzman, the private equity investor, later that day. "The last time I saw Steve was in China," where Blackstone had held a partners meeting the previous fall, Barton recalled. Barton himself was traveling to Chile later in the week, and then on to São Paolo, where McKinsey was holding a board meeting. Schwarzman, meanwhile, was about to move his primary residence to Paris for six months (he already owned one home in that country, in the south of France, of course), the better to oversee what he believed would be significant investment opportunities in Europe and Asia.

Schwarzman spends about half his time traveling. Blackstone, which he cofounded, has offices around the world in cities including Shanghai, Mumbai, London, Paris, and Düsseldorf, and the firm both invests in and raises money outside the United States.

"There is an emergent power in people whose shared experiences are more to each other than to their local context and their local governments. I think that's basically true," Schmidt told me. "The people you're describing see themselves as global citizens first. That's a relatively new phenomenon. So, while they're certainly patriotic about their countries and patriotic about where they grew up, and they love their mothers and so forth—but they see themselves as global citizens. And so, when something happens in the globe that's bad, it bothers them."

"This is the new wave, the new trend," Wang Huiyao, founder and president of Beijing's Center for China and Globalization, told me. "We had the globalization of trade, we had the globalization of capital, and now we have the globalization of talent.

"It is no longer about brain drain, or even brain gain," Dr. Wang said. "It is about global brain circulation."

Dr. Wang recalled that three decades ago, when he first came to North America as a student, there was only one flight a day to China. Today, he said, "there are two or three dozen, if not more."

As a result, instead of immigration being a single journey with a fixed starting point and end point, Dr. Wang said many Chinese have become what he calls "seagulls," going back and forth between San Francisco or Vancouver and Beijing or Shanghai. He is a seagull himself: I spoke over the phone to Dr. Wang while he was in Washington, D.C.; he is spending the academic year at Harvard's Kennedy School in Cambridge, Massachusetts; his institute is in Beijing; and he still owns an apartment in Vancouver, where he once lived.

In a similar vein, the wife of one of America's most successful fund managers offered me the small but telling anecdote that her husband is better able to navigate the streets of Davos than those of his native Manhattan. When he's at home, she explained, he is ferried around town by a car and driver; the snowy Swiss hamlet, which is too small and awkward for limos, is the only place where he actually walks. One international media executive, who traveled 120 nights out of the past 365 days, described the group this way: "We are the people who know airline flight attendants better than we know our own wives." An investment banker born and educated in Scandinavia, who built his career working as an investment banker with multinational firms in London and New York and who today works for an emerging markets plutocrat, told me that his family's recent move from London to Hong Kong was easier than moving from one borough of New York to another.

The globalization of the super-elite starts before the deals do—in school. The plutocracy doesn't have its own passport, but it does have its alma maters—America's Ivy League, plus Stanford and Oxbridge, and the world's top business schools, mostly an American group, but also including Europe's INSEAD. This is a world, as Turow puts it, where the provenance of your MBA matters more than your nationality. You can find quite a few plutocrats who were educated entirely in their home countries—this is, remember, largely a self-made group—but it is rare to come across one whose children don't attend one of these top global universities. Many start earlier, sending their children to boarding schools, especially the fancy English ones, where Russian oligarchs landing their helicopters on the sports fields for parent visiting day has become commonplace. China's plutocrats, who devote more than a fifth of their annual spending to their children's education, are enthusiastic globalizers. According to Rupert Hoogewerf, publisher of the Hurun Report and the premier chronicler of the culture of the Chinese super-elite, "Four out of every five Chinese entrepreneurs today are considering sending their children to school overseas." Middle Kingdom billionaires prefer to send their children abroad for high school, where British public schools are the preferred destination. For college, when the children of Chinese millionaires join the plutonomy, too, the most elite universities are America's Ivy League. As a European multimillionaire explained to an eastern European billionaire, over a meal I shared with them at Davos, the advantage of the British public school their children both attended (thanks to the help of the same international education placement adviser) was that, "in addition to learning the language, they will make the right international friends."

The global takeover of these elite international institutions is beginning to be reflected in the name above the door—Oxford is today home to both the Blavatnik School of Government, a would-be rival to Harvard's Kennedy School, endowed with a £75 million gift from Russian-born metals and oil baron Len Blavatnik (a truly global plutocrat who was born in Odessa, earned an MBA from Harvard, and has homes in New York and London), and the Saïd Business School, founded with a £20 million gift from Wafic Saïd, who was born in Syria, made his fortune in Saudi Arabia, and maintains his primary homes in Paris as well as tax-friendly Monaco.

CITIZENS OF THE WORLD

Like any country, the plutonomy is not uniform: its tribes have distinct national customs and its individual members make their own choices about how to live. The plutocrats whose native countries are repressive or volatile, like the Russians or the Middle Easterners, tend to be the most thoroughly global. Some, like the Chinese or the Indians, cultivate powerful community networks even when they live and work outside their home country. Some countries have built their national economy in large part by providing a physical haven for the globe-trotting members of the plutocracy—this has been the business of Switzerland and Monaco for generations. More recently, Singapore and Hong Kong have gotten into the act. Dubai is a newly minted, air-conditioned contender. English is the lingua franca of the super-elite, which means that, along with its elegant buildings and favorable tax treatment of foreigners, Britain, too, is a popular spot: nearly 60 percent of the properties in London worth more than £2.5 million are owned by foreigners.

America's business elite, by contrast, is something of a latecomer to this transnational community. In a study of British and American CEOs, for example, executive headhunter Elisabeth Marx found that almost a third of the former were foreign nationals, compared to just 10 percent of the latter. Similarly, more than three-quarters of the Brits had worked abroad for at least two years, whereas just a third of Americans had done so.

But despite the slow start, American business is catching up. Today's American chief executives are twice as likely to have worked abroad as their predecessors of a decade ago, and the number of foreign and foreign-born CEOs of U.S. companies, while still relatively small, is rising. The shift is particularly evident on Wall Street. In 2006, each of the eight leading banks on the Street was run by a native-born CEO; today, their number is down to five, and two of the survivors—Citigroup and Morgan Stanley—are led by men who were born abroad.

In fact, Jeff Immelt, the CEO of General Electric, recently told me his successor might well come from an emerging market, because that's where GE's future, and the future of American business more generally, lies.

In Immelt's view, the financial crisis marked the end of the age of America's economic dominance. "I came to GE in 1982," Mr. Immelt told me. "For the first twenty-five years, until the bubble crashed in 2007, the American consumer was the definitive driver of the global economy." But the future will be different, Mr. Immelt said. For the next twenty-five years, he said, the U.S. consumer "is not going to be the engine of global growth. It is going to be the billion people joining the middle class in Asia, it is going to be what the resource-rich countries do with their newfound wealth of high oil prices. That's the game."

"There are going to be one billion consumers joining the middle class in Asia. I think for us to reduce unemployment, exports are going to be a key way to do it," Immelt told me. "It's this country's only destiny just because most of the consumers are some place other than here."

As a cautionary counterexample, Immelt cited inward-looking Japanese firms. "Look, when I was a young guy, when I first started with GE, Jack Welch sent us all to Japan because in those days Japan was gonna crush us," he said. "And we learned a lot about Japan when we were there. But over the subsequent thirty years the Japanese companies all fell behind. And the reason why they fell behind is because they didn't globalize. They didn't have to go out and sing for their dinner in every corner of the world. That's not the case with GE. It's not the case with other American multinationals."

At the 2010 Aspen Ideas Festival, Michael Splinter, CEO of the Silicon Valley green-tech firm Applied Materials, confessed that if he were starting from scratch, only 20 percent of his workforce would be domestic. "This year, almost 90 percent of our sales will be outside the U.S.," he explained. "The pull to be close to the customers—most of them in Asia—is enormous." Speaking at the same conference, Thomas Wilson, CEO of Allstate, told a similar story: "I can get [workers] anywhere in the world. It is a problem for America, but it is not necessarily a problem for American business. . . . American businesses will adapt."

Paul Volcker, the legendary inflation-fighting former head of the Federal Reserve, told me that at a 2012 dinner with a group of chief financial officers in Manhattan he had been struck by the global outlook of what he described as "so-called American companies": "Implicitly, they don't think of themselves as American anymore," he said. "They are international companies. If the American government doesn't treat them right they will move their headquarters abroad. These companies are more likely to man their foreign branches with foreigners than they are Americans, and they send foreigners to run their American operations."

Mohamed El-Erian, the CEO of Pimco, the world's largest bond manager, is typical of the global nomads gradually rising to the top echelons of U.S. business in this international age. The son of an Egyptian father and French mother, El-Erian had a peripatetic childhood, shuttling between Paris, Cairo, New York, and London. He was educated at Cambridge and Oxford and now works for a U.S.-based company that is owned by the German financial conglomerate Allianz SE.

Though El-Erian lives in Newport Beach, California, where Pimco is headquartered, he says that he can't name a single country as his own. "I have three passports," El-Erian told me on a recent visit to New York. "I don't belong to any one country. I belong to many and to the world." As he talked, we walked through midtown, which El-Erian remembered fondly from his childhood, when he'd take the crosstown bus each day to the United Nations School. That evening, El-Erian was catching a flight to London. Later in the week, he was due in St. Petersburg.

Indeed, there is a growing sense, at GE and beyond, that American businesses that don't internationalize aggressively risk being left behind. For all its global reach, Pimco is still based in the United States. But the flows of goods and capital upon which the super-elite surf are bypassing America more often than they used to. Take, for example, Stephen Jennings, the fifty-two-year-old New Zealander who cofounded the investment bank Renaissance Capital. Renaissance's roots are in Moscow, where Jennings maintains his primary residence (he also has farms in Oxfordshire and New Zealand, and his children go to school in England), and his business strategy involves positioning the firm to capture the investment flows between the emerging markets, particularly Russia, Africa, and Asia. For his purposes, New York is increasingly irrelevant. In a 2009 speech in Wellington,

New Zealand, he offered his vision of this post-unipolar business reality: "The largest metals group in the world is Indian. The largest aluminum group in the world is Russian. . . . The fastest-growing and largest banks in China, Russia, and Nigeria are all domestic."

As it happens, one of the fellow tenants in Jennings's high-tech, high-rise Moscow office building recently put together a deal that exemplifies just this kind of intra-emerging-market trade. In the spring of 2010, Digital Sky Technologies (DST), Russia's largest investment firm, entered into a partnership with the South African media corporation Naspers and the Chinese technology company Tencent. All three are fast-growing firms with global vision—in the fall of 2010, a DST spin-off named Mail.ru went public and instantly become Europe's highest-valued Internet company, with a market capitalization of $5.71 billion—yet none is focused on the United States. A similar example of the intra-emerging-market economy was Indian telecom giant Bharti Enterprises' acquisition of most of the African properties of Kuwait-based telecom Zain. A California technology executive—himself a global nomad who has lived and worked in Europe and Asia—explained to me that a company like Bharti has a competitive advantage in what he believes will be the exploding African market: "They know how to provide mobile phones so much more cheaply than we do. In a place like Africa, how can Western firms compete?"

ARISTOCRACY OF IDEAS

Just as the railroad created new cities, private jets and private jet time-shares like NetJets have contributed to the globalization of the super-elite—owning homes and doing deals around the world becomes feasible when you can travel the planet as easily as the middle class steps into a car. New technologies have helped, too—instant and mobile communication makes it possible to live on the move and around the world. So have the political revolutions that have opened up so many of the world's borders over the past twenty years.

The most important shift, however, was the one foreseen by Adam Smith in *The Wealth of Nations*. Writing in 1776 at the very beginning of the industrial revolution, he predicted that as fortunes shifted from acres to shares they would become more mobile: "The proprietor of land is necessarily a citizen of the particular country in which his estate lies. The proprietor of stock is properly a citizen of the world, and is not necessarily attached to any particular country."

Smith could see that manufacturing companies, and the disaggregated owners of their stock, would eventually eclipse land as the engine of the economy. The technology revolution, which has created a new and powerful sphere of economic activity that has almost no physical manifestation at all, has taken that trend exponentially further. The result, as Smith anticipated, is an elite driven by its economic interests to think global: "He [the owner of stock] would be apt to abandon the country in which he was exposed to a vexatious inquisition in order to be assessed to a burdensome tax, and would remove his stock to some other country where he could either carry on his business or enjoy his fortune more at his ease." But while capital—and capitalists—have gone global, governments and most of their middle-class citizens operate within national boundaries. Figuring out how the plutocrats are connected to the rest of us is one of the challenges of the rise of the global super-elite.

Harry Mount, the *Spectator* essayist, is grudgingly grateful to the global super-elite for "buying" the traditional summer social calendar of English high society and sprucing it up—"the rackety, amateurish, faded charms of English high summer have been replaced by a professionalised, slick operation, supercharged by oceans of international cash."

But the irony of this overseas acquisition is that while the debutante balls and hunts and regattas of yesteryear may not be quite obsolete, they are certainly headed in that direction. The real community life of the twenty-first-century plutocracy occurs on the international conference circuit. "We don't have castles and noble titles, so how else do you indicate you're part of the elite?" Andrew Zolli of PopTech, an ideas forum and social innovation network, told *New York* magazine.

The best known of these events is the World Economic Forum's annual meeting in Davos, Switzerland, invitation to which marks an aspiring plutocrat's arrival on the international scene—and where, in lieu of noble titles, an elaborate hierarchy of conference badges has such significance that one first-time participant remarked that the staring at his chest made him realize for the first time what it must be like to have cleavage. The Bilderberg Group, which meets annually at locations in Europe and North America, is more exclusive still—and more secretive—though it is more focused on geopolitics and less on global business and philanthropy. The Boao Forum, convened on Hainan Island each spring, offers evidence both of China's growing economic importance and of its understanding of the culture of the global plutocracy. Bill Clinton is pushing hard to win his Clinton Global Initiative a regular place on the circuit. The annual TED conference (the acronym stands for Technology, Entertainment, Design) is an important stop for the digerati, as is the DLD (Digital-Life-Design) gathering Israeli technology entrepreneur Yossi Vardi cohosts with publisher Hubert Burda in Munich each January (so convenient if you are en route to Davos). Herb Allen's Sun Valley gathering is the place for media moguls, and the Aspen Institute's Ideas Festival is for the more policy-minded, with a distinctly U.S. slant. There is nothing implicit, at these gatherings, about the sense of belonging to a global elite. As Chris Anderson, the curator of the TED talks, told one gathering: "Combined, our contacts reach pretty much everyone who's interesting in the country, if not the planet."

Recognizing the value of such global conclaves, some corporations have begun hosting their own. Among these is Google's Zeitgeist conference, where I have moderated discussions for several years. One of its recent gatherings was held in May 2010 at the Grove, a former provincial estate in the English countryside whose three-hundred-acre grounds have been transformed into a golf course and whose high-ceilinged rooms are now decorated with a mixture of antique and contemporary furniture. (Mock Louis XIV chairs—made, with a wink, from high-end plastic—are much in evidence.) Cirque du Soleil offered the five hundred guests a private performance in an enormous tent erected on the grounds; the year before that, to celebrate its acquisition of YouTube, Google flew in overnight Internet sensations from around the world.

Yet for all its luxury, the mood of the Zeitgeist conference is hardly sybaritic. Rather it has the intense, earnest atmosphere of a gathering of college summa cum laudes. This is not a group that plays hooky: the conference room is full from nine a.m. to six p.m. on conference days, and during coffee breaks the lawns are crowded with executives checking their BlackBerrys and iPads.

The 2010 lineup of Zeitgeist speakers included such notables as Archbishop Desmond Tutu, London mayor Boris Johnson, and Starbucks CEO Howard Schultz (not to mention, of course, Google's own CEO, Eric Schmidt). But the most potent currency at this and comparable gatherings is neither fame nor money. Rather, it's what author Michael Lewis has dubbed "the new new thing"—the insight or algorithm or technology with the potential to change the world. Hence the presence of three Nobel laureates, including Daniel Kahneman, a pioneer in behavioral economics. One of the business stars in attendance was then thirty-six-year-old entrepreneur Tony Hsieh, who had sold his Zappos online shoe retailer to Amazon for more than a billion dollars the previous summer. And the most popular session of all was the one in which Google showed off some of its new inventions, including the Nexus phone.

This geeky enthusiasm for innovation and ideas is evident at more intimate gatherings of the global elite as well. Take the elegant Manhattan dinner parties hosted by Marie-Josée Kravis, the economist wife of private equity billionaire Henry Kravis in their elegant Upper East Side apartment. Though the china is Sèvres and the paintings are Old Masters, the dinner table conversation would not be out of place in a graduate seminar. Mrs. Kravis takes pride in bringing together not only plutocrats such as her husband and Michael Bloomberg, but also thinkers and policy makers such as Richard Holbrooke, Robert Zoellick, and *Financial Times* columnist Martin Wolf, and leading them in discussion of issues ranging from global financial imbalances to the war in Afghanistan.

In fact, the idea conference is so trendy that a couple of New Yorkers recently hosted an ideas wedding. When David Friedlander and Jacqueline Schmidt married in Brooklyn in December 2011, their guests were issued name tags that asked them to declare a commitment. Another card urged, "Name one action you can take in the next twenty-four hours that is aligned with your commitment." Instead of boozy speeches about the bride and groom delivered by nervous family and friends, the main entertainment was a series of TED-style talks, complete with PowerPoint presentations, about issues the couple cares about—neuroscience, the environment, and holistic healing.

A thought-leadership wedding just might be going a step too far—the Friedlander/Schmidt nuptials were snarkily chronicled in the *New York Times* and panned by *Gawker*, although the more earnest *Huffington Post* gave the pair a thumbs up. But in this age of elites who delight in such phrases as "out of the box" and "killer app," arguably the most coveted status symbol isn't a yacht, a racehorse, or a knighthood; it's a philanthropic foundation—and, more than that, one actively managed in ways that show its sponsor has big ideas for reshaping the world.

George Soros, who turned eighty in the summer of 2010, is a pioneer and role model for the socially engaged billionaire. Arguably the most successful investor of the postwar era, he is nonetheless most proud of his Open Society Foundations, through which he has spent billions of dollars on causes as diverse as drug legalization, civil society in central and eastern Europe, and rethinking economic assumptions in the wake of the financial crisis.

Inspired and advised by the liberal Soros, Pete Peterson—himself a Republican and former Nixon cabinet member—has spent $1 billion of his Blackstone windfall on a foundation dedicated to bringing down America's deficit and entitlement spending. Bill Gates, likewise, devotes most of his energy and intellect today to his foundation's work on causes ranging from supporting charter schools to combating disease in Africa. Facebook founder Mark Zuckerberg has yet to reach his thirtieth birthday, but last fall he donated $100 million to improving Newark's public schools. Insurance and real estate magnate Eli Broad has become an influential funder of stem cell research and school reform; Jim Balsillie, a cofounder of BlackBerry creator RIM, has established his own international affairs think tank; the list goes on and on. It is not without reason that Bill Clinton has devoted his postpresidency to the construction of a global philanthropic "brand."

The super-wealthy have long recognized that philanthropy, in addition to its moral rewards, can also serve as a pathway to social acceptance and even immortality. Andrew "The Man Who Dies Rich Dies Disgraced" Carnegie transformed himself from robber baron to secular saint with his hospitals, concert halls, libraries, and universities; Alfred Nobel ensured that he would be remembered for something other than the invention of dynamite. What is notable about today's plutocrats is that they tend to bestow their fortunes in much the same way they made them: entrepreneurially. Rather than merely donate to worthy charities or endow existing institutions (though they of course do this as well), they are using their wealth to test new ways to solve big problems.

Their approach is different enough to have inspired a new phrase, "philanthro-capitalism," which is also the title of a book by Matthew Bishop and Michael Green. Bishop and Green explain: "The new philanthropists believe they are improving philanthropy, equipping it to tackle the new set of problems facing today's changing world. . . . [They] are trying to apply the secret behind their money-making success to their giving."

"What they are doing is much more trying to copy business techniques and ways of thinking," Bishop told me. "There is a connection between their ways of thinking as businesspeople and their ways of giving. If you compare it with previous eras, in each era going back to the Middle Ages the entrepreneurs have been among the people leading the response to the destruction caused by the economic processes that made them rich. You saw it in the Middle Ages, you saw it with the Victorians, you saw it with Carnegie and Rockefeller. What is different is the scale. Business is global and so they are focusing on global problems. They are much more focused on how do they achieve a massive impact. They are used to operating on a grand scale and so they want to operate on a grand scale in their philanthropy as well. And they are doing it at a much younger age."

A measure of the importance of public engagement for today's super-rich is the zeal with which even emerging market plutocrats are developing their own foundations and think tanks. When the oligarchs of the former Soviet Union first burst out beyond their own borders, they were a Marxist caricature of the nouveaux riches: purchasing yachts and sports teams and surrounding themselves with couture-clad supermodels. Fifteen years later, they are exploring how to buy their way into the world of ideas.

One of the most determined is the Ukrainian entrepreneur Victor Pinchuk, whose business empire ranges from pipe manufacturing to TV stations. With a net worth of $4.2 billion, Pinchuk is no longer content merely to acquire modern art. In 2009, he launched a global competition for young artists run by his Pinchuk Art Centre in Kiev, conceived as a way of bringing Ukraine into the international cultural mainstream. Pinchuk hosts a regular lunch on the fringes of Davos (Chelsea Clinton was the celebrity moderator in 2012) and has launched his own annual "ideas" forum, a gathering devoted to geopolitics that is held, with suitable modesty, in the same Crimean villa where Stalin, Roosevelt, and Churchill conducted the Yalta Conference. The September 2010 meeting, where I served as a moderator, included Dominique Strauss-Kahn, then head of the International Monetary Fund; Polish president Bronislaw Komorowski; and Alexei Kudrin, then the Russian deputy prime minister and finance minister. At a gala dinner, keynote speaker Bill Clinton addressed, ironically enough, the economic consequences of growing inequality.

As an entrée into the global super-elite, Pinchuk's efforts seem to be working. On a visit to the United States in 2010, the oligarch met with top Obama adviser David Axelrod in Washington and schmoozed with Charlie Rose at a New York book party for *Time* magazine editor Rick Stengel. On a previous trip, he'd dined with Caroline Kennedy at the Upper East Side town house of HBO chief Richard Plepler. Back home, he has entertained fellow art enthusiast Eli Broad at his palatial estate outside Kiev (which features its own nine-hole golf course and Japanese garden, built by Japanese carpenters), and has partnered with Soros to finance Ukrainian civil society projects.

CHARITY STARTS AT HOME AND WHERE IS THAT?

One of the tensions in the life of the plutocrat that philanthropy lays bare is how hard it can be figuring out where to give back. If you are a global nomad, do you direct your charitable efforts at the place where you were born, the place where you live now (if that is even possible to define), or the place where you do the most business? Or perhaps the right approach isn't to think about tribal or emotional connection; rather it is to use the same objective logic you would apply to a business investment and to try to find the place in the world where you can make the biggest difference.

I listened to a couple of members of the global 0.1 percent think through these issues over supper in Dar es Salaam. We were there, appropriately enough, thanks to the World Economic Forum, which was hosting one of its regional summits over a few muggy days in May 2010 in the Tanzanian city. One participant in the conversation was an Australian who lived in Hong Kong and had made a career largely working in Southeast Asia and China. The second was an Asian-born technologist who had earned a fortune working in Silicon Valley.

The Australian had no doubts about where it was best to target one's philanthropy, and that was neither birthplace nor adopted city: "I always focus on where you have the biggest impact and where people need it the most—so that is always, always poor, uneducated girls in the developing world." The Asian entrepreneur felt a greater obligation to the communities with which he had a personal connection, so his philanthropy was directed in two places: building schools in his native country and supporting the education of poor children in California.

This dual focus, working with the poorest of the poor abroad and also doing something for the people at the bottom in your own neighborhood, is the balance a lot of the plutocrats strike. You could see another example on the lawns of Kensington Palace. The redbrick mansion was once home to Princess Diana and today is a home for her sons, but the most lavish celebration held on its grounds in the summer of 2011 was the annual gala auction hedge fund manager (and supermodel-dater) Arpad Busson organizes to raise money for ARK, the children's charity he founded.

Busson is a vocal proponent of philanthro-capitalism. ARK stands for Absolute Return for Kids, a play on the language of the hedge funds and their pursuit of absolute returns, often using aggressive techniques such as short selling, in contrast with generally more conservative mutual funds and their pursuit of relative returns, which is to say they aim to keep abreast of the wider investment pack. Busson thinks ARK needs to be run like a hedge fund. "If we can apply the entrepreneurial principles we have brought to business to charity, we have a shot at having a really strong impact, to be able to transform the lives of children," he told *The Observer*.

When it comes to picking which children, Busson, a true global nomad—he was born in France of a French father and an English mother, he has worked in New York and Paris as well as London, and his own two boys are the sons of Australian model Elle Macpherson—targets his efforts at the children of the world. ARK has projects in eastern Europe, Africa, and India, as well as in the UK. That mix would not have occurred to philanthropists of a previous generation, for whom poor neighbors belonged to a very different category from the poor of the third world. But to the globetrotting plutocrat, there isn't much difference between the poor child in the London estate (Britspeak for housing projects) and the New Delhi slum.

PHILANTHRO-CAPITALISM

Busson's belief in applying business techniques to philanthropy is characteristic of the global super-elite's approach to doing good. No one does this more effectively than Bill Gates, whose foundation, with its $33 billion war chest and rigorously analytical mind-set, has transformed charity, and sometimes public policy, around the world.

Within the plutocracy, the Gates Foundation has had a decisive cultural impact. Gates and his co-donor Warren Buffett—not accidentally two of the world's most visible and most admired billionaires—have made it de rigueur not only to give away a lot of your money but to be actively engaged in how it is spent. Gates has become an evangelist for this idea that capitalism must do good, and do-gooders must become more capitalist. He even has a name for it, "creative capitalism," a term he unveiled in a speech at Davos—where else?—at the 2008 meeting of the World Economic Forum.

Marx famously observed that early generations of philosophers had sought to describe the world; he wanted to change it. Gates and his plutocratic peers are having a similarly dramatic impact on the world of charity. They don't want to fund the social sector, they want to transform it. One example is their impact on education in America. With their focus on measurable results, Gates and his fellow education-focused billionaires have spearheaded a data-driven revolution. The first step was to put tests at the center of education, so that the output—student learning—could be measured. The next step is to try to make the job of teaching more data- and incentive-driven. As Gates said in a speech in November 2010, "We have to figure out what makes the great teacher great." That effort includes videotaping teachers in the classroom and paying them based on how they perform.

Strikingly, the ambition of the philanthro-capitalists doesn't stop at transforming how charity works. They want to change how the state operates, too. These are men who have built their businesses by achieving the maximum impact with the minimum effort—either as financiers using leverage or technologists using scale. They think of their charitable dollars in the same way.

"Our foundation tends to fund more of the up-front discovery work, and we're a partner in delivery, but governmental funding is the biggest," Gates told students at MIT on a visit there in April 2010.

"Take delivering AIDS medicine. We did the pilot studies in Botswana to prove that you could deliver ARBs [angiotensin II receptor blockers] in Africa, and then PEPFAR [the U.S. President's Emergency Plan for AIDS Relief], the U.S. government program, which is five billion [dollars] a year, which is way more than our whole foundation, just that one U.S. government help program—just one country—came in and scaled up based on some of the lessons from that."

It is a measure of the financial and intellectual power of plutocrats in the world economy that their goal is to guide the state. Indeed, the muscle of the philanthro-capitalists is such that they can sometimes unintentionally distort the social safety nets of entire nations. That has been a complaint in some African countries, where the richly funded, relentlessly focused Gates programs on AIDS medicine and tuberculosis and malaria vaccines have lured local doctors and nurses away from providing desperately needed, but less glamorous, everyday care. Dr. Peter Poore, a pediatrician who has worked in Africa for three decades, warned *Los Angeles Times* investigative reporters, "They can also do dangerous things. They can be very disruptive to health systems—the very things they claim they are trying to improve." Rachel Cohen, a Western aid worker in Lesotho, agreed: "All over the country, people are furious about the incentives for ART staff [as the Gates-funded health workers are known]," who can earn more than double what other health care workers are paid.

The impact of the philanthro-capitalists on global health and U.S. education is occasionally controversial—not everyone believes in more testing in schools, or the particular approaches to AIDS care in Africa. But there is little debate about the aims—it is hard to find anyone who argues that U.S. schoolchildren need less education or that Africans deserve fewer doctors and less medicine. But some idea-driven plutocrats venture into more obviously contested terrain.

The plutocrat-as-politician is becoming an important member of the world's governing elite, ranging from pragmatic problem solvers with a yen for the public stage, such as Mike Bloomberg or Mitt Romney, to emerging market billionaires whose wealth emboldens them to challenge authoritarian rulers, like Russia's Mikhail Khodorkovsky or Egypt's Naguib Sawiris. The plutocratic politician can use his own money to bankroll his campaign directly, and also to build a network of civic support through the less explicitly political donations of his personal foundation.

Some farsighted plutocrats try to use their money not merely to buy public office for themselves but to redirect the reigning ideology of a nation, a region, or even the world. Soros's Open Society Foundations may not have toppled communism, but they had a powerful impact on the emergence of democracy and pluralism in much of Eastern Europe and the former Soviet Union. At the other end of the ideological spectrum, conservative billionaires like the Koch brothers have assiduously nurtured a right-wing intellectual ecosystem of think tanks and journals that has had a powerful impact on electoral politics and the legislative agenda in the United States and beyond.

Your own view of these explicitly political plutocratic ventures depends on your own politics. If you support drug legalization, you are probably a fan of the Soros millions dedicated to that cause. If you back gay marriage, you likely cheered Republican billionaire Paul Singer's contribution to the campaign to legalize it in New York state.

Where things get really complicated is when the philanthro-capitalists use their money to finance a political agenda that dovetails with their personal business interests or with the interests of the plutocratic class as a whole. The Koch brothers, for instance, have pushed for less government regulation of industry, including state efforts to protect the environment. They are lifelong libertarians who are genuinely skeptical about climate change. They also happen to own a company whose assets include oil refineries, oil pipelines, and lumber mills—all businesses that would benefit from a weakened EPA.

Then there are the class interests of the plutocrats more generally. Balancing the budget isn't an idea that belongs to a particular socioeconomic group or political party—the Germans, with their generous social safety net, are as hawkish about deficits as the U.S. Tea Party. But cutting so-called entitlement spending is a policy that would have a disproportionate impact on the poor, who depend most on these programs—and it is also an idea that plutocrat Pete Peterson has devoted $1 billion of his fortune to advance.

Jeffrey Winters, a political scientist at Northwestern University, believes America's super-elite has been particularly effective at using the tools of a political democracy—where, in theory, the majority should rule—to protect its minority privilege. The first permanent federal income tax in the United States was explicitly devised as a tax on plutocrats. When it was first mooted in 1894, it was to be levied on the top 0.1 percent—eighty-five thousand of the sixty-five million Americans. Resistance in Congress, whose members included two millionaires, was predictably intense. One representative warned that this "was not Democracy, it was Communism." Another fumed, "It is a shame that the successful should be made the legal prey of the un-successful." It took nineteen years and an amendment to the Constitution, but the tax did eventually become law in 1913. This was, after all, the height of the Gilded Age and the dawn of the Progressive Era. America was getting rich, but it was also getting worried about the disproportionate wealth and power of its plutocrats.

Over the subsequent century, though, the 0.1 percent fought back. Driven up by the costs of World War I, the initial tax rate on the very rich was high, reaching a peak of 77 percent in 1918. By the early twenty-first century, the effective tax rate at the very top had fallen to less than a third of that level. Strikingly, as the tax rate at the top fell, it rose on those lower down the income distribution—in the political fight over tax rates, the plu-tocrats have outfoxed the merely wealthy. In 1916, millionaires—that era's super-rich—were hit with a published income tax rate of 65 percent, nearly 35 points higher than the rate for the merely affluent. Capital gains were taxed at the same level as ordinary income, and most Americans paid no income tax at all. Today, that fiercely progressive curve has been reversed. Within the 1 percent, the richer you are, the lower your effective tax rate: in

2009, the top 1 percent paid over 23 percent of their income in tax, the top 0.1 percent paid just over 21 percent, and the top four hundred taxpayers paid less than 17 percent. Capital gains, an important source of income for the plutocrats but less significant the lower you go down the income distribution, were taxed at just 15 percent in 2012.

Winters argues that America's oligarchs have achieved these low effective tax rates thanks to the services of a professional army of lawyers, accountants, and lobbyists. Collectively, he calls this group of courtiers the "income defense industry." They certainly benefit from the intellectual anti-tax agenda elaborated over the past several decades at some of the think tanks financed by plutocrats.

But if America really is ruled by an oligarchy, it is a very badly disciplined clique indeed. After all, some of the most prominent plutocrats, most notably Warren Buffett, have highlighted the low effective tax rate they pay and have called on politicians to raise it. As he likes to put it, "There's class warfare, all right. But it's my class, the rich class, that's making war, and we're winning."

THE 0.1 PERCENT VS. THE 1 PERCENT

When Anders Aslund, a Swedish economist who has studied and advised most of the leaders in the former Soviet Union, visited Kiev in late 2004, at the height of the Orange Revolution, he returned to his home in Washington, D.C., with a surprising observation.

Most reports depicted the Orange Revolutionaries, with their determined, subzero encampment in the capital city's central square, either as western Ukrainians rebelling against the government's pro-Russian stance or as idealistic students who were unwilling to stomach political repression. Both characterizations were true, but Aslund saw a third dynamic at play. The Orange Revolution, he told me, was the rebellion of the millionaires against the billionaires. Ukraine's crony capitalism worked extremely well for the small, well-connected group of oligarchs at the very top, but it was stifling the emerging middle class. This rising petite bourgeoisie was finally fed up and it was fighting for more equitable rules of the game.

That battle of the millionaires versus the billionaires has been playing out across the world. It was a decisive factor in the Tahrir Square protests, whose most visible organizer was Wael Ghonim, an MBA-trained Google executive based in Dubai, which quickly won the support of the country's well-heeled military elite. It was on show in India, where veteran social activist Anna Hazare's anticorruption hunger strike was hailed as the political awakening of the prospering Indian middle class. And it can be seen in Moscow, where the unexpected revolt against Vladimir Putin's "party of crooks and thieves" was catalyzed by a blogging real estate lawyer and drew fur-clad professionals onto the streets.

In the United States, Occupy Wall Street has drawn the political battle lines somewhat differently—between the 99 percent and the 1 percent. But when you drill down into the data, you can see another, even steeper division inside the 1 percent itself. The ultrarich of the 0.1 percent have pulled far ahead of the merely rich, who make up the other 0.9 percent at the tip of the income pyramid. The divide is cultural and it is economic—and if it becomes political it could transform the national debate.

The wider public discussion about income inequality hasn't much touched on the divisions within the 1 percent. That is partly because it can be a little stomach churning to consider the gradations of wealth at the very top at a time when unemployment is close to 9 percent and working-class families are being hammered. But within the 1 percent, the awareness of the different tiers of wealth is as keen as an Indian matchmaker's sensitivity to the finer divisions of caste.

Holly Peterson, the daughter of Pete Peterson and herself a sly and eloquent chronicler of the 1 percent, tells a similar story of the tension at the very top.

"I think people making $5 million to $10 million definitely don't think they are making enough money," she told me. "'Wouldn't it be nice to fly private?' There are so many things you can aspire to, even making $5 million a year. For the lower rung of this crowd, these people set up lives for themselves they can't afford. These people are broke and maxed out on their credit cards in December, just like middle-class couples living on $100,000. I don't think they feel that rich. They are trying to play with the high rollers and there are things they can't do and they feel deprived, which is completely sick and absurd, but that's the truth of the matter."

One way to understand what is happening at the top of the income distribution is to look at the numbers. Brian Bell and John Van Reenen, two economists at the Centre for Economic Performance at the London School of Economics, have done a careful study of Britain's super-rich. Peering inside the top 1 percent, they found a distribution almost as skewed as that within the economy as a whole—the top 2 percent of the 1 percent took 11 percent of the wage share of that cohort in 1998 and 13 percent in 2008. Among financiers, who are disproportionately represented within the British and American 1 percent, the tilt toward the very top is even more pronounced.

Winters, the U.S. political scientist, has devised another way to appreciate the difference between the merely rich and the super-rich. He has created a "material power index," which measures the income of the top 10 percent of Americans as a multiple of the average income of the bottom 90 percent. His material power index shows that, like a mountain whose cliffs become steeper as you ascend to the peak, income polarization in America gets sharper the richer you are: the top 10 percent have an MPI of 4—meaning their average income is four times that of the bottom 90 percent—while the top 1 percent have an MPI of 15. But when you get to the top 0.1 percent, the MPI jumps to 124. That is the line, in Winters's view, that separates the affluent from the oligarchs. "There were about 150,000 Americans whose average annual incomes were $4 million and above in 2007," Winters writes of the 0.1 percent. "This is the threshold at which oligarchs dominate the landscape."

Another peek into the dynamic within the 1 percent comes from inside one of America's elite institutions. Claudia Goldin and Lawrence Katz, the Harvard economists, compiled a data set chronicling the family and career choices of twelve Harvard classes between 1969 and 1992. Their purpose was to understand the impact of gender on life and work, but their numbers turned out to tell a nuanced and unexpected story about the elite overall. One of the biggest surprises was how far, even among the gilded graduates of Harvard, the top had pulled away from everyone else—in 2005, median earnings for Harvard men were $162,000, comfortably in the top 10 percent of the national income distribution. But almost 8 percent of the men had labor market income above $1 million, putting them in the top 0.5 percent. An important driver of the gap was the split between the bankers and everyone else, with financiers earning 195 percent more than their classmates.

For the 1 percenters who didn't switch majors from art history to economics and find themselves moored at the bottom of the top, the experience can be surprisingly hard to bear. One force at work is Carol Graham's paradox of happy peasants and miserable millionaires. In international research that grew out of findings for Russia and Peru, Graham found that "very poor and destitute respondents report high or relatively high levels of well-being, while much wealthier ones with more mobility and opportunities report much lower levels of well-being and greater frustration with their economic and other situations."

One source of that frustration, Dr. Graham told me, was when "the gains around them are much bigger than their own, and bigger than they can ever achieve in their lifetime." Dr. Graham attributes this feeling of inadequacy vis-à-vis the 0.1 percent partly to greed. She points to work by economist Angus Deaton that shows the richer you are, the more covetous you become—the social science version of the biblical proverb about the eye of the needle. But she says crony capitalism is to blame, too. The middle-class achievers are the most frustrated in societies where getting to the top is seen as a function of connections rather than merit.

A more sympathetic rationale, advanced most prolifically by Cornell economist Robert Frank, is the problem of positional goods. These are products and services whose value is derived in part from their scarcity and how much everyone else wants them. If you have them, I don't. A place in the Harvard first-year class or a home in a desirable public school district is a positional good. An iPhone or a Gmail account is not. An appetite for some positional goods is easy to dismiss as part of the greed effect—a reservation at the hottest new restaurant, or buying a limited-edition handbag. But what about an organ transplant? Or the positional good that causes some of the greatest angst in the foothills of the 1 percent, an elite education?

The gap between the 1 percent and the 0.1 percent could have serious political consequences. Even in America, there were just 412 billionaires in 2007, and 134,888 taxpayers in the 0.1 percent. The 1 percent is bigger— with 749,375 taxpayers—and, with an average annual income of $486,395, it is not that far away from the wider 10 percent, with its 7.5 million taxpayers earning an average $128,560. These people at the bottom of the top of the income distribution are financially essential to the country and politically essential to those at the very top. If the super-elite lose their loyalty, it could become very isolated indeed.

Historically, in America the merely rich have strongly identified with the very rich. The strivers at the bottom of the 1 percent were just one big idea or one big job away from the very top, and, anyway, everyone belonged to the same upper middle class. They might be struggling to support their middle-class lifestyles month to month, but the 1 percent have liked to think of themselves as "soon to be rich." But there are a few signs that the nearly millionaires are starting to suspect the billionaires are getting an unfair deal. One sign is how "crony capitalism" has become the battle cry not just of Occupy Wall Street but also of Tea Party darling Sarah Palin and conservative intellectual Paul Ryan.

This nascent split between probusiness, promoney Americans of the bottom of the 1 percent and the 0.1 percent is in many ways more potentially incendiary than the antiestablishment idealism of Occupy Wall Street. We always knew the left was suspicious of high finance. What is surprising is that Wall Street's yeomen have become suspicious of their bosses.

Here's how Joshua Brown, a New York–based investment adviser to high-net-worth individuals, charitable foundations, and retirement plans responded to complaints by a number of Wall Street chiefs that they are being unjustly vilified in America today.

Brown's tirade, which he posted on his blog, *The Reformed Broker*, quickly went viral: "Not only do we not 'hate the rich' as you and other embubbled plutocrats have postulated, in point of fact, we love them," Brown wrote. "We love the success stories in our midst and it is a distinctly American trait to believe that we can all follow in the footsteps of the elite, even though so few of us ever actually do. So, no, we don't hate the rich. What we hate are the predators. . . . America hates unjustified privilege, it hates an unfair playing field and crony capitalism without the threat of bankruptcy, it hates privatized gains and socialized losses, it hates rule changes that benefit the few at the expense of the many, and it hates people who have been bailed out and don't display even the slightest bit of remorse or humbleness in the presence of so much suffering in the aftermath."

In a democratic age, the super-elite can survive if every millionaire is convinced he has a billionaire's baton in his knapsack. If that conviction breaks down, the battle of the millionaires versus the billionaires could move from Cairo and Kiev to London and New York.

WHERE ARE THE WOMEN?

For 47,745 of the 47,763 runners who competed in the New York Marathon in 2011, it was a co-ed race. Women ran alongside men, and as demanding sports such as endurance running have become socially acceptable for women, females formed an ever greater part of the pack. But for the first eighteen racers, the top 0.04 percent, the marathon is exactly as segregated as it was before 1971, when women were banned from racing more than ten miles on the theory that their delicate bodies weren't up to the strain.

Becoming a plutocrat is like being one of those eighteen men. This is not to suggest that women are somehow biologically precluded from breaking into the plutocracy, in the way that the female physique may never run a marathon as quickly as the male one. But the image is a way of illustrating a significant and rarely remarked-on aspect of the rise of the super-elite: it is almost entirely male. Consider the 2012 *Forbes* billionaire list. Just 104 of the 1,226 billionaires are women. Subtract the wives, daughters, and widows and you are left with a fraction of that already small number.

What's especially striking about this absence of women at the top is that it runs so strongly counter to the trend in the rest of society. Within the 99 percent, women are earning more money, getting more educated, and gaining more power. That's true around the world and across the social spectrum. If you aren't a plutocrat, you are increasingly likely to have a female boss, live in a household where the main breadwinner is female, and study in a class where the top pupils are girls. As the 99 percent has become steadily pinker, the 1 percent has remained an all-boys club. One way to understand the gap between the 1 percent and the rest is as a division of the world into a vast female-dominated middle class ruled by a male elite at the top.

Another window into how the gender divide sharpens at the very top comes from the Goldin and Katz Harvard study. College is one of the arenas the women of the middle class are conquering—more than half of all U.S. undergraduates are now female, and their grade point average is higher than that of their male peers. Young women are more likely to get their BAs and go on to graduate school. The recession has exacerbated the gender divide, with young women responding to a tough job market by going back to school and improving their skills. Young men have not. At Harvard, which released women from the apartheid of Radcliffe only in 1973, the incoming first-year class in 2004 included more women than men.

But as soon as they graduate, Harvard women's chances of getting to the very top decline because of the jobs they choose. Goldin and Katz found that finance and management were overwhelmingly the most lucrative fields, with financiers earning that whopping 195 percent premium. Men have responded to this incentive strongly—of the class of 1990, 38 percent of the men worked in management and finance fifteen years after graduating, compared to just 23 percent of the women. By 2007, the number of women starting off in finance or management had jumped to 43 percent, but a staggering 58 percent of the men had made that same choice. You can see the difference in their incomes: in 2005, 8 percent of Harvard men earned more than $1 million; just 2 percent of the women crossed that threshold.

Not too many people talk about the absence of women at the very top. That's partly because, in a fight that's been going on since the famous debates between Lenin and Bolshevik feminist Alexandra Kollontai, the left has a history of bullying women who dare to talk about gender at the apex of power. Doing so has been framed as a selfish concern of upper-class women, who are urged to focus their attention on the more deserving problems of their sisters at the bottom. As for the right, it has historically preferred to avoid discussion of gender and class altogether.

But the absence of women in the plutocracy is an important part of the culture of the 1 percent and a crucial way the very rich differ from everyone else. It is a powerful force in the workplace, where most plutocrats have no female peers. And it shapes their personal lives as well. The year 2009 was a watershed for the American workplace—it was the first time since data was collected that women outnumbered men on the country's payrolls. In 2010, about four in ten working wives were the chief breadwinners for their families.

The plutocracy, by contrast, still lives in the *Mad Men* era, and family life becomes more patriarchal the richer you get. In 2005, just over a quarter of taxpayers in the top 0.1 percent had a working spouse. For the 1 percent, the figure was higher, at 38 percent, but significantly lower than in the country as a whole. There's not a lot of mystery to these choices of the wives of the 0.1 percent, as I discovered at a dinner party when I sat next to a private equity investor. He was in his late thirties with no children, and as we chatted I learned that he had met his wife when they were both students at Yale Law School. But when I asked which firm she now worked at, I realized I had committed a faux pas. If your husband is earning $10 million a year, choosing the treadmill of billable hours really is rather bizarre. (It turns out she spends her time investing part of the family portfolio, studying art history, and decorating their Upper East Side town house.)

And it is graduates of Yale Law School and the like who are the housewives of the plutocrats. In 1979, nearly 8 percent of the 1 percent had spouses the IRS described as doing blue-collar or service sector jobs—governmentspeak for bosses married to their secretaries. That number has been falling ever since. What economists call assortive mating—the tendency to marry someone you resemble—is on the rise. But while the aggressive geeks of the super-elite are marrying their classmates rather than their secretaries, their highly educated wives are unlikely to work.

My own suspicion is that most plutocrats privately believe women don't make it to the top because something is missing. Most know better than to muse on this matter in public—they all remember, for instance, what that cost Larry Summers, who happens to have a sterling record of promoting the careers of his female protégés—but I can report an unguarded remark one private equity billionaire made to me. The problem, he said, wasn't that women weren't as smart or even as numerate as men; he had hired many women in starting positions who were as skilled as their male counterparts. But they still didn't have the royal jelly: "They don't have the killer instinct, they don't want to fight, they won't go for the jugular." By way of evidence, he described a subordinate who had cried when he told her she had made a mistake. You can't do that and win, he said.

———◆———

THREE

SUPERSTARS

A society in which knowledge workers dominate is under
threat from a new class conflict: between the large minority of
knowledge workers and the majority of people, who will make
their living traditionally, either by manual work, whether skilled
or unskilled, or by work in services, whether skilled or unskilled.

—Peter Drucker

It is probably a misfortune that . . . popular writers . . . have
defended free enterprise on the ground that it regularly rewards
the deserving, and it bodes ill for the future of the market order
that this seems to have become the only defense of it which is
understood by the general public. . . . It is therefore a real
dilemma to what extent we ought to encourage in the young the
belief that when they really try they will succeed, or should rather
emphasize that inevitably some unworthy will succeed and some
worthy fail.

—Friedrich Hayek

It is possible that intelligent tadpoles reconcile themselves to the
inconvenience of their position by reflecting that, though most of
them will live and die as tadpoles and nothing more, the more
fortunate of the species will one day shed their tails, distend their
mouths and stomachs, hop nimbly on to dry land, and croak
addresses to their former friends on the virtues by means of
which tadpoles of character and capacity can rise to be frogs.

—R. H. Tawney

The Intellectuals on the Road to Class Power

When Shelley described poets as "the unacknowledged legislators of the world," he was referring to the moral and imaginary power of the creative class, not suggesting that it actually controlled the machinery of the state or pulled the levers of the economy. But a samizdat manuscript written in 1973–74 and later smuggled out of communist Hungary asserted precisely that. *The Intellectuals on the Road to Class Power*, by novelist György Konrád and sociologist Ivan Szelényi, argued that Marx's vision of a communist state run by the working class, or indeed of an eventual utopia in which the state withered away entirely, had been perverted. Instead, a new class had seized power: the class of engineers, economists, physicists, and, yes, even poets—which is to say, the intellectuals.

Konrád and Szelényi's book was a revolutionary act—its authors retreated to a village in the Buda Hills to write it in an effort to evade the secret police, and they buried their manuscript in the garden every night, to protect it from being seized in a feared early morning raid. The book caused a predictable splash when it was published in the West in 1979, five years after it had been written—this was, after all, the beginning of the final triumphant chapter of the cold war, the year Ronald Reagan was elected and Leonid Brezhnev was starting the fifteenth year of his reign as general secretary of the Communist Party of the Soviet Union. Anything that discredited the so-called workers' paradise, particularly from the inside, was a geopolitical event.

The Intellectuals on the Road to Class Power built on the arguments of an even more groundbreaking work smuggled out of Eastern Europe a generation earlier: Milovan Djilas's *The New Class*. Writing in the seventies, Konrád and Szelényi were themselves members of the somewhat threadbare but socially cosseted socialist intelligentsia they described, though they were not members of the Communist Party. Djilas—Tito's right-hand man during the partisan struggle and his emissary to Stalin's Kremlin court—belonged to the earlier revolutionary generation. Djilas's book, which earned its writer a seven-year prison sentence in the same jail he had been sent to for his revolutionary activities in the 1930s, was an instant international sensation, and rightly so. It was the first time a senior Soviet bloc official publicly condemned the system he had helped to create. Written thirteen years after George Orwell had made the same charge in his allegorical *Animal Farm*, Djilas made the ideologically devastating argument that the so-called workers' state had simply replaced the old ruling bourgeoisie with a new class, the communist apparat. He even estimated the material gap between this new elite and the people it ruled, citing Soviet dissident Yuri Orlov's report that a *rayon* secretary—the head of a provincial or city party organization—earned about twenty-five times more than the average worker.

The important twist Konrád and Szelényi added to this analysis was that the rule of this new class actually amounted to a seizure of political and economic power by the intellectuals—heredity and military might determined power under feudalism; money and commercial acumen were the source of control under capitalism. Under communism, they asserted, technical skills and higher education were the most important defining characteristics of the new party elite.

There was a lot of truth to their analysis, and it is one reason some members of the old Eastern European and Soviet intelligentsias, not to mention their friends in the West, are nostalgic for the old order. But if you read *The Intellectuals on the Road to Class Power* today, the most striking paradox about this dissident dissection of Warsaw Pact socialism is how powerfully it applies to twenty-first-century global capitalism. For the intellectual class Konrád and Szelényi studied, highly educated technocrats, the collapse of communism, and the emergence of a global market economy turned out to be the true road to class power.

The language of twenty-first-century Western economists is rather less colorful than that of 1970s central European dissidents. That's why you won't find many references to the rise of the technocrats to class power in the American academic debate of the early twenty-first century. But there is intense study of the impact of "skill-biased technical change" on income distribution, particularly in the developed Western economies. The consensus, advanced most powerfully by MIT economist David Autor, is that skill-biased technical change has indeed brought the technocrats to class power. As Autor puts it, it has polarized the labor market, with huge rewards for those at the top, who have the skills and education to take advantage of new technologies, not much impact for those who do the low-paying "lousy" jobs at the bottom, and a hollowing out of the well-paying jobs in between that used to support the middle class.

There is, of course, a fierce debate about what is causing rising income inequality, and the most honest students of the phenomenon attribute it to a number of factors. But there is broad agreement that skill-biased technical change is a crucial, and possibly the crucial, factor. In a January 2012 speech about income inequality, Alan Krueger, a Princeton economist who now heads President Barack Obama's Council of Economic Advisers, reported one indicator of that consensus. In the mid-1990s he polled a non-random group of professional economists attending a conference at the New York Fed. They overwhelmingly named technological change as the main driver of income polarization—more than 40 percent said it was the chief cause. In a touching sign of humility, the second most popular explanation was "unknown." Third was globalization. Political shifts, like the decline in the minimum wage and the decline in unionization, came in behind these top three.

There's another reason the rise of the intellectuals to class power in global capitalism isn't always immediately apparent within that favored group. That's because not all of the highly educated are prospering equally. If you have a PhD in English literature, you probably don't feel you are a member of the ruling elite. And even within tribes whose training vaults them collectively into the 1 percent—like bankers, lawyers, or computer programmers—there's a twist to the impact of skills-biased technological change that lessens the sense of group prosperity. This is what economists call the "superstar" effect—the tendency of both technological change and globalization to create winner-take-all economic tournaments in many sectors and companies, where being the most successful in your field delivers huge rewards, but coming in second place, and certainly in fifth or tenth, has much less economic value.

The triumph of the nerds is intuitively obvious in the postindustrial economies of the developed West, where brains have had more value than brawn for a couple of generations. But in today's era of the twin gilded ages, the triumph of the intellectuals is a global phenomenon. The highly educated are in the vanguard of India's outsourcing miracle; the intellectuals, especially their "technical" branch, are very much in charge in communist China; and even the Russian oligarchs, who are better known in the West for their yachts and supermodel consorts, overwhelmingly have advanced degrees in math and physics.

The rise of the geeks, particularly the super-achievers among them, is a sharp break from the postwar era, when the robust economic recovery in the United States and western Europe was driven by the rise of a vast, and culturally dominant, middle class, much of it employed in blue-collar or relatively routine midlevel clerical, administrative, and managerial jobs. The disappearance of these opportunities, at a time when the super-smart are prospering as never before, is one reason for the populist antipathy toward the nerds. The impulse is strikingly bipartisan—the conservative Tea Party is every bit as hostile toward elites as is Occupy Wall Street, which has defined itself as the forum of the 99 percent.

Ironically—and frustratingly, for those in the discontented middle—the class power of the intellectuals is such that they are rising to the top of the political heap on both the left and the right. Indeed, at a time of fierce partisan conflict, one of the striking paradoxes is how much the champions of liberals and conservatives have in common: Mitt Romney and Barack Obama are both disciplined, dogged millionaires who describe their more popular wives as their better halves, hold degrees from Harvard Law School, and have a preference for data-driven arguments rather than emotional ones. Both men struggle to connect with the grassroots of their parties, coming across as cold and robotic.

You might call it the cognitive divide—the split between an evidence-based worldview and one rooted in faith or ideology—and it is one of the most important fault lines in America today. To his critics on the right, Obama is a socialist with dangerous foreign antecedents. To his critics on the left, he is a waffler with no real point of view and a craven desire to be liked. But the best explanation is that, like the rest of the rising intellectual class to which he belongs, the president is an empiricist. He wants to do what works, not what conforms to any particular ideology or what pleases any particular constituency. His core belief is a belief in facts.

Obama the empiricist is not the man who surged from behind to win the 2008 presidential election. That candidate was the Obama of soaring rhetoric, who promised hope and change. But the pragmatist has always been there. Writing in September 2008, several weeks before the presidential elections, Cass Sunstein, who has gone on to serve in the White House, had this to say about his candidate: "Above all, Obama's form of pragmatism is heavily empirical; he wants to know what will work." Word crunchers found that the president's 2009 inaugural address was the first one to use the term "data" and only the second to mention "statistics."

That cognitive approach is one reason Obama attracted so much support, especially among the younger generation, on Wall Street and in Silicon Valley. That wasn't some sentimental betrayal of class interests—what Lenin is said to have called the useful idiocy of the capitalists who bankrolled the Bolsheviks; it was a recognition that Obama was an almost perfect embodiment of the super-elite that rules today's global economy. Obama is a data-driven technocrat, and so are the traders and the Internet entrepreneurs. As one insider who is equally familiar with Wall Street and with Washington, D.C., told me: "You want your money managed by people who are responsive to evidence, who care about results, and who understand that the world is an uncertain place. Obama wants to get his economic advice from the same sorts of people."

By training, by temperament, and by life experience, Mitt Romney, too, belongs squarely to the empiricist camp; it is hard to make millions in private equity without appreciating the power of data. What looks like flip-flopping to the Republican base can equally be understood as Romney's effort to bridge the cognitive divide.

The super-geeks don't just rule Wall Street, Silicon Valley, Bangalore, and Beijing. They are in charge in Washington, too—no matter which party wins.

ELIZABETH BILLINGTON—DIVA FOR THE FIRST GILDED AGE

Elizabeth Billington was a diva, a celebrity—and a superstar. Today, many music scholars judge her to be the greatest English soprano; contemporary critics described her as "the Goddess of Song." At the invitation of the king, she sang at the Naples opera house, then the most prestigious in the world, where she was the heroine of a new opera, *Ines di Castro*, written especially for her. Her Italian tour was such a success that after her recovery from an illness in Venice the opera house was illuminated for three nights. In Milan she was warmly received by the empress Joséphine.

At the height of her fame, Sir Joshua Reynolds, at the time Britain's most popular portraitist, painted Mrs. Billington as Saint Cecilia, about to be crowned with laurels by one cherub, and listening to the singing of four others. The woman on the canvas has a gleaming mane of hair, a perfect oval face, and large, expressive eyes, but her fans complained that it didn't do her justice. "How could I help it?" Reynolds is said to have challenged his critics. "I could not paint her voice." When Haydn, a lifelong friend, saw the painting, he told Reynolds: "It is like, but there is a strange mistake. You have made her listening to the angels; you should have made the angels listening to her."

Mrs. Billington was famous among the hoi polloi, too. When an unauthorized biography of her was published on January 14, 1792, it sold out by three p.m. The sensational highlight: intimate letters she had written to her mother, containing vivid accounts of, as Haydn described them, "her amours," a group rumored to include the Duke of Sussex and even the Prince of Wales.

Her talent and her celebrity and the international demand for her performances gave her pricing power. In 1801, when Mrs. Billington returned to Britain after seven years in Italy, the managers of both Drury Lane and Covent Garden, London's two most prestigious opera houses, fought a bidding war for her voice. Mrs. Billington finessed that struggle with an unprecedented compromise: she sang alternately at both houses, and was paid £3,000 for the season, plus a £600 bonus, and a £500 contract for her violinist brother to lead the orchestra whenever she performed. Her total income that year was believed to exceed £10,000, enough to employ five hundred farm laborers, and as much as the annual rents collected by Elizabeth Bennet's opulently wealthy Mr. Darcy, who made his fictional debut twelve years later.

Writing nearly a century later, in 1875, Alfred Marshall, the father of modern economics, used Mrs. Billington as an example of one of the consequences of the unprecedented increase in national GDP that Britain was just beginning to experience at the turn of the nineteenth century, thanks to the industrial revolution. Growing prosperity, Marshall believed, meant richer paydays for the most skilled practitioners of every trade and profession, even as the industrial revolution drove down the incomes of ordinary artisans. He was watching the birth of the superstar economy.

Here's how Marshall, the first truly sympathetic student of the economic impact of the industrial revolution, described what was happening: "The relative fall in the incomes to be earned by moderate ability . . . is accentuated by the rise in those that are obtained by men of extraordinary ability. There was never a time at which moderately good oil paintings sold more cheaply than now, and . . . at which first-rate paintings sold so dearly."

One cause of this premium on super-talent, Marshall believed, was the "general growth of wealth" created by the industrial revolution. The national tide was rising, and the boats of the superstars were rising the most quickly with it. This broader economic transformation, Marshall argued, "enables some barristers to command very high fees; for a rich client whose reputation, or fortune, or both, are at stake will scarcely count any price too high to secure the services of the best man he can get: and it is this again that enables jockeys and painters and musicians of exceptional ability to get very high prices."

Of course, the painters, musicians, jockeys, and barristers Marshall describes weren't the first talented artists and professionals to command a premium for their talents. China's Ming Dynasty, which ruled the Middle Kingdom from the fourteenth to the seventeenth centuries, prized painting; Qiu Ying was once paid one hundred ounces of silver to paint a long hand scroll as an eightieth-birthday gift for the mother of a wealthy patron. Artists were the superstars of Renaissance Italy, profiting from the rise of a new commercial elite much as Mrs. Billington did. Nor has culture been the only arena in which the superstars can earn huge rewards: the lords and princes of the Middle Ages bid for the services of Europe's best mercenary knights; modernizing Russian sovereigns, such as Peter and Catherine, paid top ruble for Western technical and military expertise.

But Marshall was one of the first to point out that the industrial revolution had made superstars shine more brightly than ever, both by increasing the prices top talent could command and by pushing down the relative wages of many of the artisans and professionals lower down the ladder, through new technologies and more widely diffused skills.

As the industrial revolution gathered strength, the later phenomenon was part of the conventional wisdom about what was happening in English society. One of Marshall's examples—sound familiar?—was the declining wages of the clerical class: "A striking instance is that of writing . . . when all can write, the work of copying, which used to earn higher wages than almost any kind of manual labour, will rank among unskilled trades." Most of us are more familiar with a more violent episode in the redundancy of once valuable skills—the machine-busting revolt of the Luddites, hand-loom weavers who protested the introduction of wide-framed, automated looms that made their trade pointless. The Luddite protests began in 1811, a decade after Mrs. Billington's £10,000 triumph.

Marshall had the brilliance to understand that the two processes were connected—the mechanization that put the hand-loom weavers out of work was a tragedy for those individuals, but it was part of a broader economic transformation that greatly enriched the country as a whole. Among the beneficiaries of that growing national wealth were superstars like Mrs. Billington.

Already in the nineteenth century, the most successful superstars capitalized on—and, indeed, cultivated—an international market for their services: Mrs. Billington started her serious professional career in Ireland, and then made the jump back home to London. Her debut in Italy, the most prestigious music market in the world at the time, was carefully orchestrated with the help of the aristocratic English friends her London fame had won her. Mrs. Billington's subsequent Italian success increased her cachet even further, and when she returned to London she was able to command a much higher fee.

But even though Mrs. Billington was a beneficiary of globalization, Marshall believed there was a physical limit to how much she, or any other superstar, could capitalize on the international market for her services. After all, as he observed with the asperity of someone pointing out the obvious, "The number of persons who can be reached by a human voice is strictly limited."

Marshall's remark about the natural constraint on the income Mrs. Billington and her successors could demand is just a footnote on page 728 of his magnum opus. But it has had a much cited afterlife in the economic literature because it is the rousing conclusion to a seminal 1981 paper by University of Chicago economist Sherwin Rosen, in which he explained how the twentieth-century technology revolution had further magnified the income of superstars. After quoting Marshall's reference to Mrs. Billington and the impossibility of scaling her work, Rosen argued: "Even adjusted for 1981 prices, Mrs. Billington must be a pale shadow beside Pavarotti. Imagine her income had radio and phonograph records existed in 1801!"

CHARLIE CHAPLIN—IT GETS BETTER

In fact, when it came to capitalizing on the financial potential of new technology, Pavarotti came late to the game. The shift had begun nearly a century earlier, with the invention of the phonograph, the radio, and, crucially, movies. Consider the career of Charlie Chaplin. Born in 1889, roughly 125 years after Elizabeth Billington, he was, like her, a native Londoner with a prodigy's talent for performance. Mrs. Billington had made her debut at age nine; by the time Chaplin was nine years old he was on the road, rehearsing and performing in two or three shows a day. His appeal, too, was international—he made his first U.S. tour in 1910, traveling the country for two years. But, for all his energy, like Mrs. Billington, in his live performances he was constrained by the physical reach of the human voice and the distance the human eye could see.

But Chaplin was lucky. In 1867 American inventor William Lincoln patented a device he called "the wheel of life," through which animated pictures could be viewed. The motion picture era really took off after 1895 (six years after Chaplin's birth), when French brothers Louis and Auguste Lumière invented the *cinématographe*, the first portable motion picture camera, projector, and printer. Public adoption wasn't immediate—a disappointed Louis Lumière fretted that "the cinema is an invention without a future"—but within a generation, the way people were entertained had been transformed. In 1900, nearly all spectator entertainment was provided by live performers. By 1938, live acts accounted for just 8 percent of all public entertainment. In the mid-1920s, before the introduction of sound in movies, Americans spent $1.33 per capita on theater, versus $3.59 on movies; by 1938, the spending had further tilted in the direction of film—down to $0.45 on live performances and up to $5.11 at the movies.

Chaplin became the first global superstar of this new medium. He had an uncertain start—Mack Sennett, Chaplin's first studio boss, deemed the actor's film debut in the 1914 picture *Making a Living* "a costly mistake." But that same year Chaplin also created the character of "the Tramp" for a series of Keystone movies. The character and the actor almost instantly became global celebrities—elsewhere in the world the Tramp took on such names as Charlot, Der Vagabund, and Carlitos. Just two years after the Tramp's debut, Chaplin was enough of a superstar to command $670,000 to produce a dozen two-reel comedies over the next year for the Mutual Film Corporation. Adjusted for inflation, that was roughly double Mrs. Billington's £10,000 fee in 1801.

Technology had created a new way for live performers to become superstars. In Alfred Marshall's world, superstars had emerged thanks to the increased wealth of society as a whole, particularly its richest members. That meant lawyers, doctors, jockeys, painters, and opera singers could demand higher fees of their ever wealthier clients.

But Marshall's superstars couldn't benefit from one of the great innovations of the industrial revolution—mass production. They were limited by the reach of the human voice. (Thanks to the printing press, writers were something of an important exception. In 1859, Anthony Trollope, a successful writer but not quite a superstar, was paid £1,000 for the novel that became *Framley Parsonage*, provided he could write it in six weeks.) That was why, in Marshall's view, the bigger winners of the industrial age were businessmen. They were the ones who could take advantage of "the development of new facilities for communication, by which men, who have once attained a commanding position, are enabled to apply their constructive or speculative genius to undertakings vaster, and extending over a wider area, than ever before."

Sherwin Rosen understood that, in the twentieth century, culture had been industrialized, too. Advances in communications technology had allowed talented individuals to take advantage of the same economies of scale: "The phenomenon of Superstars, wherein relatively small numbers of people earn enormous amounts of money and dominate the activities in which they engage, seems to be increasingly important in the modern world." The key to the shift, Rosen argued, was "personal market scale" and the power of new technologies to increase the size of that personal market. Like nineteenth-century industrialists, the superstars of the twentieth century reached vast markets, and because technology and volume drastically reduced the cost per unit or per performance, they created new markets, too.

New technology squeezed out the old, but it also increased the overall size of the market. Live performance—Mrs. Billington's only profession, and Charlie Chaplin's first one—accounted for a smaller piece of the entertainment pie. But thanks to movies and the radio, people devoted more of their time to commercial entertainment, creating a bigger market for the top performers.

Writing in 1981, Rosen, the inventor of the modern theory of what he called "the economics of superstars," knew the technology revolution was still unfolding. He ends his paper wondering what impact the coming wave of technology would have on his superstars: "What changes in the future will be wrought by cable, video cassettes and home computers?"

The Internet wasn't featured on Rosen's list—its commercial introduction was still a few years away—but once it began to make itself felt as a mass phenomenon, there were a lot of good reasons to think this new technology would be the one that would bring an end to superstar economics. This, in the term popularized by its most visible advocate, Chris Anderson, is the theory of the long tail. As Anderson argued in his 2004 essay of that name, the long tail is "an entirely new economic model for the media and entertainment industries, one that is just beginning to show its power. . . . If the 20th century entertainment industry was about hits, the 21st will be equally about misses." Anderson's point was that technology meant the end of the era of the blockbuster and the superstar; instead the new century would be the golden age of the niche artist and small audience.

It hasn't quite worked out that way. While a great business can be built by bringing together millions of sales along the long tail—think Google— for individuals, the income gap between the superstars and everyone else is greater than ever. We see that in the overall income distribution, with the top 1 percent earning around 17 percent of the national income, and we see it within specific professions—in banking, in law, in sports, in entertainment, even in a quotidian profession like dentistry—those at the top are pulling ahead of everyone else. This superstar economics is one of the reasons we are seeing the emergence of the global super-elite.

ALFRED MARSHALL IS VINDICATED

Part of what is happening is an intensification of the rising-tide effect first noticed by Marshall more than a century ago. As the world economy grows, and as the super-elite, in particular, get richer, the superstars who work for the super-rich can charge super fees.

Consider the 2009 legal showdown between Hank Greenberg and AIG, the insurance giant he had built. It was a high-stakes battle, as AIG accused Greenberg, through a privately held company, Starr International, of misappropriating $4.3 billion worth of assets. For his defense, Greenberg hired David Boies. With his trademark slightly ratty Lands' End suits (ordered a dozen at a time by his office online), his midwestern background, his proud affection for Middle American pastimes like craps, and his severe dyslexia (he didn't learn how to read until he was in the third grade), Boies comes across as neither a superstar nor a member of the super-elite. But he is both.

Boies and his eponymous firm earned a reputed $100 million for the nine-month job of defending Greenberg. That was one of the richest fees earned in a single litigation. Yet, for Greenberg, it was a terrific deal. When you have $4.3 billion at risk, $100 million—only 2.3 percent of the total—just isn't that much money. (Further sweetening the transaction was the judge's eventual ruling that AIG, then nearly 80 percent owned by the U.S. government, was liable for up to $150 million of Greenberg's legal fees, but he didn't know that when he retained Boies.)

It is this logic of big numbers that is driving up the fees of Boies and a small cadre of elite lawyers. The willingness of richer clients, with more at stake, to pay higher fees is why even those superstars who aren't directly affected by globalization or the technology revolution can nevertheless benefit from them. Boies has never lived outside the United States, speaks only English, travels overseas for an annual biking holiday in southern Europe, and has never appeared in a non-American court. He is something of a Luddite, as well—he sends fewer than a dozen e-mails a week and was only recently persuaded by his wife to adopt an iPad, which he mostly uses to check stock prices. But because globalization (Hank Greenberg is one of the pioneers of globalization, nearly as at home in Beijing as he is in Manhattan) and technology have made his clients rich, they have made Boies a superstar, too.

If you are a plutocrat, there is a sound economic rationale for paying a brilliant litigator like David Boies such a premium. But it is not just the stellar providers of business services, like lawyers, who profit from the rise of the super-elite. Purveyors of luxury, like interior designers, are becoming superstars, too. Michael Smith redecorated the Oval Office and the East Wing of the White House in 2009, but his most famous commission to date turned out to be his $1.2 million face-lift of the Manhattan waterfront office of John Thain, then the CEO of Merrill Lynch. The job made headlines in 2009, when Bank of America, which had rescued a struggling Merrill, got a $45 billion bailout from the U.S. government. Suddenly, Smith's $800,000 fee, and some of his big-ticket purchases, including $87,000 for "area rugs" and a $35,000 antique commode—paid for by the company— became symbols of plutocratic excess. Those infamous furnishings are also an example of how the emergence of the global plutocracy is creating a class of superstar artists and professionals, the best and luckiest of whom can become plutocrats in their own right.

Another pair of winners is Candy and Candy, the London-based brothers whose opulent interior design business expanded into property development. Property is the ultimate local good, but it has also allowed Candy and Candy to surf the waves of the twin gilded ages. Candy and Candy's star 2011 venture turned out to be a play on the rise of the global super-elite. The list of buyers at One Hyde Park, a 385,000-square-foot apartment building next to the Mandarin Oriental and overlooking London's Hyde Park, is a better directory to the international plutocracy than the fat, bricklike facebooks distributed each year to attendees at the World Economic Forum. The biggest place, occupying some twenty-five thousand square feet, was sold for $223 million to Rinat Akhmetov, a coal and metallurgy oligarch from eastern Ukraine. Other buyers include Vladimir Kim, who made his money in Kazakh copper; Sheikh Hamad bin Jassim bin Jabr al-Thani, the prime minister of Qatar; Irish property developer Ray Grehan; and Russian real estate magnates Kirill Pisarev and Yuri Zhukov.

Candy and Candy are an example of how the twin gilded ages—the rise of the plutocrats not just in the West but also in the emerging markets—has expanded the market for the superstars who work for them and thus driven up the prices those at the very top of their professions can command. You can see the power of globalization in the divergent careers of two North American architects born just twenty years apart. Gordon Bunshaft was born in 1909 in Buffalo, New York. Frank Gehry was born in 1929, a hundred miles to the north, in Toronto. Both had Eastern European roots—Bunshaft's parents were Russian Jews; Gehry's people were Polish Jews. Both went on to win the Pritzker Prize, architecture's highest honor. But you have almost certainly heard of Gehry, and you probably haven't heard of Bunshaft. The difference is the emerging markets and their first gilded age.

Bunshaft's signature construction is Lever House, a clean-lined modernist rectangle that presides over Park Avenue just across the street from the Four Seasons restaurant, the lunchtime canteen of Manhattan's princes of finance. The architect designed just a few buildings outside North America, and one of those, the National Commercial Bank in Jeddah, was built at the very end of his career, in 1983, when he was seventy-four. Globalization had arrived, but too late to make much of a difference to Gordon Bunshaft. But for Gehry, who began his work just twenty years later, globalization was the making of his career. His first foreign commission, the Vitra Design Museum in Germany, was in 1989, six years after Bunshaft's big international gig. But what was a nightcap for Bunshaft was the main course for Gehry. Since 1989, half of his work has been outside the United States, including landmark buildings like the Guggenheim Museum in Bilbao.

Gehry is more than an architect—he is a starchitect, a neologism coined to describe the small band of elite international architects whose personal brands transcend their buildings. He has appeared in Apple's iconic black-and-white "Think Different" ad campaign, parodied himself on the *Simpsons*, and helped Arthur and his friends build a tree house on the children's cartoon. He has even designed a hat for Lady Gaga. The difference between Bunshaft, an award-winning North American architect, and Gehry, a multimillionaire global starchitect, is the difference between living in the postwar era of the Great Compression, when the gap between the 1 percent and everyone else shrank, and living during the twin gilded ages, when globalization and the technology revolution are creating an international plutocracy and therefore a fantastically wealthy global clientele for superstars like Gehry.

Here's how Eric Schmidt, then the CEO of Google, explained the impact of the global plutocracy on the prices of luxury goods, and on the fortunes of those who produce and sell them. "I'm a pilot, so I understand airplane economics very well. For a while, high-end private air jets went up 50 to 80 percent higher than they should be by any modeling, because the Russians all entered the market," he recalled. "In these wealth markets, the numbers are small enough that you can watch the real economics. You know, there's three bidders for one property kind of thing. . . . In California ten years ago, during the bubble, there was a specific street in Atherton where all the prices doubled because of a set of offers that a number of executives who no longer live in the Bay Area made. They had so much discretionary income at the time, and they needed a house, so boom, right?"

If you understand the economic cycles of the plutocrats, Schmidt explained, you can become pretty rich yourself: "There's another IPO cycle going to happen off companies like Facebook. And those companies are predominantly headquartered in a number of cities. Those cities will have scarcity of some things those people, newly arrived, need. The first thing you need is a house, okay? So, if you want to make some short-term money, buy the assets that will be bid up by the people when they get their money six months after the IPO.

"There's obviously negative consequences from all of this. I'm not endorsing it. I'm just trying to describe it."

Already in the nineteenth century, Marshall noticed that the rising tide of prosperity wasn't lifting the boats of all artists and professionals—those "moderately good oil paintings" had never been as cheap while the "first-rate" ones had never "sold so dearly." More than a century later that winner-take-all effect has become even more pronounced in the professions whose superstars are prospering from the rise of the global super-elite.

A good example is the law. In 1950, the median salary for American lawyers working in private practice was $50,000 in today's dollars. Lawyers working at firms with nine or more partners enjoyed a median income of around $200,000 in today's dollars.

By today's standards, though, that differential feels practically socialist. In 2011, the highest-paid partners at America's top firms earned more than $10 million a year; the average salary of a partner in a law firm was $640,000. A similar chasm is opening between partners within firms. In the 1950s, the highest-paid partner at a Wall Street law firm earned double, or maybe triple, what his lowest-paid partner earned, and the main difference was seniority. In 2011, America's most aggressively expanding law firms paid their stars ten times what the average partner earned.

That is just the gap between partners within a single elite firm. The difference between star partners and those lower down in the legal profession has become a chasm. In 2011, a year when top partner paydays exceeded $10 million and more than one hundred U.S. lawyers were on the record as charging more than $1,000 an hour (David Boies's hourly rate is reportedly more than $1,220), the average starting salary for a law school graduate was $84,111 and the average lawyer earned $130,490. This trend is increasing. More and more law firms are adopting a "permanent associate" or domestic outsourcing model, in which they employ experienced lawyers at associate pay rates in non-partner-track jobs. (One firm, DLA Piper, will bill its domestic outsourced lawyers at around a hundred dollars an hour.)

Part of what is going on is the economics of the plutonomy. As the global super-elite pulls ahead of everyone else, the demand for luxury services is exceeding the demand for low-rent ones. This, remember, was the investing thesis the Citigroup inventors of "plutonomics" devised—Gucci is doing better than Walmart; outstanding oil paintings are appreciating in value more quickly than moderately good ones; the demand for David Boies is outstripping the demand for associates.

And even as the growing demand for high-end services is putting a premium on legal superstars, some of the other forces at work in the twenty-first-century economy are pushing down the incomes of those in the middle.

Technology helps David Boies—mostly by making his clients richer. But it is driving down the incomes of more junior lawyers and creating less of a demand for their services as law firms discover ways to computerize work that was once done by well-paid lawyers. The most advanced example of this trend is e-discovery. In 2010, DLA Piper faced a court-imposed deadline of searching through 570,000 documents in one week. The firm, which has expanded from its Baltimore base to become the biggest law firm in the world, hired Clearwell, a Silicon Valley e-discovery company. Clearwell's software did the job in two days. DLA Piper lawyers spent one day going through the results. After three days of work, the firm responded to the judge's order with 3,070 documents. A decade ago, that job would have eaten up hundreds of billable hours and taken weeks if not months. (Meanwhile, DLA Piper, one of the law firms with a nine-to-one differential between its star partners and the rest, in 2011 poached Jamie Wareham, a high-profile Washington lawyer, partly thanks to compensation of reportedly about $5 million in his first year.)

Globalization is having a similar, two-speed impact on lawyers. For the superstars, it is one of the forces creating richer clients, bigger cases, and fatter fees. But at the bottom, cheaper emerging market lawyers are undercutting the salaries of Western lawyers, just as outsourcing has brought down costs—and wages—in manufacturing and more routine services like call center work. One example is Pangea3, an Indian legal process outsourcing firm, which recently opened offices in the United States. Employing hundreds of lawyers who work around-the-clock shifts, Pangea3 does basic, repetitive legal work like drafting contracts and reviewing documents. Its clients have included blue-chip companies like American Express, GE, Sony, Yahoo!, and Netflix. This is "Manhattan work at Mumbai prices," as the *American Bar Association Journal* put it in a recent headline.

In the age of the global super-elite, even dentists can be superstars. That's the only way to describe Bernard Touati, the Moroccan-born French dentist who has parlayed fixing the teeth of the plutocrats, starting with the Russian oligarchs, into a superstar career of his own. Roman Abramovich, the Siberian oil oligarch, paid Touati to fly regularly to Moscow to fix his teeth—and installed a dentist's chair in his office specially for the job. Dr. Touati treated Mikhail Khodorkovsky, once Russia's richest man before Putin sent him to Siberia, and he brightens the smiles of oligarchs' wives, like oil and banking baron Mikhail Fridman's. He treats the Western super-elite, too—New York–based designer Diane von Furstenberg is a patient, as is Madonna.

Touati's super-rich patient list is an example of how, thanks to the Marshall effect, the plutonomy is a self-sustaining global economy, largely insulated from the rest of us. Russian oligarchs create a superstar French dentist; Wall Street bankers and Arab sheikhs, superstar interior designers. Whether your skill is tooth enamel or fabric swatches, if you make it into the superstar league you can benefit from the concentration of wealth in the hands of a small, global business elite. And whether you got your start in western Siberia or the American Midwest, once you join the super-elite you patronize the same dentist, interior designer, art curator. That's how, from the inside, the plutonomy becomes a cozy global village.

Sherwin Rosen Is Vindicated, Too

Providing superstar services to the plutocrats is one way to join them. But an even more powerful driver of twenty-first-century superstar economics is the way that globalization and technology have allowed some superstars— the Mrs. Billingtons—to achieve global scale and earn the commensurate global fortunes. This is the superstar effect that Sherwin Rosen was most interested in, and it is both the most visible and the easiest to understand. These superstars are the direct beneficiaries of the twin gilded ages.

Thanks to the Internet, Lady Gaga reaches hundreds of millions more listeners than Mrs. Billington did. Her 2011 single "Born This Way" sold one million copies in five days. In 2011, when Lady Gaga topped the *Forbes* Celebrity 100 list, she had sold some twenty-three million albums and sixty-four million singles worldwide. Between May 2010 and May 2011, she performed in 137 shows in twenty-five countries, earning $170 million in gross revenue. *Forbes* estimated Lady Gaga's 2010 earnings at $90 million, over eighteen hundred times the typical U.S. family income. Mrs. Billington's fabulous £10,000 income in 1801—a fee so extravagant that Alfred Marshall used it as shorthand for superstar remuneration nearly a century later—was two hundred times the average British farm laborer's income at the time.

There isn't much mystery to why Lady Gaga is worth several Mrs. Billingtons. Each one was the leading diva of her time, and each one had an international reputation. But the only way to listen to Mrs. Billington was in person; Lady Gaga can be heard and seen by anyone with an Internet connection. Technology and globalization have given Lady Gaga access to a much bigger audience and she is consequently a much bigger star.

Superstar actors and athletes are beneficiaries of the same forces. In his own lifetime, Charlie Chaplin went from the physical stage to the silver screen and his earnings accordingly multiplied a thousandfold. But he was underpaid compared to today's movie stars. Contrast Chaplin's $670,000 income in 1916–1917 with Leonardo DiCaprio's $77 million payday in 2010–2011—adjusted for inflation, DiCaprio earned six times as much. Economies of scale have similarly enriched sports stars. Mickey Mantle, the New York Yankees star hitter, earned about $100,000 a season in the mid-1960s. Compare that with Alex Rodriguez, the Yankees star fifty years later, who made $30 million in 2012. Adjusted for inflation, Rodriguez's earnings are fifty times more than Mantle's. The gap between the superstars and the rank and file has increased, too. Mantle earned less than five times the baseball average; Rodriguez earns ten times more than the average major leaguer.

What is particularly striking about these Rosen superstars is that they have become richer even as the Internet has weakened the businesses that once supported them. Singers like Lady Gaga have never done better, yet the music business has been eviscerated by the Internet. Movie studios have also been weakened even as their stars do better than ever. Athletes can earn millions while their teams go broke.

Superstars have stayed on top partly by cashing in on their technology-driven celebrity with lucrative in-person performances. Lady Gaga earns much of her income from her live acts. The same is true of the other best-paid singers of 2011—U2, Bon Jovi, Elton John, and Paul McCartney. All of them earned more than $65 million, and all of them depended heavily on the revenues from live shows.

What we are seeing is the Rosen effect and the Marshall effect enhancing each other. Cheap and effective communication has allowed a few performers to achieve global celebrity more quickly and at a greater scale than ever. At twenty-five, Lady Gaga had sold sixty-four million singles around the world. But she had a slow start compared to Justin Bieber, who, at sixteen, produced a video that has now been viewed nearly 750 million times.

The paradox is that much of the technology that has made Justin Bieber and Lady Gaga famous doesn't make them rich. In 2012, the most powerful way the two stars connected with their fans was Twitter—Lady Gaga had more than twenty-five million followers (known as "little monsters"); Bieber had more than twenty-three million "Beliebers." Those tweets don't make money, but they create an audience for the live acts, which do.

And those in-person performances are an example of the Marshall effect on a global scale. Just as an England that was growing rich could afford to fund lavish productions at Drury Lane and Covent Garden—and a competition between the two that drove up Mrs. Billington's fees—so the rising middle class in emerging markets and the rising global super-elite are creating affluent audiences for today's celebrity performers. Global scale is essential to the economics of today's superstars: in 2010, Lady Gaga performed in twenty-nine countries, U2 in fifteen, Elton John in sixteen, and Bon Jovi in fifteen. We may think of these musicians as products of mass culture, but their shows are elite events. The average ticket price at Lady Gaga's *Born This Way* show was more than a hundred dollars.

In a study of concert ticket prices, economist Alan Krueger found that in the two decades between 1982 and 2003, a time when first music videos, especially as celebrated on MTV, and then digital sharing technology, as pioneered by Napster, extended the reach of top performers, the share of concert revenue taken by the top 5 percent of entertainers increased by more than 20 percent, from 62 percent to 84 percent. The top 1 percent did even better: their share more than doubled, from 26 percent in 1981 to 56 percent in 2003. (By contrast, the top 1 percent in the United States overall earned 14.6 percent of the income in 1998.)

More intimate deals with the billionaire class are a smaller, but significant, source of income for superstar performers. Arkady, a Russian businessman in his thirties, reportedly paid Lady Gaga $1 million to appear in her "Alejandro" music video. And even stars a little past their prime can earn fat fees for personal appearances for the plutocrats. This seems to have become the standard for the big birthdays of private equity chiefs, their equivalent of baking themselves a homemade birthday cake. In 2011, Leon Black, the founder of private equity group Apollo, celebrated his sixtieth with a birthday bash that included a million-dollar performance by Elton John. (In a global economy, these gigs can sometimes go badly wrong, as Hilary Swank discovered when she agreed to attend Chechen strongman Ramzan Kadyrov's thirty-fifth birthday celebrations in Grozny, in exchange for a six-figure fee. She was roundly—and rightly—denounced for sharing a stage with a warlord notorious for torturing and killing his opponents.)

The people a previous generation might have called public intellectuals also make much of their living by leveraging the Rosen effects of mass popularity and the Marshall effect of earning lavish fees from a plutocracy that can afford to pay them. Malcolm Gladwell, the world's most influential business writer, is an example. He is paid millions to write books. But he makes almost as much—and with less effort—by giving $100,000 speeches. Groups he has addressed include a gathering of Blackstone's investors and the Pebble Beach legal conference, the Davos of the world's top lawyers.

You don't have to top the bestseller list to profit from the super-elite speaking circuit. Charlie Cook, the political analyst and editor of the twenty-eight-year-old *Cook Political Report*, "subsidizes" his journalism by giving speeches, an activity he says is "very, very lucrative," even if it can be wearing to "haul my tired old ass to three different cities a week."

This interplay of Marshall effects—in-person performances for a society growing more affluent—and Rosen effects—the power of technology-driven scale—is creating a superstar effect beyond what we are accustomed to thinking of as the performing arts.

Consider chefs. The rise of culinary superstars is certainly an example of Alfred Marshall's trickle-down wealth from the super-rich. Plutocrats not only insist on the best barristers and the finest jockeys, they also want to dine at El Bulli, with its €250 prix fixe meal (or at whatever its successor turns out to be). And there, you might think, it would end. After all, preparing a delicious meal, like arguing a case in court or riding a racehorse, is a hands-on service, which can't be duplicated and scaled in the way an aria or a drama can be.

For superstars, that is a serious financial constraint. One way celebrity chefs are getting around it is by transforming their trade from a high-end personal service to a scalable mass performance. Thus Mario Batali first shot to fame as the iconoclastic founder of Po, a trattoria in New York's West Village. But, even at fifteen dollars a plate, physical dishes of ravioli can get you only so far. Batali became a real superstar in 1997, when he signed a contract to host his own show, *Molto Mario*, on the Food Network. The celebrity his TV show created not only sent diners to his restaurants, it allowed Batali to go mass retail—as the author of bestselling books, producer of his own line of pasta sauces, co-owner of a vineyard, and partner in

Eataly, an Italian grocer, wine store, and cluster of restaurants kitty-corner to Manhattan's Flatiron building. If your client is visible enough, superstar cooks don't even need a retail presence to build a second career in the mass media. Consider Art Smith, Oprah Winfrey's personal chef until 2007, who used that pedigree to publish three cookbooks, open three restaurants, and rent out his celebrity by writing menus for other restaurants.

You could observe how superstar chefs benefit from both the Rosen and Marshall effects at a super-elite meal hosted by consulting firm Booz Allen Hamilton on a balmy late June evening in 2011 at the Aspen Meadows Resort during the Aspen Ideas Festival, where this evening's guests included, among others, Alan Greenspan. "Curated" food has become part of the super-elite lifestyle, so for this "meal of a lifetime" the consulting firm flew in Craig Stoll, co-owner and cofounder of the Delfina group of restaurants in San Francisco, so he and his kitchen staff could prepare supper. Each course was "narrated" by Corby Kummer, a senior editor and food writer at the *Atlantic*.

There was a lot to narrate. The second course, for example, of Berkshire pork *arista* with butter beans and grappa-preserved cherries, was served along with the commentary that the meat came from Niman Ranch, a producer so ethical its founder's third wife was a vegetarian and author of a book called *Righteous Porkchop*. The sour cherries had been purchased at the San Francisco farmers' market by Delfina staff—a particular coup because this year's crop was poor and cherries were therefore scarce—and marinated in homemade Delfina grappa. The blackberries and raspberries served for dessert—the *frutti del bosco* accompanying Delfina's buttermilk panna cotta—had traveled from San Francisco to Aspen that morning in carry-on bags packed into the overhead luggage compartments by Delfina staff. Most of the diners applauded when Kummer related that final detail.

Cooking a private meal for Booz Allen Hamilton and its guests is one way that Craig Stoll and superstar chefs like him benefit from the broader rise of the super-elite. But in an aside that revealed the extent to which simultaneously catering to a mass audience has become part of the everyday menu for celebrity cooks, Kummer concluded the meal by informing the replete audience that Stoll hadn't written a book "yet," so as a keepsake of their meal of a lifetime—their *ricordi del soggiorno*—the diners would have to make do with colorful Italian-style ceramic plates depicting a signature Delfina seafood dish. The wife of one diner, who was traveling back to Westchester the following morning on a private plane ("wheels up at nine a.m."), was persuaded to take the dish home when she was shown that Delfina had encased it in bubble wrap and packed it tightly in an air-travel-friendly cardboard box.

Cooks are just the latest tradesmen to understand that the most powerful way to cash in on superstar talent is to strike the right combination of very expensive personal service for the elite with a cheaper, mass-produced version. Tailors probably got there first. Their first revolutionary was Charles Frederick Worth. An Englishman who moved to Paris in 1825, Worth was the Elizabeth Billington of the clothing industry—a superstar who cashed in on the emergence in the nineteenth century of a super-rich European elite. To do that, Worth had to invent a new profession. Born in 1826, Worth started out in London and then in France as a draper. He saw an opportunity to expand the business by sewing clothes for his clients, not just selling them fabrics. Worth persuaded his initially hesitant employers to back his idea, and they opened a small dressmaking department. It became increasingly profitable, and Worth was made a partner in the firm. That success emboldened him to set up his own venture in 1858, financed by Otto Gustav Bobergh, a Swedish investor. Before long Worth had created a new superstar profession—haute couture—and become its first practitioner.

Worth sewed his label into his dresses. Rather than sewing clothes created by his clients, he invented modern fashion design by presenting his own styles four times a year, then custom producing them for his clients. Worth was an avid adopter of technology. The first reliable sewing machine was patented in Boston by Isaac Singer in 1851, seven years before Worth opened his dressmaking shop, and his seamstresses used sewing machines wherever that was quicker and more efficient than stitching by hand. Worth also enthusiastically used factory-made decorations such as ribbons and lace.

Worth made his name by assiduously courting the European aristocracy. An early client was Princess Pauline von Metternich, wife of Austria's ambassador to France, and his success was assured when Empress Eugénie, wife of Napoléon III, began to wear his designs. But financially he was as much a beneficiary of America's Gilded Age as were the Astors, Carnegies, and Vanderbilts, who sent their ladies to Paris to order their entire wardrobes. They would also make the transatlantic journey to buy dresses for special occasions, such as weddings or the lavish masquerades that, as with the 1897 Bradley Martin ball, were a fixture of late nineteenth-century elite social life.

Worth was more than a superstar tradesman. He was an innovator who created a new way of making and selling clothes to the rising European and American super-rich. In the 1870s, at the peak of his career, he was making $80,000 a year; some of his dresses sold for as high as $10,000. That was a fortune, to be sure. But just as Mrs. Billington's earnings were limited by the number of people who could hear her perform in person, the six thousand to seven thousand gowns the House of Worth produced a year were each tailored to the body of a specific client.

But just as Charlie Chaplin's superstardom dwarfed Elizabeth Billington's since he could perform for the masses, fashion designers became exponentially richer when they expanded from the haute couture business to prêt-à-porter. That revolution happened in 1966, when Yves Saint Laurent opened his first Rive Gauche ready-to-wear store on the rue de Tournon in the sixth arrondissement of Paris, less than two miles away from the original home of Worth and Bobergh, where Charles Worth had gone into business just over a century earlier.

It took the couturiers a long time to reap the benefits of mass production. That was partly because the sewing machine didn't immediately translate into well-made and cheap clothes for women—the most lucrative designer market. The sizzle of mid-nineteenth-century inventive genius devoted to the sewing machine—call it the smartphone of the 1850s—almost immediately translated into mass production of military uniforms, for the U.S. Civil War and Europe's Franco-Prussian War.

But factory-produced women's clothes remained a difficult value proposition. As late as 1920, a study found that it was still cheaper to sew a dress at home, for an average cost of twenty dollars, than to buy it ready-made, for an average cost of thirty dollars; buying a dress from a dressmaker, at thirty-five dollars, was the priciest of all. This was partly because the big technology advance in clothes production—the sewing machine—could be used almost as effectively at home as it could be in the sweatshops of the garment district. As long as your wife's or daughter's labor was cheaper than that of an immigrant in midtown Manhattan, and for very many Americans it was, buying ready-made clothes was a luxury—hence Laura Ingalls Wilder's remembered envy in *Little House on the Prairie* of the wealthy classmate who could afford a "store-bought" dress. The second problem was fit, more of an issue for women's clothes than for men's because they were often tighter and subject to more quickly changing styles.

We still don't have a perfect answer to the problem of fit—female readers can sigh here—but there was a tipping point in 1941, when, in a government project funded to employ casualties of the Great Depression, the U.S. Department of Agriculture measured almost fifteen thousand women and published the results, creating the first standard dress sizes. Industrial sewing technology made advances, too, and by the 1950s a factory-made dress could be produced in a fraction of the time it took for a lone seamstress using a sewing machine.

As Yves Saint Laurent realized, these two innovations made it possible for superstar designers to benefit from economies of scale. More than acting or singing or cooking, modern fashion design (as opposed to mere dressmaking) was invented as a very expensive service for the Gilded Age elite. Saint Laurent understood that his move into ready-to-wear was a break with that paradigm, and he sought to make his populism a virtue. Fashion, he liked to say, would be incredibly upset if its sole purpose was to dress rich women. (Note, however: the first highly visible client of Rive Gauche, the YSL ready-to-wear was Catherine Deneuve. And in 1987, a few days after the Black Monday stock market crash, the collection included a $100,000 jeweled jacket.)

Many of Saint Laurent's fellow elite couturiers were horrified. They had, after all, punished another designer's earlier flirtation with the mass market with high fashion's equivalent of excommunication. In 1959, when Pierre Cardin designed a ready-to-wear line for department store Printemps he was expelled from the couturiers' club, the Chambre Syndicale.

Before long, however, it became clear that by producing both an haute couture line and a prêt-à-porter line—offering very costly personal service to the super-rich, and using technology to scale their talent—the fashion designers at the very height of their profession could benefit from both Marshall and Rosen effects. In 1975, Yves Saint Laurent earned $25 million, a hundred times what Charles Worth earned at the peak of his career (when taking inflation into account). Worth was richer than his French seamstresses; YSL, however, is a veritable plutocrat compared with the foreign garment workers who sewed his prêt-à-porter line. As in the law, the performing arts, and cooking, in fashion the chasm between the superstars and everyone else is only getting bigger.

THE MARTIN EFFECT—TALENT VS. CAPITAL

The Marshall superstars and the Rosen superstars—and those who benefit from both effects—are getting richer in two ways.

The first is because they are being served from a larger pie—their super-rich clients are richer than ever, and economies of scale now allow them to reach a mass audience. The second is because they are getting a bigger share of the pie relative to their less elite peers (whether those peers are any less talented is open to debate). Their clients—both the super-rich and the masses—prefer to listen to the "very best" singer, and wear clothes created by the "very best" designer. Even where the service can't be scaled—

as in a courtroom appearance or an original painting—the same force is at work.

Roger Martin, a management consultant and business school dean, thinks that over the past three decades another force has come into play: superstars aren't just earning more from their clients, they are increasingly able to extract a greater amount of the value of their work from their employers. In Martin's view, this dynamic, which he describes as the struggle between talent and capital, is tilted in favor of the "talent," or the superstars. Just as the fight between labor and capital defined the first stage of industrial capitalism in the nineteenth and twentieth centuries, Martin argues that the battle between capital and talent is the central tension in the knowledge-based postindustrial capitalism of the twenty-first century.

Here is how Martin laid out his theory in the *Harvard Business Review*: "For much of the twentieth century, labor and capital fought violently for control of the industrialized economy and, in many countries, control of the government and society as well. Now . . . a fresh conflict has erupted. Capital and talent are falling out, this time over the profits from the knowledge economy. While business won a resounding victory over the trade unions in the previous century, it may not be as easy for shareholders to stop the knowledge worker–led revolution in business."

Martin's thesis helps explain one of the most striking contrasts between today's super-elite and their Gilded Age equivalents: the rise, today, of the "working rich." As Emmanuel Saez found, the wealthiest Americans these days are getting most of their income from work—almost two-thirds— compared to a fraction of that, roughly one-fifth, a century ago.

Martin's theory about the growing power of "the talent" builds on the ideas of Peter Drucker, the Austrian-born scholar who laid the intellectual foundations for the academic study of management. That means you can probably blame Drucker for far too many soul-destroying PowerPoint presentations, peppy but hollow business books, and inspirational corporate "coaches" with lots of energy but no message. But Drucker also, more than half a century ago, predicted the shift to what he dubbed a "knowledge economy" and, with it, the rise of the "knowledge worker."

Drucker made his name in America, but he was a product of the Viennese intellectual tradition—Joseph Schumpeter was a family friend and frequent guest during his boyhood—of looking for the big, underlying social and economic forces and trying to spot the moments when they changed. Accordingly, he saw the emerging knowledge worker as both the product and beneficiary of a profound shift in how capitalism operated. "In the knowledge society the employees—that is, knowledge workers—own the tools of production," Drucker wrote in a 1994 essay in the *Atlantic*. That, he argued, was a huge shift and one that would, for the first time since the industrial revolution, shift the balance of economic power toward workers— or, rather, toward one very smart, highly educated group of them—and away from capital.

As Drucker explained: "Marx's great insight was that the factory worker does not and cannot own the tools of production, and therefore is 'alienated.' There was no way, Marx pointed out, for the worker to own the steam engine and to be able to take it with him when moving from one job to another. The capitalist had to own the steam engine and control it." Hence the power of the robber barons and the complaints of the proletariat.

But that logic collapses in the knowledge economy: "Increasingly, the true investment in the knowledge society is not in machines and tools but in the knowledge of the knowledge worker. . . . The market researcher needs a computer. But increasingly this is the researcher's own personal computer, and it goes along where he or she goes. . . . In the knowledge society the most probable assumption for organizations . . . is that they need knowledge workers far more than knowledge workers need them."

Here, then, is another way that some of the highly talented are catapulted into the super-elite: when it becomes possible for them to practice their profession independently. Or, to put it another way, when the tool of their trade is a personal computer, rather than a steam engine.

Of course, even during the first machine-driven thrust of the industrial revolution, there were some superstars who remained beyond the thrall of the capitalists. A painter needed only oil and canvas; a lawyer needed only his education, wits, and admission to the bar. It is no accident that it was the superstars of these two professions that Marshall, writing in 1890, singled out as benefiting disproportionately from the Western world's economic transformation.

In the knowledge economy, more and more professions use a laptop rather than a steam engine, and that means that the superstars in these fields are earning ever greater rewards. The intellectuals are on the road to class power.

THE STREET AND THE SUPERSTARS

The biggest winners are the bankers. They did well enough, to be sure, in the industrial revolution. They were among that era's plutocrats—think J. P. Morgan in New York, or Siegmund Warburg in the City of London. But these were the owners of capital. Their employees, the salaried financial professionals, weren't nearly as richly rewarded. Their job was just to keep score.

In the postwar era, with the steady rise of the knowledge economy, the bankers' role has been dramatically transformed. Instead of working for the owners of capital—whether they are industrial magnates or the shareholders of publicly traded companies—financiers have discovered they can themselves own the capital and, with it, the companies. Critically, this shift from wage earner to owner has been accomplished not just by one or two stars at the very top of the field—the Oprah Winfreys or the Lady Gagas—but by thousands. In 2012, of the 1,226 people on the *Forbes* billionaires list, 77 were financiers and 143 were investors. Of the forty thousand Americans with investable assets of more than $30 million, a group described by Merrill Lynch, which produces the premier annual study of the wealthy, as "ultra high net worth individuals," 40 percent were in finance. Of the 0.1 percent of Americans at the top of the income distribution in 2004, 18 percent were financiers. Bankers are even more dominant at the very tip of the income pyramid. In a study of the 0.01 percent, Steven Kaplan and Joshua Rauh found Wall Street significantly outearned Main Street. Collectively, the executives at publicly traded Wall Street firms earned more than the executives of nonfinancial companies. Wall Street investors, such as hedge fund managers or private equity chiefs, did even better. "In 2004," Kaplan and Rauh write, "nine times as many Wall Street investors earned in excess of $100 million as public company CEOs. In fact, the top twenty-five hedge fund managers combined appeared to have earned more than all five hundred S&P 500 CEOs combined."

You can trace this transformation of bankers from accountants and clerks to the dominant tribe in the plutocracy to three new forms of finance pioneered in the decade after the Second World War, and to three very different men who lived within five hundred miles of one another on the East Coast stretch running from Boston to Baltimore.

The first was Alfred Winslow Jones, a patrician New Yorker (his father ran GE in Australia), who invented the modern hedge fund in 1949 when, as a forty-eight-year-old journalist with two children and two homes, he decided he needed to make more money. The second was Georges Doriot, a French-born Harvard Business School professor who invented the modern venture capital business in 1946 as a way to encourage private investment in start-ups founded by returning GIs. The third was Victor Posner, the teenage school dropout son of a Baltimore grocer who pioneered the hostile takeover business (now usually known by the more genteel name of "private equity") in the 1950s.

Together, this trio spearheaded the transformation of finance from an industry dominated by large institutions whose job was the conservative stewardship of other people's money into a sector whose moguls were iconoclastic entrepreneurs who specialized in risk, leverage, and outsize returns. The broader economic impact of this revolution remains debatable—you could argue that these three men are the fathers of the instability of modern financial capitalism—but it was clearly crucial in the rise of the super-elite. Hedge funds, venture capital, and private equity transformed finance— previously the dependable plumbing of the capitalist economy—into an innovative frontier where smart and lucky individuals could earn nearly instant fortunes.

The biggest beneficiaries are those who strike out on their own. And the would-be masters of the universe know that. David Rubenstein, the billionaire cofounder of the Carlyle Group, one of the world's biggest private equity firms, told me that when he visited America's top business schools during their spring recruiting season in 2011, he discovered that everyone wants to be an entrepreneur. "When I graduated from college, you wanted to work for IBM or GE," he told me." Now when I talk to people graduating from business school, they want to start their own company. Everyone wants to be Mark Zuckerberg; no one wants to be a corporate CEO. They want to be entrepreneurs and make their own great wealth." That quest starts earlier and earlier. Jones and Doriot were both nearly fifty when they started their businesses. Nowadays, would-be plutocrats want to be well on their way to their fortune by their thirtieth birthday.

THE BILLIONAIRE'S CIRCLE

But the real mass revolution sparked by the rise of entrepreneurial finance is in the way that it reshaped the big institutions it threatened to usurp. Civilians—which is to say anyone who doesn't work on Wall Street (or maybe in Silicon Valley)—tend to think of the $68 million earned by Lloyd Blankfein in 2007, just before the crash, or the $100 million bonus earned by Andrew Hall, Citigroup's star energy trader, in 2008—as princely fortunes. On the Street itself, though, even the most successful and lavishly compensated employees of the publicly listed firms see themselves as also-rans compared to the principals of hedge funds, venture capital firms, and private equity companies.

We got a glimpse of that way of thinking when federal agents were allowed to tap the telephones of Raj Rajaratnam, a billionaire hedge fund founder, and his network of contacts. In one of those conversations, Rajaratnam and Anil Kumar discuss their mutual friend Rajat Gupta, the Indian-born former head of McKinsey, a company that epitomizes the rise of the managerial aristocracy. Gupta was on the board of Goldman Sachs, one of the most prestigious in the world. But he had been invited to the board of KKR, one of the four biggest private equity firms. Serving on both would be a "perceived conflict of interest," because KKR and Goldman often compete for the same business. That left Gupta with a tough decision, but he was leaning toward KKR. Here, according to Rajaratnam, is why: "My analysis of the situation is he's enamored with Kravis [one of the three founders of KKR] and I think he wants to be in that circle. That's a billionaire's circle, right? Goldman is like the hundreds of millionaires' circle, right? And I think here he sees the opportunity to make $100 million over the next five or ten years without doing a lot of work."

That phrase—the billionaire's circle—is the key to how the entrepreneurs of finance transformed the wider culture of Wall Street, and thus of the global banking business. Thanks to Jones, Doriot, and Posner, being in the "hundreds of millions" circle isn't enough. To understand how that sentiment has ratcheted up individual compensation for Wall Street's salarymen—not just the entrepreneurs who take the risk of going it alone— consider this fact: in 2011, 42 percent of Goldman Sachs's revenues were spent paying its employees, who earned an average of $367,057. Nor is that princely compensation restricted to the über-bankers at Goldman Sachs. At Morgan Stanley, which made a $4 billion mistake on the eve of the financial crisis and whose recovery from it has been lackluster, compensation accounted for 51 percent of revenue in 2010. At Barclays, which now owns Lehman, the figure was 34 percent; at Credit Suisse, it was 44 percent. To put it another way, on Wall Street, in the battle between talent and capital, it is the talent that is winning. Wall Street is the mother church of capitalism. But its flagship firms are run like Yugoslav workers' collectives.

THE MATTHEW EFFECT

Matthew of Capernaum was a Galilean tax collector and the son of a tax collector. He became one of Jesus Christ's apostles, the patron saint of bankers—and one of the first thinkers about superstars. What he noticed was the ratchet effect of superstardom: "For unto every one that hath shall be given, and he shall have abundance; but from him that hath not shall be taken away even that which he hath."

The Marshall effect, the Rosen effect, and the Martin effect are all about the ways in which superstars are able to be better paid for the value they create—thanks to richer clients (Marshall), more clients (Rosen), and better terms of trade with their financial backers (Martin). The multiplier effect that Saint Matthew observed is what makes all these drivers of superstardom so powerful: the superstar phenomenon feeds on itself.

We are all familiar with the Matthew effect in pop culture, where it is so apparent that it seems as inevitable and unremarkable as gravity. Celebrities are famous for being famous. And fame is its own achievement and currency. One reason we know that is because of fame production machines, like reality TV shows, and the intense popular desire to participate in them. (In Philadelphia in August 2007, twenty thousand people competed for twenty-nine spots on *American Idol*, a far tougher ratio than being admitted to Harvard.)

Here's what might surprise you: The intrinsic power of superstardom—making an impact because of who you are, not what you do—operates not only in the skin-deep world of entertainment. It also applies to what we like to think of as the empirical universe of science. In fact, the term "Matthew effect" was coined by sociologist Robert Merton to describe how prestigious awards, in particular the Nobel Prize, influenced the perception of scientific work. Merton discovered that science had its own superstars, and that those stars' discoveries were considered more important or original just because of who had made them.

Merton found that scientists who published frequently and worked at "major" universities gained more recognition than scientists who were equally productive but worked at lesser institutions. In cases where several researchers made the same discovery at roughly the same time, the more famous scientist was usually credited with the breakthrough while his or her unknown peer became "a footnote." Writing more than four decades ago, Merton predicted that the superstar phenomenon would accelerate, partly because science was at the beginning of a shift from "little science," with an investigator and a microscope, to "big science, with its expensive and often centralized equipment needed for research." The superstars, he believed, would be the only ones to get the tools to do "big science," giving them a further advantage relative to their less recognized peers.

What is striking about Merton's scientific superstars is how conscious they are of the inequities of the celebrity from which they benefit. One Nobel Prize–winning physicist pointed out: "The world is peculiar in this matter of how it gives credit. It tends to give credit to [already] famous people." A Nobel Prize–winning chemist admitted: "When people see my name on a paper, they are apt to remember it and not to remember the other names." Another physics laureate went so far as to worry he was getting kudos for discoveries made by others: "I'm probably getting credit now, if I don't watch myself, for things other people figured out. Because I'm notorious and when I say [something], people say: 'Well, he's the one that thought this out.' Well, I may just be saying things that other people have thought out before."

The scientist who best exemplifies the self-fulfilling power of fame is, ironically, the one most of us would immediately name as the twentieth century's brightest example of pure intellectual genius: Albert Einstein. Einstein was indeed a groundbreaking physicist, whose theory of relativity ushered in the nuclear age and transformed the way we think about the material world. But why is he a household name, while Niels Bohr, who made important contributions to quantum mechanics and developed a model of atomic structure that remains valid today, or James Watson, one of the discoverers of the double helix structure of DNA, is not?

According to historian Marshall Missner, Einstein owes much of his power as one of the most influential men of the twentieth century less to his theoretical papers and more to the trip he made to the United States in April 1921 as part of a Zionist delegation led by Chaim Weizmann. Before the ship made landfall, Einstein was already known—and feared. His theory of relativity, first put forward in 1905, had been dramatically confirmed in 1919 by the observation of the deflection of light during the solar eclipse in May of that year. The discovery captured the American popular imagination, but not in a good way. The twenties were a fraught decade. The Bolsheviks were consolidating their power in the Soviet Union. Germany was struggling under the weight of punitive World War I reparations. The U.S. economy was still booming, but income inequality was higher than it had ever been and elites were frightened both of homegrown populist protesters and of revolutionary ideas crossing the Atlantic. It was also a time of intense xenophobia and mounting anti-Semitism.

In that climate, America's arbiters of public opinion decided that Dr. Einstein and his theory of relativity were sinister and subversive. It became a truth universally acknowledged that only "twelve men" in the world understood the theory of relativity. Pundits worried that this small, foreign cabal could use its knowledge to bend space and time and to enter a "fourth dimension" and thereby achieve "world domination." Even the *New York Times* warned of "the anti-democratic implications" of Einstein's discovery: "The Declaration of Independence itself is outraged by the assertion that there is anything on earth, or in interstellar space, that can be understood by only the chosen few."

Then came the Weizmann delegation. Zionism was growing in popularity among New York Jews, and thousands came to the pier to greet the visitors. But the press thought the crowds were Einstein groupies. The *Washington Post* reported there were "thousands at pier to greet Einstein." The *New York Times* wrote that "thousands wait four hours to welcome theorist and his party to America." Its interest piqued, the press pack descended on Einstein. Instead of the "haughty, aloof European looking down on boorish Americans" they had expected, he turned out to be a modest, likable guy who "smiled when his picture was taken, and produced amusing and quotable answers to their inane questions." No longer a threat to the Declaration of Independence, "Professor Einstein," the *New York Times* editorial page declared, "improves upon acquaintance." The scribblers loved him, and they loved the frisson of overturning their readers' expectations, and a scientific legend was born. From that moment on, a great deal of Einstein's power in the world, particularly outside the lab, but also within it, was derived from his celebrity.

You can see the same power of accidental celebrity at work in other fields. One is bestselling fiction. Thanks to the inevitable mistakes in bestseller lists (in 2001 and 2002, 109 books that should have been on the *New York Times* bestseller list according to their sales were left off), Stanford Business School professor Alan Sorensen was able to show that for books of equal initial popularity, being left off the list—not getting the Nobel Prize, not enjoying Einstein's superstar treatment on that 1921 visit to the United States—meant fewer subsequent sales.

The same is true of classical musicians. The most important contest for pianists is Belgium's Queen Elisabeth Competition. Looking at eleven years of the competition, economists Victor Ginsburgh and Jan van Ours found that the top three players went on to become successful professional musicians. Less than half of the others were able to find work of any sort as musicians. But is that a reward for talent or for the celebrity of winning the competition? One clue that officially being named a superstar—winning the competition—had more value than pure talent was an unexpected discovery Ginsburgh and van Ours made when they studied the winners. Placing first, second, or third correlated closely with the randomly determined order in which contestants had competed. So, unless you believe that the random order of participating in the competition is linked to talent, the more obvious conclusion is that the music world celebrity brought by winning the Queen Elisabeth Competition, independent of how good you are, has a powerful effect on your professional success as a musician.

But what about the long tail? One of the promises of the Internet has been that it can weaken the Matthew effect: the Web has low barriers to entry, and we all start out equal online. Matthew Salganik and Duncan Watts tested that premise in 2005 on 12,207 Web-based participants. The research subjects were offered a menu of forty-eight songs. Some participants were shown the songs ranked by popularity in the research group and told how often each song had been downloaded. Others were shown the songs in random order. A separate group was shown the songs in a meek-shall-inherit-the-earth order—the least popular songs were presented as most popular and vice versa. The results largely confirmed Merton's thesis: being presented as popular, whether that information was true or not, strongly increased a song's subsequent popularity. The impact was strongest for the songs that were the "worst" as measured by the unmanipulated judgment of listeners. Nor was the effect absolute. Even when presented as the least popular in the "inverted" world, the best songs gradually climbed up the rankings. If you are very, very good, you can break into the superstar league, but it's an uphill battle.

CAPITAL FIGHTS BACK

On January 11, 1991, Jeffrey Katzenberg, then CEO of Walt Disney Studios, sent a memo to his thirteen top executives titled "The World Is Changing: Some Thoughts on Our Business." Despite its bland title, the twenty-eight-page note was instantly leaked to the press, probably by Katzenberg himself, and it swiftly became the most read prose in Hollywood. "We are entering a period of great danger and ever greater uncertainty," the memorandum began. The change Katzenberg was worried about? The rise of superstars.

In 1984, when Katzenberg and his team arrived at Disney with a mandate to turn around the venerable but troubled moviemaker, Disney had been "the most cost-conscious of all studios." It had saved money mostly "by avoiding the reigning stars of the moment." Katzenberg wrote, proudly: "Instead we featured stars on the downward slope of their career or invented new ones of our own. Robin Williams suggested to *Newsweek* magazine that we recruited talent by standing outside the back door of the Betty Ford Clinic. The first instance of this approach to moviemaking was *Down and Out in Beverly Hills*, a film that reignited the careers of its three stars, Bette Midler, Richard Dreyfuss, and Nick Nolte."

But as the decade progressed, Disney found itself paying its stars more. What particularly distressed Katzenberg was the Matthew effect—paying stars not just for their talent, but also for their fame, something Katzenberg called the "celebrity surcharge": "In 1984, we paid Bette only for her considerable talent. Now, we must also pay her for her considerable and well-earned celebrity. This is what might be called the 'celebrity surcharge' that must be ante'd up when hiring major stars."

Katzenberg's biggest complaint was the signal achievement of "talent" in the second half of the twentieth century: the shift from earning a wage to having a stake in the business. Hedge managers and private equity investors call their stake "the carry." Movie stars call it "participation." Katzenberg called it "extremely threatening": "Unreasonable salaries coupled with giant participations comprise a win/win situation for the talent and a lose/lose situation for us. It results in us getting punished in failure and having no upside in success."

Actors weren't the only talent Katzenberg worried about. Writers, he complained, were starting to be paid "$2–$3 million for screenplays." Instead, Katzenberg thought Disney should be paying "young" writers $50,000 to $70,000 or "proven writers" $250,000 to develop a screenplay for an idea suggested by Disney. Katzenberg admitted that in the new world of superstar scripts, persuading writers to agree to these skimpier rations, ideally on long-term contracts, wouldn't be easy: "I know many will argue that this just isn't feasible anymore. Agents won't let their clients sign long-term contracts because the spec script market is too lucrative. All this means is it will be tougher. It doesn't mean it's impossible."

Katzenberg's solution was for Disney executives to seek out actors and writers who were talented but either hadn't achieved or had lost the superstardom that allowed those at the very top to charge a celebrity surcharge. "All the big-time writers have one thing in common," Katzenberg wrote. "They were all once unknown and thrilled just to make a sale. The future big-time writers are out there and would be grateful just to be considered by our studio. To find them, we have to search harder, dig deeper . . . and be there first."

As for actors, Katzenberg urged his team to "be aggressive . . . at the comedy clubs searching for future stars, and at the back door of the Clinic picking up the stars that once were and can be again."

Katzenberg is not alone. As superstars have become more powerful, bosses in every field have struggled to find ways to avoid paying them the celebrity surcharge. In addition to haunting the back door of the Clinic, studio chiefs have shifted resources to animated films—illustrators, technologists, and voice actors don't yet command a superstar premium—and to serials in which the character is the star, and the actor who plays him or her in one installment can be replaced by a cheaper successor if the original becomes too famous. Reality television and competition shows are another way to avoid paying the celebrity premium, by making the hoi polloi the stars and, as *Pop Idol* does, binding them to contracts that prevent them from demanding any of the upside if their shows make them famous.

Some sports team owners are on a similar quest to pay for talent, not stardom. That is the story of the Oakland A's and their general manager, Billy Beane, as lionized in Michael Lewis's *Moneyball*. Beane is Lewis's underfunded, underdog hero, but his is really the story of capital—the baseball team owners—looking for a way to avoid paying the celebrity premium to its stars—the players—in this case by looking for athletes whose skills were crucial to the team's success but were undervalued by the market.

Even in finance, whose superstars are less well known but even better paid than film and sports celebrities, some bosses have been looking for ways to avoid the celebrity premium. Harvard Business School professor Boris Groysberg became the hero of Wall Street's HR departments in 2010 when he published *Chasing Stars*, a study that has become the banking industry's *Moneyball*. After interviewing more than two hundred Wall Street analysts, Groysberg concluded that recruiting stars from rival firms was a waste of money, because poached analysts tended to falter when they were plucked from their native culture. Warren Buffett famously agrees. He emerged from his Omaha fastness to join the battle between capital and talent on Wall Street in the 1990s, when he briefly chaired struggling investment bank Salomon Brothers—a period he described in the next year's letter to shareholders as "far from fun"—and slashed the bonus pool by $110 million.

But here is the catch in management's fight to rein in superstar salaries, and one institutional reason the super-elite continue to rise: in the age of the vast, publicly traded joint-stock company, where ownership is widely dispersed and boards lack the time, expertise, and gumption to weigh in on the specifics of how companies operate, the managers themselves are superstars, too. Entertainers and athletes are the most visible superstars, but they are hugely outnumbered by the army of business managers who in the past four decades have been transformed from salarymen to multimillionaires.

The ideas Katzenberg laid out in his 1991 memo have been largely vindicated by subsequent academic research. Mostly strikingly, in a 1999 study analyzing the economics of two hundred movies, Abraham Ravid found that stars had no impact on box office revenue. Katzenberg had a powerful incentive to sniff out the financial danger of paying the celebrity surcharge— as Disney's CEO, his job was to turn a profit. But the checks on soaring salaries of chief executives and their top teams are much weaker. Even superstars have bosses, but as Jack Welch, the first CEO to become a celebrity, said in a conversation at the 92nd Street Y in the spring of 2011, what the chief executive needs is "a generous compensation committee."

Or a smart lawyer. Katzenberg's big complaint about "the talent" was "participations," or contracts that gave actors a share in a movie's revenue. It turned out he had cut a similar deal himself, earning a share of the entire studio's profits in addition to his cash salary and CEO perks. That package was big enough to make a dent not just in one movie's profits but in the entire company's bottom line, as Disney shareholders learned when the company settled a legal battle with Katzenberg over his severance package. The terms of the deal were undisclosed, but Hollywood lawyers estimated it was at least $200 million—more than four times the production costs of *Dick Tracy*, the overbudget movie that inspired Katzenberg's 1991 *cri de guerre*.

Sometimes the title says it all. That was certainly the case in March 1986, when the *Harvard Business Review* published an essay headlined "Top Executives Are Worth Every Nickel They Get." *HBR* is owned by the Harvard University, and its readers are the aforementioned top executives and their ambitious underlings. So one purpose of the essay was inevitably service journalism's accustomed function of flattering its constituency. But the piece had a less cynical motivation, too. Its author, Kevin J. Murphy, was in the vanguard of a small group of business school academics who had spent the previous decade trying to solve one of the big problems of twentieth-century market economies: How do you have capitalism without capitalists? Or, to put it another way, who manages the managers?

This is not a new problem. In *The Wealth of Nations*, Adam Smith compared the executives of a joint-stock company to "the stewards of a rich man" and warned that "being the managers rather of other people's money than their own, it cannot well be expected, that they should watch over it with the same anxious vigilance with which the partners in a private copartnery frequently watch over their own. . . . Negligence and profusion, therefore, must always prevail." Writing just over a hundred years later, Alfred Marshall bemoaned the feebleness of the staid British joint-stock company, compared to an America dominated by owner-entrepreneurs: "The area of America is so large and its condition so changeful, that the slow and steady-going management of a great joint-stock company on the English plan is at a disadvantage in competition with the vigorous and original scheming, the rapid and resolute force of a small group of wealthy capitalists, who are willing and able to apply their own resources in great undertakings."

That small group of wealthy capitalists laid the foundations for America's astonishing economic ascent in the twentieth century. But as the American economy matured, control of its private businesses began to pass from the hands of the vigorous, scheming, and resolute founders of Marshall's age to a new generation of stewards. That shift was documented in a seminal paper published in 1931 by Gardiner Means, a New England farm boy and steely-nerved World War I pilot who'd eventually made his way to economics and the Ivy League faculty. Means showed that of the two hundred largest U.S. companies at the end of 1929, 44 percent were controlled by managers rather than by their owners. An even greater share of the wealth of America's top companies was in the hands of the managerial class—58 percent of the top two hundred companies, as measured by market capitalization, was manager ruled.

Means saw this ascendant managerial class as self-selecting and self-perpetuating: the only institutional parallel he could come up with was the clergy of the Catholic Church. In a book he and Adolf Berle, a professor of corporate law at Columbia, cowrote the next year, they described the rising managerial elite as "the princes of industry." Berle and Means saw the shift from owners to managers as comparable in its significance to the switch from independent worker-artisans to wage-earning factory employees.

Berle and Means worried about how to keep this managerial aristocracy in check. Thanks to the ability of the publicly traded company to attract capital from millions of retail investors, this managerial class presided over firms of unprecedented scale and power. But the market incentives that governed the actions of owners didn't necessarily apply to their stewards. In fact, their interests were "different from and often radically opposed to" those of the owners—the hired managers "can serve their own pockets better by profiting at the expense of the company than by making profits for it."

Berle and Means were leading architects of the New Deal—Berle was an original member of FDR's "Brain Trust," and Means, working as an economist in the Roosevelt administration, waged a campaign against price fixing in the steel industry. Their prescription, accordingly, involved state and social intervention. Government should regulate managerial princes who overstepped the mark, and a new set of social conventions should be developed requiring managers to be "economic statesmen" who ran their companies in the collective interest.

Murphy's "Worth Every Nickel" essay was a robust public statement of a radically different solution to the problem Berle and Means had identified. Like the New Dealers, Murphy and his confreres believed that managing the managers was the central problem of twentieth-century capitalism. But instead of trying to get corporate executives to behave more like public-spirited civil servants, Murphy and his fellow business school professors thought the answer lay in the opposite direction: the stewards needed to be turned into the red-blooded founder-owners they had replaced. To do that, their financial incentives needed to be aligned as closely as possible with the success or failure of the companies they ran. That wouldn't give them as powerful a profit motive as owning the whole company, to be sure, but it would be a close second-best.

The "Worth Every Nickel" movement was in part a response to the success of the New Dealers' efforts to create a social and political order in which managers were constrained. Thirty years after Berle and Means worried that managers would be tempted to profit at the expense of the companies they ran, here is how John Kenneth Galbraith, hardly an apologist for the C-suite, described the ethos of corporate America: "Management does not go out ruthlessly to reward itself—a sound management is expected to exercise restraint. . . . With the power of decision goes opportunity for making money. . . . Were everyone to seek to do so . . . the corporation would be a chaos of competitive avarice. But these are not the sorts of things that a good company man does; a generally effective code bans such behavior."

In a follow-up to his *Harvard Business Review* cri de coeur, Murphy, along with his coauthor Michael Jensen, found that the culture of restraint in the postwar era could be quantified. During the three decades after the Second World War, the U.S. economy grew at a faster, more consistent pace than ever before, and American companies were ascendant around the world. The acknowledged social and economic leaders of this golden age were the country's captains of industry, yet during that period their salaries actually fell. In our honey-tinged, *Mad Men* memories of the postwar era, we may imagine it to be a time of the triumph of the company man. But in fact it was an era when the managerial aristocracy was trammeled by the rest of society, even as the companies they oversaw prospered. As Jensen and Murphy concluded in their 1990 paper: "The average salary plus bonus for top-quartile CEOs (in 1986 dollars) fell from $813,000 in 1934–38 to $645,000 in 1974–86, while the average market value of the sample firms doubled."

Jensen and Murphy agreed with Galbraith's explanation of what was going on—social pressure was limiting CEO salaries: "Political forces operating both in the public sector and inside organizations limit large payoffs for exceptional performance."

The Means and Berle solution to the rise of the managerial class had prevailed, and it seemed to be working. America's companies were no longer run by their vigorous and self-interested robber baron founder-owners, but the new salaried stewards who had replaced them weren't looting the corporate kitty. Governed by a "remarkably effective code," their incomes were actually falling. They seemed to be doing a pretty good job, too. The companies under their stewardship doubled in size between 1932 and 1976, the total real compound annual return on the S&P 500 was 7.6 percent, and America's GDP had quintupled.

But by the late seventies and the eighties, when Jensen, Murphy, and their like-minded peers began to investigate CEO pay, the economic picture was starting to darken. Economic growth seemed to stall even as inflation rose—remember stagflation. Corporate America, too, seemed sluggish, risk averse, and under threat from more innovative foreign rivals. These were the conditions that inspired the liberal economic revolution more generally, and also a rethinking of what was happening in the corner office.

As Berle and Means had warned in the 1930s, the problem started with the twentieth-century fact that the economy was largely run by "stewards" rather than owners. But the New Dealers' fear that these managerial aristocrats would line their own pockets hadn't come true—indeed, the opposite was the case. And that, Jensen and Murphy warned, was the problem. The social constraints that prevented executive looting also meant executives had weak economic incentives to do an outstanding job. The New Dealers had transformed hired-gun CEOs into capitalist civil servants—public-spirited and self-restrained. The "Worth Every Nickel" business school professors wanted to turn the managerial class into red-blooded capitalist owners.

Their solution was "pay for performance." Managerial compensation should be more tightly tied to how well they did their jobs and, in particular, to how well their companies performed.

By one measure, the academic advocates of pay for performance were remarkably effective. After falling steadily during the postwar years, CEO salaries began to soar. The real takeoff was during the 1990s: by the end of that decade they were growing by 10 percent a year. As Roger Martin has calculated, for CEOs of S&P firms, the median level of pay soared from $2.3 million in 1992 to $7.2 million in 2001. That's a lot of money, and a growing share of the overall income of corporate America. Between 1993 and 2003 the top five executives of America's public companies earned $350 billion. Between 2001 and 2003, public companies paid more than 10 percent of their net income to their top five executives, up from less than 5 percent eight years earlier.

These were, of course, the decades when the 1 percent broke away from the rest of the pack in society as a whole. That happened inside corporations, too. Rising CEO compensation pulled the boss ever further from the factory floor or the cubicle rows. In the early 1970s, CEOs earned less than thirty times what the average worker made; by 2005, the median chief executive made 110 times what the average worker did. And just as income inequality in society overall has become more pronounced at the very, very top, the gap has grown between CEOs and their direct reports. Until the early 1980s, the chief executive earned about 40 percent more than the next two most highly paid managers; by the early twenty-first century, he made more than two and a half times as much.

This gap is no accident—it is inevitable in an economic model in which the CEO has gone from being the company man of Galbraith's postwar account to the free-agent superstar of the pay-for-performance era. That shift was made starkly apparent when two economists at the London School of Economics asked a simple question: "Does it matter whether you work for a successful company?" The answer from HR is—of course! And our corporate Web sites duly urge us to be team players and to root for our firm's overall success. But when Brian Bell and John Van Reenen looked at what actually happens in a sample of companies covering just under 90 percent of the market capitalization of Britain's publicly listed firms, they came up with a chilling reply. CEOs and executives at the very top are rewarded for corporate success, but almost no one else is: "A 10 percent increase in firm value is associated with an increase of 3 percent in CEO pay, but only 0.2 percent in average workers' pay."

These growing chasms within companies didn't just mirror the broader rise of the 1 percent, they also drove it. Executives working outside finance (a category all its own) were 31 percent of the 1 percent in 2005, the single largest group. They account for an even larger share of the 0.1 percent—42 percent in 2005.

A couple of decades earlier, György Konrád and Ivan Szelényi had revealed the politically uncomfortable truth that in the so-called workers' states the real winners—and the real bosses—were the intellectuals, particularly their technocratic branch. They are coming out on top in market economies, too. It is the MBAs on the road to class power.

Under communism, the rise of the intelligentsia was undeniably a political process. But the academic theory underpinning the rise of the MBA class in the West is all about market forces. The goal of the pay-for-performance revolution, after all, wasn't to raise CEO compensation, although that was certainly one of its consequences. The point was to get the managerial aristocrats to do a better job by more closely tying their paychecks to their impact. On this reading, the soaring salaries of CEOs, and the growing gap between them and their senior lieutenants, is one chapter in the broader story of superstar economics. Once companies began to do a better job of tying pay to performance, they discovered that some managers were more talented than others, and those stars, like the best singers or lawyers or chefs, could command a significant financial premium.

For the CEO to be a superstar—and to be paid like one—he has to stop being a company man. The executives of the postwar era were corporate lifers. They were the creations and the servants of their companies, and a great deal of their value came from their knowledge of the particular corporate cultures that had created them and the specific business they did. The superstar CEO cannot be tied to a single corporation and, ideally, not even to a single industry. He must be an exemplary talent whose skill is in "management" or in "leadership." He is more likely to have an MBA—28.7 percent of CEOs did in the 1990s, compared to 13.8 percent in the 1970s—and less likely to be a loyalist of a specific firm. If these are the general skills we believe it takes to lead successful businesses, the world's companies will engage in a bidding war to secure the services of the men and women who are the world's best managers and leaders.

That is exactly what has happened. The surge in CEO salaries coincided with a rise in bosses hired from outside the firm. In the seventies and eighties, when CEOs were paid less than they had been in the 1930s, 85.1 percent and then 82.8 percent of chief executives were company men. But in the 1990s, as CEO compensation came to vault upward by 10 percent a year, more than a quarter of chief executives were appointed from outside their firm. Jumping to a new company was a good way to get a raise— external hires, according to research by Kevin Murphy, one of the leaders of the pay-for-performance school, made 21.6 percent more than chiefs appointed from inside. In sectors where these portable general managers are most valued, all CEOs earn more—a premium of 13 percent.

One of the drivers of superstar incomes in other professions is the economics of scale—singers who can perform for millions, designers whose styles can be sold around the world. Size can be a reason to pay CEOs more, too. As companies get bigger thanks to the globalization and technology revolutions, the economic impact of good management increases. The world's very best CEO may be only marginally better than the hundredth best. But if your company's annual revenues are, say, $10 billion, then just a 1 percent difference in performance is worth $100 million. Sure enough, as economists Xavier Gabaix and Augustin Landier found in a 2008 paper, "The six-fold increase of U.S. CEO pay between 1980 and 2003 can be fully attributed to the six-fold increase in market capitalization of large companies during that period."

But there is one very big problem with the superstar CEO model, and it goes back to the challenge posed by the rise of the managerial aristocracy that first Berle and Means and later the pay-for-performance school grappled with. It is what economists call the agency problem, and it means that CEOs are a very special sort of superstar: the one who is in charge of the company that pays his salary. Superstar athletes are paid by the owners of sports teams, superstar chefs by their diners, and even superstar hedge fund managers are paid by their investors. But CEOs are paid by the companies they run. Their compensation, to be sure, is determined by the board of directors, but, particularly in the United States, the chairman of the board is often the CEO.

"In the U.S., you can more or less do whatever you want, without having the support of the owners," Mats Andersson, the chief executive officer of the Fourth Swedish National Pension Fund and critic of corporate governance in the United States, told me after speaking at a conference on the issue convened in Washington by the Securities and Exchange Commission. "Because of the composition of the boards in Sweden, the company's big decisions all have to be based on the mandate or the support of the owners.

"Who is actually responsible for executive remuneration in U.S. companies?" Mr. Andersson said. "If I could decide on my own salary, I would certainly love that system."

Adam Smith forthrightly warned that the consequence of the agency problem was "negligence and profusion." Academic economists today use a more delicate term: "skimming." A decade ago, two young economists, Marianne Bertrand and Sendhil Mullainathan, came up with an original way to investigate whether CEOs were superstars, being rewarded by their firms for exceptional performance, or whether they were stewards who were rigging the rules of the game in their own favor. The test was to see whether performance-based CEO pay responded as strongly to external good fortune as it did to managerial prowess. Two of the examples of outside luck were changes in the price of oil and changes in the exchange rate. Bertrand

and Mullainathan found that luck matters: "CEO pay is as sensitive to a lucky dollar as to a general dollar," which is to say for overall good company performance. They found, for instance, that a 1 percent increase in the revenues of oil companies because of an increase in the price of oil led to a 2.15 percent increase in CEO pay. Better still, from the perspective of the oil chief, while an increase in the price of oil always correlated with an increase in the CEO's paycheck, when the price fell, the CEO's salary didn't necessarily decline: "While CEOs are always rewarded for good luck, they may not always be punished for bad luck."

Thanks to the financial crisis and the global recession it triggered, public opinion and politics in much of the world are catching up to this ivory tower critique. Consider Britain, where a Conservative-dominated coalition government began 2012 with a proposal to rein in executive pay. "We cannot continue to see chief executives' pay rising at 13 percent a year while the performance of companies on the stock exchange languishes well behind," Vince Cable, the business secretary, told parliament as he announced the new measures. "And we can't accept top pay rising at five times the rate of average workers' pay, as it did last year."

Cable's reference to the gap between CEO salaries and those of average workers is telling. We may frame our complaints about rising executive compensation with arguments about skimming—that the millions are unearned. But part of our unease stems from something entirely different—that the final outcome, the gap between CEOs and the rank and file, is wrong.

This second concern may very well not be solved by doing a better job of coping with the agency problem. Bertrand and Mullainathan's finding that there is a lot of skimming going on in the corner office doesn't, it turns out, make them complete skeptics of the pay-for-performance revolution. Pay for performance actually works, but only in companies where the board is strong enough to truly oversee the chief executive. Boards are best able to do that, Bertrand and Mullainathan discovered, when they have a large shareholder. "An additional large shareholder on the board reduces pay for luck by between 23 and 33 percent"—a big number, especially when you consider how tricky it is in real life and in real time to distinguish between lucky profits and hard-earned ones.

There's a reason for CEOs to position themselves as superstars—highly talented people being paid for their skill—that goes beyond getting a great deal from the comp committee. Even in an age of tension between the 99 percent and the 1 percent, we love our superstars. That's because, as the *New York Times*'s David Carr put it in a deft analysis of the popularity of basketball player Jeremy Lin, in aspirational America, we all like to think that we are superstars-in-waiting, on the verge of our big break: "The Lin story has broken out into the general culture because it is aspirational in the extreme, fulfilling notions that have nothing to do with basketball or race. Most of us are not superstars, but we believe we could be if only given the opportunity. We are, as a matter of practicality, a nation of supporting players, but who among us has not secretly thought we could be at the top of our business, company or team if the skies parted and we had our shot?" That's the irony of superstar economics in a democratic age. We all think we can be superstars, but in a winner-take-all economy, there isn't room for most of us at the top.

———◆———

FOUR

RESPONDING TO REVOLUTION

It is better to lead revolutions than to be conquered by them.

—*Otto von Bismarck*

A lesson from the technology industry is that it's better to be in front of a big change than to be behind it.

—*Reid Hoffman, cofounder and chairman of LinkedIn*

He who does not risk, does not drink champagne.

—*Russian proverb*

On August 9, 2007, BNP Paribas froze withdrawals from three of its funds. Fearing that move would halt interbank lending, the world's worried central bankers, led by the European Central Bank's Jean-Claude Trichet, pumped billions into global money markets. Those twin steps eventually came to be viewed as the opening shot in the global credit crisis.

Eight days later, George Soros hosted twenty of Wall Street's most influential investors for lunch at his Southampton estate, on the eastern end of Long Island. It was a warm but overcast Friday afternoon. As the group dined on Long Island striped bass, fruit salad, and cookies, their tone was serious and rather formal. The meal was one of two annual "Benchmark Lunches," held on successive Fridays in late August and organized by Byron Wien, a Wall Street veteran who had befriended Soros four decades earlier thanks to a shared interest in then obscure Japanese stocks.

James Chanos, the influential short hedge fund manager, was one of the guests. It was a group, Chanos told me, of "pretty heavyweight investors." Other diners included Julian Robertson, legendary founder of the Tiger Management hedge fund; Donald Marron, the former chief executive of PaineWebber and now boss of Lightyear Capital; and Leon Black, cofounder of the Apollo private equity group.

In a memo about the luncheon discussion he distributed a few weeks later, Wien wrote that the talk focused on one issue: "Were we about to experience a recession?" We all know the answer today. But just over a year before the collapse of Lehman Brothers definitively plunged the world into the most profound financial crisis since the Great Depression, the private consensus among this group of Wall Street savants was that we were not. According to Wien's memo, "The conclusion was that we were probably in an economic slowdown and a correction in the market, but we were not about to begin a recession or a bear market."

Only two of the twenty-one participants had dissented from that bullish view. One of the bears was Soros. "George was formulating the idea that the world was coming to an end," Wien recalled. Far from being won over by his friends, Soros saw their optimism as reinforcing his fears. He left the lunch convinced that the global financial crisis he had been predicting prematurely for years had finally begun.

His conclusion had immediate and practical consequences. Soros had been one of the world's most successful and most influential investors: for the thirty years from 1969 through 2000, Soros's Quantum Fund returned investors an average of 31 percent a year. Ten thousand dollars invested with Soros in 1969 would have been worth $43 million by 2000. According to a study by LCH Investments, a fund owned by the Edmond de Rothschild Group, during his professional career Soros has been the world's most successful investor, earning, as of 2010, a greater total profit than Warren Buffett, the entire Walt Disney Company, or Apple.

But in 2000, following the departure of Stan Druckenmiller, who had been running Quantum, Soros stepped back from active fund management. Instead, he recalled, "I converted my hedge fund into a less aggressively managed vehicle and renamed it an 'endowment fund' whose primary task was to manage the assets of my foundations."

On August 17, 2007, he realized he had to get back in the game. "I did not want to see my accumulated wealth be severely impaired," Soros told me during a two-hour conversation in December 2008 in his thirty-third-floor conference room in midtown Manhattan, with views overlooking Central Park. "So I came back and set up a macro account within which I counterbalanced what I thought was the exposure of the firm."

Soros complained that his years of semiretirement meant he didn't have the kind of "detailed knowledge of particular companies I used to have, so I'm not in a position to pick stocks." Moreover, "even many of the macro instruments that have been recently invented were unfamiliar to me." At the moment he made his crisis call, Soros was so disengaged from daily trading that he didn't even know what credit default swaps—the now notorious derivatives that brought down insurance giant AIG—were. Even so, his intervention was sufficient to deliver a 32 percent return for Quantum in 2007, making the then seventy-seven-year-old the second-highest-paid hedge fund manager in the world, according to Institutional Investor's *Alpha* magazine. He ended 2008 up almost 10 percent, the same year that saw global destruction of wealth on the most colossal scale since the Second World War, with two out of three hedge funds losing money, and he was ranked the world's fourth highest-paid hedge fund manager. Druckenmiller, his former first lieutenant and a self-confessed admirer of Soros's approach to investing, came in at number eight.

The twenty more bullish guests at the Soros table that August afternoon weren't outliers. They reflected the consensus view of corporate America's top economists. When the *Wall Street Journal* reviewed the 2008 predictions of America's fifty-two leading economic forecasters, it found that only one of them had foreseen a fall in GDP. As Dick Fuld, the once lionized Lehman chief, told a congressional committee in October 2008, a month after his firm's bankruptcy and more than a year after Soros's lunch: "No one realized the extent and magnitude of these problems, nor how the deterioration of mortgage-backed assets would infect other types of assets and threaten our entire system."

Alan Greenspan was so wrong-footed by the crash of 2008 that he admitted intellectual defeat. "I made a mistake," he told a congressional committee on October 23, 2008. "Something which looked to be a very solid edifice, and indeed a critical pillar to market competition and free markets, did break down. And I think that, as I said, shocked me."

Hindsight makes all of us Einsteins. With the wisdom it bestows, it is easy to mock and malign the actions and the explanations of the Fulds and the Greenspans. But in 2007 and early 2008, inertia—whether you believe it to have been motivated by avariciousness or incompetence—was the normal response. While the bubbles are easy to identify in retrospect, when we are caught up in them, most of us find it difficult to imagine they will ever burst. And even those of us who are intellectually honest and experienced enough to appreciate that, one day, the boom is bound to end, find it tough to act on that realization.

It is not just financial crashes we have a hard time anticipating. Significant paradigm shifts more generally—revolutions in politics and society, as well as those in business and the markets—are notoriously hard to foresee. The CIA famously failed to predict the collapse of the Soviet Union. Less than a year before Hosni Mubarak was toppled, the IMF published a report lauding his economic reforms and the stability they had created. Mike McFaul, a political scientist who was appointed U.S. ambassador to Russia in 2011, believes that "we always assume regime stability and when it comes to authoritarian regimes we are always wrong."

Even after the revolution has begun—after the first overleveraged bank freezes withdrawals from its riskiest fund, after the protesters win their first important standoff against the soldiers of the ruling regime—most of us are reluctant to admit that the world has changed. As historian Richard Pipes observed, after the Bolsheviks seized power in 1917, prices on the Petrograd stock exchange remained stable. And once we recognize that the world has changed, most of us are very bad at adapting our behavior to the new reality.

Instead, according to London Business School professor Donald Sull, most companies respond to revolutionary change by doing what they did before, only more energetically. Sull calls this "active inertia" and he believes it is the main reason good companies fail: "When the world changes, organizations trapped in active inertia do more of the same. A little faster perhaps or tweaked at the margin, but basically the same old same old. . . . Organizations trapped in active inertia resemble a car with its back wheels stuck in a rut. Managers step on the gas. Rather than escape the rut, they only dig themselves in deeper."

Clayton Christensen, the Harvard Business School professor whose book *The Innovator's Dilemma* is the corporate bible on disruptive change, has found that established companies almost always fail when their industries are confronted with disruptive new technologies or markets. And that is not, he argues, because their managers are dumb or lazy. It is because what works in ordinary times is a recipe for disaster in revolutionary ones. "These failed firms," he writes, "were as well run as one could expect a firm managed by mortals to be—but there is something about the way decisions get made in successful organizations that sows the seeds of eventual failure."

The rare ability—like Soros's—to spot paradigm shifts and to adapt to them is one of the economic forces creating the super-elite. That's because moments of revolutionary change are also usually moments when it is possible to make an instant fortune. And, thanks to the twin gilded ages, we are living in an era of a lot of revolutionary shifts.

One set of changes is in the emerging markets. The broad secular trend since the late 1980s has been for authoritarian regimes to give way to more democratic ones and for closed, state-controlled economies to become more open. Sometimes the transition happens with a bang, as it did in Eastern Europe in 1989 and North Africa in 2011; sometimes it happens more gradually, as in India, China, and parts of sub-Saharan Africa. But in much of the world, the late eighties and the nineties were a time of privatization, deregulation, and the lowering of trade barriers. The result was economic windfalls for the locals and foreigners with the skills, the smarts, and the psyche to take advantage of them.

A second set of revolutions is in technology. New technologies, especially computers and the Internet, then mobile and wireless, are disrupting existing businesses and opening up the chance to create new ones. Like the industrial revolution, which started with mechanization of the textile industry, then the invention of the steam engine, followed by the combustion engine and electricity, the technology revolution isn't a single discovery; it is wave after wave of related transformations. In 2012, the hot new areas were big data—our ability to collect and analyze massive amounts of information—and machines talking to machines, creating what W. Brian Arthur, the economist who studies technological change, describes as the second, digital economy—"vast, silent, connected, unseen, and autonomous."

Finally, these two big revolutions, together with a broader global trend toward more open markets in money, goods, and ideas, combine to reinforce each other and create a faster-paced, more volatile world. Twitter and Facebook are the offspring of the technology revolution, but they turn out to have made political revolutions easier to organize. Before the invention of the personal computer, the securitization of mortgages—which turned out to be part of the kindling for the financial crisis—would not have been possible. Nor would the algorithmic trading revolution, in which machines are replacing centuries-old stock exchanges and a couple of lines of corrupt code can trigger a multibillion-dollar loss of market value in moments, as occurred during the "flash crash" on May 6, 2010.

Revolution is the new global status quo, but not everyone is good at responding to it. My shorthand for the archetype best equipped to deal with it is "Harvard kids who went to provincial public schools." They got into Harvard, or, increasingly, its West Coast rival, Stanford, so they are smart, focused, and reasonably privileged. But they went to public schools, often in the hinterlands, so they have an outsider's ability to spot the weaknesses of the ruling paradigm and don't have so much vested in the current system that they are afraid of stepping outside it.

Facebook's Mark Zuckerberg (New York State public school, Harvard), Blackstone cofounder Steve Schwarzman (Pennsylvania public school, Yale undergraduate, Harvard MBA), and Goldman Sachs CEO Lloyd Blankfein (Brooklyn public school, Harvard) are literal examples of this model. Most of the Russian oligarchs—who were clever and driven enough to get degrees from elite Moscow universities before the collapse of the Soviet Union, but were mostly Jewish and therefore not fully part of the Soviet elite—have a similar insider/outsider starting point. Soros, the worldly and well-educated son of a prosperous Budapest lawyer, who was forced by war and revolution to make his own way in London and New York, is another representative of the genre.

The Citigroup analysts who coined the term "plutonomy" go one step further. They argue that responding to revolution is a biological trait, genetically inherited, and that one way to be sure your society is good at it is to open your borders to immigrants, on the theory that moving to a new country is an example of responding to revolution. They write, "Dopamine, a pleasure-inducing brain chemical, is linked with curiosity, adventure, entrepreneurship, and helps drive results in uncertain environments. Populations generally have about 2% of their members with high enough dopamine levels with the curiosity to emigrate. Ergo, immigrant nations like the United States and Canada, and increasingly the UK, have high dopamine-intensity populations." Responding to revolution—and the economic rewards it brings today—they argue, isn't just something we can learn by reading the works of business school professors like Christensen or Sull, or the result of an insider/outsider background. It is, they believe, hard-coded in our DNA.

The economic premium on responding to revolution not only helps to create the super-elite, it is one of the forces widening the gap between the super-elite and everyone else. The revolutions that those Harvard public school kids capitalize on create outsize rewards for the winners and, in the medium term, usually make the world a better place for everyone.

But in the short run, they also create a lot of losers: new technologies destroy old jobs and, according to extensive research by MIT's David Autor, have significantly hollowed out the U.S. middle class; Russia's market transition created seventeen billionaires in a decade, but also led to a 40 percent drop in GDP; Soros profited from the 2008 crash and it made John Paulson a billionaire, but millions lost their jobs, homes, and retirement savings. For the winners, revolutions can bring a windfall; for the losers, disaster.

By any measure, private equity tycoon David Rubenstein is a plutocrat. *Forbes* estimated his personal fortune in 2012 to be $2.8 billion. Carlyle, the private equity group he cofounded, manages $150 billion. The atrium of New York's premier cultural venue, Lincoln Center, is named after him. Former president George H. W. Bush served as a senior adviser to Carlyle; James Baker, the former secretary of both the Treasury and state, was a partner. John Major, the former British prime minister, was chairman of Carlyle Europe.

One afternoon in 2007, when Rubenstein noticed that the last privately held copy of the Magna Carta was being auctioned off by Sotheby's, he was suddenly struck by the idea that the Magna Carta wasn't just the founding document of Britain's constitutional monarchy, it was the founding document of American democracy, too. The United States, he thought, really should have its own copy of this seminal agreement. So he bought it. For $21.3 million. When he tells this story, with a mixture of pride and lingering incredulity at his own impetuosity, Rubenstein's favorite moment is talking to his wife at the end of the day and offering a humdinger of a punch line to the classic conjugal question "What did you do today, darling?" Rubenstein's answer: "I bought the Magna Carta."

All of which is to say that Rubenstein is no stranger to super-wealth. But the first time I met him, he was fascinated by the years I had spent chronicling the rise of the Russian oligarchs. Now that, he told me, was a time and place where you could make some real money.

Rubenstein is right. Responding to revolution has been particularly profitable in those parts of the world where there has been a real revolution, either overthrowing the ancien régime, as in the former Soviet bloc, or just a shift in the economic system, from central planning to the market. The most dramatic transition—and the biggest opportunity to earn a windfall—was in Russia, where twenty years of capitalism has created around a hundred billionaires, 8 percent of the world's total. The personal wealth of this group of Russians could buy roughly 20 percent of their home country's annual economic output.

Russia, of course, gives plutocracy a bad name. The Kremlin version of capitalism has been exceptionally good at producing billionaires—Russia has the world's highest ratio of billionaires relative to the size of the economy—but the country's overall performance has been less impressive. The economy shrank by 40 percent in six years and male life expectancy dropped nearly to the levels of sub-Saharan Africa in the 1990s—the decade when most of today's oligarchs got their start. It has been growing more robustly for the past ten years, but has been outpaced by China, India, and Brazil, and remains largely dependent on natural resources. By 2011, per capita income was $12,993, well above emerging markets like China and India but below Lithuania, Chile, and Barbados, and male life expectancy is a mere sixty-two. Russia remains a tough place to do business: the World Bank rates it at 120, below Nicaragua, Yemen, and Pakistan.

But, as Rubenstein recognized, if you knew how to respond to revolution, there was no better place to be than Moscow in the 1990s. The conventional wisdom, even in Russia, is that the winners of the great privatization windfalls were Kremlin insiders. But that isn't quite true. Of course, onetime apparatchiks have done extremely well in Russia's transition to a market economy—one of the country's richest men is probably Vladimir Putin. But in the former Soviet Union, as in the United States, many of the plutocrats have turned out to be the Russian equivalent of public school kids who went to Harvard: close enough to the levers of power to take advantage of the market transition, but also far enough away that they understood that the regime was crumbling.

Mikhail Fridman, an oil, banking, and telecom magnate worth $13.4 billion in 2012, is an archetypal oligarch. He was born and raised in L'viv, in western Ukraine, one of the Soviet Union's freest and most cultured cities, but also far from the center of political power. Fridman was smart enough to make it to an elite Moscow polytechnic institute, where he earned a degree in physics. But Fridman was both unconnected and Jewish, which blocked him from becoming a total insider. He wasn't allowed to do graduate research work, as he wanted, and was instead assigned a job in a provincial factory 150 miles outside Moscow.

With hindsight, that exclusion was a blessing. Fridman had been an energetic college entrepreneur, organizing ventures ranging from window washing to a theater ticket purchasing system, and he had accumulated enough rare goods (mostly jeans and caviar) to bribe his way into a choicer work assignment in Moscow. But the experience made him skeptical about his chances to prosper inside the Soviet system and determined to focus on opportunities outside it. By the time the Soviet Union collapsed, and the really big business opportunities materialized, he was already a millionaire, a powerful starting position.

"What I really, really wanted to do, my childhood dream, was to be a physics professor," Fridman once told me. "If I had been born in America, that is what I would be. Thank goodness for Soviet anti-Semitism."

The early biographies of the other oligarchs are uncannily similar. Viktor Vekselberg, a metals and oil oligarch, is another Jew from western Ukraine who got a PhD in math from an elite Moscow polytechnic. But he was enough of an outsider that in the late 1980s he decided to supplement his family income—"I really wanted a car," he told me—by writing and selling computer programs. Again, by the time the Soviet Union collapsed, he was poised to pounce. Boris Berezovsky, an oil, industrial, and media magnate before he lost a power struggle with Putin, was an obscure mathematician and apparatchik when perestroika was first declared, bringing its attendant business opportunities. Vladimir Gusinsky, Russia's most powerful media baron before he, too, lost a power struggle with Putin, was a Jewish theater impresario who never made it into the first circle of state-supported Soviet cultural intellectuals and who supplemented his income by trading consumer goods like jeans, copper bracelets, and Sony Walkman players in the black market.

In fact, of the seven men who between them controlled half of the entire Russian economy in 1998, and who became known as the oligarchs, six were Jewish and few of them were privileged. The only oligarch who was a real insider, a member of a group known as "the gilded youth" because of their privileged upbringing as the children of the nomenklatura, was Vladimir Potanin, the son of an official in the Ministry of Foreign Trade. Ultimately, that network and that pedigree were a great help to Potanin as he built his metals and banking empire, including control of Norilsk Nickel, the world's largest nickel producer. And it is no accident that Potanin is the only oligarch who served in the cabinet.

But at the moment of transition, Potanin's elite background almost blinded him to the biggest economic opportunity in his country's history. In the late eighties and early nineties, while men like Fridman, Vekselberg, and Gusinsky were experimenting in the small space for private business permitted by Gorbachev, Potanin was still climbing the Soviet political ladder, earning his degree in foreign relations, and winning a coveted job at the Ministry of Foreign Trade. He sensed that the world was changing, and he had just about summoned the courage to start his own trading firm when he was offered a post in Brussels, a plum assignment at a time when travel to the West was highly restricted.

"I was proud and excited and I accepted the assignment," Potanin told me. "But then, at the last minute, I realized things were changing so quickly in Russia and I had to be part of the change. Everyone thought I was crazy."

A lot of responding to revolution is about luck. Not just being at the right place at the right time, but also reading the one book or having the single conversation that allows you to spot a nascent opportunity in a fast-changing world. And sometimes, you might have the misfortune to read the wrong book or watch the wrong movie. That is what happened to Kakha Bendukidze, a Georgian-born biologist (yes, another smart outsider) who parlayed his scientific skills and connections into a small manufacturing empire, including ownership of Uralmash, a legendary Soviet heavy machine–building factory.

Bendukidze became a multimillionaire, but he never became an oligarch. Why? "I blame *Wall Street*," he told me—the film, not the Manhattan neighborhood. "We watched that movie in 1992 and we didn't understand any of it. I thought to myself, If I can't even understand as much finance as an ordinary American moviegoer understands, it would be crazy for me to start my own bank." But at a moment of hyperinflation and slightly lower state interest rates, banking offered an opportunity to make the first big post-Soviet windfall. Even more important, the fortunes earned using state credits provided the future oligarchs with the capital and the connections to muscle their way into the real windfall, the 1995 loans-for-shares giveaway of Russia's natural resources. Because of Gordon Gekko, Bendukidze missed out.

Soros learned about revolutions the hard way. He compares 2008, with its cataclysmic events and his survival of them, with 1944, when as a Jewish fourteen-year-old in Nazi-occupied Budapest he and his family eluded the Holocaust. The Soroses and their circle of friends had lived comfortable, largely secular lives before the Germans arrived. Many in their community were unable to grasp that that life was over and they needed to flee at once. An exception was Tivadar, Soros's beloved father, whose experience of the Russian Revolution as an Austro-Hungarian officer had taught him the necessity of responding to revolutionary change with equally radical behavior. Over the objections of his wife and mother-in-law, Tivadar immediately sent the family into hiding—a decision that saved all their lives. Now a fit, often tanned eighty-two-year-old who favors beautifully tailored suits and has a thick, graying head of hair as well as a hearing aid, George Soros thinks his father's "formative" experience of revolutionary change helped him to anticipate and respond to the current crisis.

"I recognize that sometimes survival requires a positive effort. I think that is really a childhood experience, and it was partly taught and partly experienced. . . . I had his [my father's] experience of where the normal rules don't apply and that if you abide by the rules, you're dead. So your survival depends on recognizing that the normal rules don't apply. . . . Sometimes not acting is the most dangerous thing of all."

That early life training shaped Soros's investing style and his investing philosophy. "My theory of bubbles was a translation of this real-time experience. I became a kind of specialist in boom and bust."

That is certainly the view of his son Jonathan, a triathlete, Harvard Law School grad, and married father of two—but also, as the child of American prosperity and stability, someone who, in his father's opinion, is not a leader of radical change. Jonathan says of his father: "That experience has allowed him to see through artifice. He can see the things that look like they are very stable—things that look like marble are not marble, they are plaster—and the institutions that we have built are human institutions and aren't necessarily permanent."

Although many CEOs and regulators say the crash had been impossible to predict, among professional traders it was commonplace as early as 2005 to believe that inflated house prices and turbocharged derivatives were creating the next asset bubble.

"Whenever I read about people not seeing it coming, I get a kick out of it," Keith Anderson, Soros's former chief investment officer, told me. Tall, burly, and soft-spoken, with a modest office decorated largely with photos of his smiling children, Anderson has a friendly, unpretentious air—more Little League dad than Davos man—and a blue-chip money management CV. "Most every intelligent person—we all understood and knew that there was a housing bubble, that the CDOs and the derivatives were creating distortions."

The difficulty was knowing when the bubble would burst. "What the problem was," he said, was "that many of us had thought that for too long and were wrong. We knew it was occurring, but you wouldn't want to be betting against it, because you weren't getting satisfaction.

"There are multiple versions of history," Anderson explained. "The common one, in the normal newspaper, is 'What fools! No one saw it coming.' Lots of people saw it coming. The question was: When was it going to stop? What was going to cause it to stop? How do you profit from it?"

In mid-2007, when Soros decided he needed to actively manage his money again, Quantum's funds were mostly entrusted to outside managers. They, and the smaller number of inside managers, operated with "total discretion," Soros recalled. "They have their own style and their own exposure and some of them have money for extended periods of time."

Soros "didn't interfere in the running of their accounts, because that's not the way we operate," so he set up an account to counterbalance their positions, which he ran himself. "Basically, it involved a large amount of hedging. It was neutralizing market exposure [of his external and internal managers] and then taking market exposure on the negative side." Soros was not only unfamiliar with fancy new derivatives; by his own admission, he didn't know much about individual stocks anymore, either. So one of the world's great investors set about protecting himself from the coming crash with tools so simple your average booyah Jim Cramer watcher would scorn to use them: S&P futures and other exchange-traded funds. He made simple bets, too: "Basically, I went short—the stock market and the dollar."

Soros didn't get it exactly right. "In a time like this, where the uncertainty is so big and the volatility is so big, you must not bet on a large scale," Soros told me at the end of 2008. "One of the mistakes I made is that actually I bet too much this year, too large positions, and therefore I had to move in and out to limit the risk. I would have actually done better had I taken my basic positions on a smaller scale and not allowed the market to scare me out of those positions. I would have done much better."

That's because Soros's radar for revolution is a way of thinking about the world, not a foolproof algorithm. "That's what makes this macro investing difficult," Anderson told me. "People like George can see the disequilibrium, but there is always the question of what catalyst is going to cause the change."

The biggest disequilibrium of the twentieth century was the economic gap between the developed Western economies and everywhere else. And the single biggest catalyst for change was the collapse of Soviet communism. But the opportunities created by that monumental revolution weren't limited to Russia. Across the Warsaw Pact as well as in Asia and in Latin America, a global wave of economic liberalization opened up huge opportunities for the people who figured out how to respond to revolution. As in the former Soviet Union, this wasn't something you could teach in business school—talent and an appetite for risk were essential, but most of all you needed to be in the right place at the right time.

Azim Premji is the chairman of Wipro, the pioneering Bangalore-based IT company. The first revolution in Premji's life was personal. He was studying engineering at Stanford University in 1966 when his father died suddenly. The twenty-one-year-old had to drop out of college and return from Palo Alto to Bangalore to run the family vegetable oil company. Premji turned out to be an energetic, talented, and omnivorous businessman. A decade after he took over, Wipro was still producing vegetable oil, but it also made lightbulbs in a partnership with GE, as well as shampoo, soap, and hydraulic cylinders. The really big break came in 1978, when IBM was forced out of India. Premji saw the opportunity to return to his first passion—computer science, whose pioneers he had met as a student at Stanford. By 1991, when Manmohan Singh's liberalization opened up India to the world economy, Premji and Wipro were perfectly poised to seize the opportunity—and the Indian outsourcing revolution was born.

"I was very lucky," Premji, today a dignified patriarch with a quiff of white hair, told me when I asked him how he did it. "I had the right education, at the right moment, in the right country."

"India is growing at 8 percent per annum," explained Ashutosh Varshney, the Brown professor who spends half his time in his hometown of Bangalore. "But the main point was that when an economy grows at 7 to 8 percent, then some sectors grow at 18 to 20 percent—8 percent is an average."

If you are good at responding to revolution, you figure that out and start a business in one of the 18 to 20 percent sectors: "It is the possibility of multimillionaires overnight."

You hear the same story in China. Lai Changxing was born and raised in a small village outside Xiamen, on China's southeast coast, less than two hundred miles from Taiwan.

When in the early 1980s Deng Xiaoping told the brutalized Chinese people it was okay to make money, Xiamen was one of the first provinces where the market experiment was launched, and Lai responded to that revolutionary opportunity. Starting with an auto parts company, by the middle of the next decade he had diversified into everything from umbrellas to textiles to electronics—and he had become a billionaire.

"You could start a business in the morning and make money by the evening," he told a journalist. "Everything was so free and open back then that everyone had lot of businesses. You would be stupid not to."

If you have the right skills and the right connections and the right appetite for risk, surfing the wave of emerging market revolution is thrilling— and even feels easy.

David Neeleman is a serial entrepreneur. He has founded two U.S. airlines and a touch-screen airline reservation system that was acquired by HP. When Neeleman was eased out of the CEO's chair at JetBlue, his most successful creation, it was less than a year before he announced the launch of a third big entrepreneurial venture. That was no surprise—starting companies is simply what Neeleman does. And it made sense that it was an airline, the business Neeleman knows. But for his third big play, Neeleman left the United States for Brazil.

"Well, the U.S., like I said, it's kind of tapped out," Neeleman told me in the fall of 2010. "We're growing [in Brazil], us and our competitors, 25 percent a year. That's three times GDP growth, which in the first half of last year was almost 9 percent. And we're growing traffic 27 percent. So that's exciting. You know, if I was here in the U.S., we would be still trying to fight it out with other established carriers, whereas down there, I'm flying routes that had never had nonstop flights. We will be serving cities that haven't had airline service for years."

That's the real secret of the emerging markets. If you aren't scared of uncertainty or of leaving home, making money in these frontier economies is a lot simpler than battling for 1 percent more market share in the developed world.

"The next ten years is going to be the most exciting time in our lives! The Indian economy will double! You will only see that once in a lifetime! It will be incredible!" Tejpreet Singh Chopra, then a forty-year-old Indian businessman, told me in the spring of 2010. A few weeks before we met, he had taken the bold decision to jump from the managerial aristocracy to try to become one of the entrepreneurs who have figured out how to respond to the emerging market revolution.

Chopra had just the right inside/outside CV. Born and educated in Chennai, India, he landed his first two jobs working for Lucas Diesel Systems in the UK and France. He got his MBA in the United States, from Cornell University, and spent the next decade at GE in Stamford, Connecticut, and Hong Kong, before moving back to India. Chopra met his wife, a fellow Indian, while he was working in the United States; she has a law degree from NYU and worked as an M&A lawyer for white-shoe Wall Street firm Weil, Gotshal and Manges.

In 2007, when he was just thirty-seven, Chopra was chosen as the first Indian to run GE's Indian business. That job put Chopra at the center of the globalization and technology revolutions, which are transforming our world as dramatically as the industrial revolution did two centuries ago.

Consider the Mac 400, a portable electrocardiograph made and designed in India in 2008, which Chopra touts as one of the flagship achievements of his tenure in the GE India job. The Mac 400 is a cheaper, cruder, and lighter version of its American parent—it weighs less than three pounds, rather than fifteen; sells for around $800 (already barely half of the $1,500 it cost when it hit the market), rather than $10,000; and costs $500,000 to develop, rather than $5.4 million. Eight of the nine engineers who created it were based at GE's Bangalore research lab.

Selling Western technology and brands into emerging markets is an old story. So is selling cheap emerging market labor—in the form of manufactured goods, electronics, or commodity white-collar services like call centers—into developed markets.

The Mac 400 is an example of the next stage—emerging market engineers, employed by a Western company, creating a product inspired by a Western prototype, and redesigned for emerging market consumers.

The world's smartest megacorporations—GE, Google, Goldman Sachs—are finding ways to profit from the great economic shift of our times. The biggest winners, though, are individuals, not institutions; globalization and technology have dramatically lowered barriers to entry, and the beneficiaries are the people smart enough and lucky enough to make it on their own.

Chopra was aware of the perks of working for a highly respected global behemoth like GE—"If you are the CEO of GE, anyone anywhere in the world will take a meeting with you," he said—but he couldn't resist the lure of responding to revolution.

Following the model of Nucor, which revolutionized the U.S. steel business by building mini-mills, Chopra is working to create an Indian power company based on small, twenty- to forty-megawatt plants using environmentally friendly sources of energy. With Bharat Light and Power, his new firm, Chopra is hoping to surf at least three revolutionary transformations at once. The first is the shift from big factories to small ones. Nucor—one of Professor Christensen's case studies of the impact of disruptive technologies on legacy competitors—is the textbook example of this transition in the steel business. By building mini-mills, which can be constructed at less than a tenth the cost of large, integrated steel mills and operated more efficiently, Nucor outflanked North America's steel giants. Chopra hopes to apply the same approach to power generation. The second revolutionary wave he hopes to surf is the shift to renewable sources of energy. And finally, he hopes to take advantage of the liberalization of the Indian economy and the country's consequent burst of economic growth. An example of Chopra's approach is Bharat's decision in 2012 to invest in a rooftop solar power project in Gandhinagar, the capital city of Gujarat, in western India, constructed after World War II. This pilot plan lets power companies rent roof space for solar panels from the buildings' owners—a way of getting around the shortage of space and the logistical and bureaucratic difficulties of new construction in India.

"I've helped so many entrepreneurs when they were just a piece of paper, and I thought, 'I could do that,'" Chopra said. "When you work in a corporation, when you retire, you only look back. As an entrepreneur, you are always looking forward. I wouldn't be happy in my life if I was always looking back."

Wherever you go in the emerging markets—or the fast-growing markets, as their boosters are trying to rebrand them—you hear a variation on this theme.

Stephen Jennings grew up in New Zealand's Taranaki territory, where the sheep really do outnumber the people. When New Zealand flirted with an antipodean version of the liberal economic reforms being championed by Thatcher and Reagan in the 1980s, Jennings, with his freshly minted degree in economics, was a young member of the team that enacted them. That took him to Credit Suisse First Boston, first in Auckland, then London, and then, as Russia plunged into its own radical reforms, Moscow, in 1992.

Jennings was one of the Westerners who most adeptly surfed the waves of Russia's revolution. By the beginning of the next century, the investment bank he cofounded, Renaissance Capital, had expanded aggressively into Eastern Europe and Africa and had ambitions of becoming the first global emerging market bank. In April 2009, while most of the world was still in a deep recession set off by the financial crisis, Jennings went home to New Zealand to deliver his country's most prestigious annual economic lecture. The theme he chose, naturally, was the rise of the emerging markets, and he urged his countrymen to dive in and take part in what he described as the most important and fastest economic transformation in human history.

"Yes, you need to be bold and extremely committed, but you *can* participate fully in an historically unique opportunity for value creation," Jennings told the gathering of New Zealand's top businesspeople. "And it is a lot more fun than watching others do it on CNN!"

But to thrive in revolutionary environments, Jennings warned his audience, you need different skills and a different attitude from those who work in slower-growing societies.

"In economies growing at 2 to 3 percent a year, industrial change is relatively gradual," Jennings explained. "In these countries, explosive change is usually associated with rapid technological change, such as with the information technology industry in the 1980s and '90s. In fast-growing emerging markets all industries are like IT. Market growth and changes in competitive dynamics are explosive. For Russian retailers or Nigerian banks, 100 percent–plus growth in revenues or profits is totally normal. Small businesses can become multibillion-dollar enterprises in just a few years. Losers rapidly disappear without a trace. Needless to say, with these stakes, the winners tend to be highly organized and extremely aggressive in their business style and strategies."

This chaotic, messy, high-risk, high-reward world is anathema to many of the managerial aristocrats of the developed world. Jennings recalled how "Credit Suisse First Boston's elite European bankers had a nickname for our tiny group camped out in borrowed office space in Moscow. We were called the 'smellies,' a reference to sanitary conditions in Eastern Europe at the time."

The "smellies" had the last laugh. "By the beginning of 1999, you could not mention Russian finance in polite company, but you could buy shares in Gazprom for five cents. Six months ago, the stock was trading at US$10."

This contrast between the Moscow smellies and the elite European bankers of Zurich, Frankfurt, and London isn't confined to CSFB. Jennings argued it was an example of the wider difference between emerging markets entrepreneurs, whose defining characteristic was their ability to respond to revolution, and the slower-moving corporate princes of Western multinationals.

"Slow or hesitant business leaders are quickly weeded out in high-growth emerging markets. The survivors are typically able to think on a big canvas, to make bold decisions and have the resilience to withstand extreme volatility and market setbacks," he explained. "It is virtually impossible for multinationals to operate in this manner. . . . Their advantages in terms of know-how and capital have been neutralized by their inability or reluctance to grow explosively in complex, foreign environments. . . . Their key decision makers usually live in a distant part of the world; they think they fully understand the risks but cannot grasp the upside."

One of the rising emerging markets champions that Jennings cites is Mittal Steel. Aditya Mittal, son of Lakshmi, the company's founder, and his partner in business and heir apparent, describes an embrace of change that dovetails with Jennings's theory of the case.

"Some people, when the trends are smacking them right in the face, they don't wake up and realize it," Mittal told me. "When I was head of M&A [mergers and acquisitions] and focused on expanding in Central and Eastern Europe, where there were a lot of good opportunities, I kept thinking, when is everyone else going to wake up and start competing with the U.S. for these assets, particularly the other European steel companies. But I didn't have competition for five years. I was like, 'What is wrong with these guys?' I'm in their backyards buying steel companies in Poland, the Czech Republic, Romania, and they are nowhere to be seen."

For Mittal, crisis is always an opportunity: "Historically we've found opportunity from a crisis. . . . A crisis doesn't change the long-term trajectory that the economies will industrialize, right? And if they are not performing well for a short time, that's when you go and buy them, and not cloud your judgment of the future. Provided you're confident in the medium- to long-term investment case and you are confident you can create value for share-holders, then it can be a good thing to do. That's what we've done in the past and it's what we'd do again in the future if we saw the right opportunities."

Responding to revolution is how you become a plutocrat. "Change is great," Mittal told me. "Change is fantastic. That's how you create value because you participate in the change that you see. Now, it can be wrong, or it can be right—that is your own judgment call. But change is how you create value. If there is no change, how else do you create value?"

It is back to Budapest in 1944. In some environments—like today's emerging market economies—not acting is the greatest risk. You may not need to be bold to survive, but you certainly must be bold to thrive.

Jennings was selling his countrymen on the rewards of jumping into the emerging markets—his speech was titled "Opportunities of a Lifetime." But the risks are real, too. Six months before his triumphant hometown lecture, Jennings's firm was on the brink of bankruptcy. To survive, he had to sell a 50 percent stake at a fire sale price to Russian oligarch Mikhail Prokhorov.

Lai, the Xiamen entrepreneur who gloried in the moneymaking opportunities in 1980s China, spent a decade evading Beijing in Canada, but was finally deported back home in 2002. In 1999 China accused him of smuggling, bribery, and tax evasion in one of its periodic high-profile anticorruption campaigns.

"If Lai Changxing were executed three times over, it would not be too much," Zhu Rongji, the former premier who led the attack, said after the verdict. Mikhail Khodorkovsky, the biggest winner in the loans-for-shares privatization and in 2003 the richest man in Russia, has been in jail, mostly in a Siberian labor camp, for nearly a decade.

This volatility at the top is a defining characteristic of the new plutocracy and one reason it is less secure and less homogeneous than its bank balances might suggest. The biggest winners in today's economy are the experts in responding to revolution, but that means that they live in a world in which, as another Hungarian adept famously put it, "only the paranoid survive."

Yuri Milner is another smart, driven Russian who missed out on the privatization windfall. He suffered from the Bendukidze problem. Like the Georgian industrialist, Milner didn't think he knew enough to succeed in an advanced capitalist economy. So after graduating from Wharton, where he was the first non-émigré Russian to get an MBA there, instead of returning home, he went to Washington to work for the World Bank. Unfortunately for him, his job in America—a position whose perks and prestige would have been unmatchable just five years earlier—coincided with Russia's privatization bonanza. He calls that period his "lost years." By the time Milner got back home, the choicest spoils had been divided. Instead of becoming an oligarch, he went to work for one: Mikhail Khodorkovsky.

But the experience taught Milner the value of capitalizing on paradigm shifts, and he began to look for the next one. He found it not in a political revolution but in a technological one. Milner was one of the first Russians to understand the impact of social networks. His first step was the classic developing market technique of copying what was working elsewhere: he bought and invested in Mail.ru, the Russian equivalent of Hotmail, and Odnoklassniki, Russia's Facebook. The Cyrillic alphabet, which had sometimes been a barrier to Russia's success in the global economy, turned out to be a boon for Milner, making it harder for Silicon Valley to conquer his domestic market.

But winning in the Russian technology market wasn't enough for Milner. He decided that his failure in Russia had taught him to be faster and hungrier than the Americans he had met at Wharton. Now that he understood how to respond to revolution, he would take that talent to the place where the biggest transformation in the world was happening: Silicon Valley. Milner was the first major outside investor in Facebook, a coup he pulled off in May 2009 by agreeing to terms that seemed ridiculous to the Valley: $200 million for a 1.96 percent stake, valuing the five-year-old company at nearly $10 billion, and with no board seats. When Facebook made an initial public offering in 2012, Milner's group's expanded stake was valued at more than $6 billion. The day the Facebook investment was announced, one of Milner's colleagues approached the founder of Zynga, the online gaming company, at a conference; a few months later Digital Sky Technologies led a $180 million investment round. Groupon was easier— by the time the online coupon company was looking for investors, Milner's prescience with Facebook and Zynga had made him a prestige investor.

In the United States, the technology revolution is the radical paradigm shift that is yielding windfalls for those with the skill, the luck, and the chutzpah to take advantage of it. The scale of the change is tremendous. Randall Stephenson, the CEO of AT&T, told me the shift was the biggest economic change since the discovery of electricity and the internal combustion engine.

And like Russia's transition from communism to capitalism, the technology revolution is driving a paradigm shift that creates the opportunity to reap a windfall. Dan Abrams, founder of the Mediaite group of Web sites, describes it as a frontier moment. Whoever has the courage and the vision to claim that frontier, he believes, will lay the foundation for the business empires of the future. Actually, the opportunity is even richer and more complicated: the technology revolution isn't a single moment of revolutionary change, the way Russian privatization was. Instead, like the industrial revolution, it is a series of paradigm shifts, each of which offers a financial windfall for those who are in the right place at the right time—and who have the ability to respond to revolution.

One example is the generation of app inventors who made a fortune by riding on Facebook's coattails. In 2007, as that social network was taking off, it threw its platform open to developers as a way to multiply its own reach. That approach worked so well that by 2009 Facebook decided to close the floodgates a little bit, by controlling how apps spread virally. But for the developers who got their timing right, it was a windfall.

"There was a period of time when you could walk in and collect gold," B. J. Fogg, a specialist in technology and innovation who taught a class at Stanford in the fall of 2007 that challenged students to build a business on Facebook, told the *New York Times*. "It was a landscape that was ready to be harvested." And as Mike Maples, a Silicon Valley investor, told the reporter, "The Facebook platform was taking off and there was this feeling of a gold rush."

Another wavelet is the shift from broadcast and cable television to Web-based video. Now that we have seen what the Web has done to the print and music businesses, that revolution seems inevitable. But to capitalize on it, the big question is timing. In 2011, when YouTube announced a big push to open up its platform to producers of Web-based videos, Michael Hirschorn, a writer and former head of programming at VH1, decided the digital television revolution was about to begin—and he was determined not to miss out. "I felt, having been late to several revolutions previously, that we needed to go all out for this," Hirschorn told a journalist. He called his future partner and insisted, "We need to start a company now!"

If you have a PhD in math or statistics, the revolution you are probably trying to capitalize on today is big data—a term for the vast amounts of digital data we now create and have an increasing ability to store and manipulate.

If wonks were fashionistas, big data would be this season's hot new color. When I interviewed him before a university audience in late 2011, Larry Summers named big data as one of the three big ideas he is most excited about (the others were biology and the rise of the emerging markets). The McKinsey Global Institute, the management consultancy's research arm and the closest the corporate world comes to having an ivory tower, published a 143-page report in 2011 on big data, touting it as "the next frontier for innovation, competition, and productivity."

To understand how much data is now at our fingertips, consider a few striking facts from the McKinsey tome. One is that it costs less than six hundred dollars to buy a disk drive with the capacity to store all of the world's recorded music. Another is that in 2010 people around the world stored more than six exabytes of new data on devices like PCs and notebook computers; each exabyte contains more than four thousand times the information stored in the U.S. Library of Congress.

McKinsey believes that the transformative power of all this data will amount to a fifth wave in the technology revolution, building on the first four: the mainframe era; the PC era; the Internet and Web 1.0 era; and, most recently, the mobile and Web 2.0 era.

Big data will create a new tribe of highly paid superstars. McKinsey estimates that by 2018 in the United States alone there will be shortfall of between 140,000 and 190,000 people with the "deep analytical talent" required to use big data. And it will probably create a handful of billionaires who understand and capitalize on the revolutionary potential of big data before the rest of us do—indeed, one way to understand Facebook's $100 billion market capitalization is as a bet on big data.

The technology revolution isn't just about the nerds of the West Coast. We think of the computer revolution as a Silicon Valley phenomenon. But while most of the technology is invented there, many of its biggest beneficiaries are on Wall Street. Here is how Larry Fink, the billionaire founder of Black-Rock, the world's largest asset manager, with nearly four trillion dollars under management in the spring of 2012, described the impact of computers on finance.

"People have always asked me, 'What happened in '83? Why in '83 did all of this intellectualism create mortgage securitization?'" Fink explained to me in his office just off Park Avenue in a 2010 conversation. "It was the technology revolution, which put computers on our desks. . . . It was really the advent of the PC and the availability of having individuals to use a computer, the capabilities of computers to analyze securities, risks, a lot of data . . . And that had never happened before. . . . And in my mind that was the beginning of the trading desk becoming more profitable. If you start looking at the profitability of Wall Street, Wall Street was never that profitable before '83."

And when computers arrived on traders' desktops, Wall Street understood the rise of the knowledge worker had begun in earnest and went out to get the best ones. "Most of what Wall Street did is they understood," Fink told me. "So where did they go? They went to the top schools, they went to engineering. They got these really smart quants. . . . They got some really smart people who could intellectualize a lot of data and come up with trends and formulas. To me a lot has to do with that."

The Citigroup analysts writing about "plutonomy" describe it as the triumph of the "managerial aristocracy," and that is certainly true. But, at its apex, the plutonomy is even more about the triumph of the entrepreneurs—a 2011 Capgemini/Merrill Lynch report estimated that 46 percent of the world's high-net-worth individuals had founded their own businesses.

And while these individualists are fewer in number than the company men, their gains are much more spectacular—and their windfalls are one reason the super-elite are pulling away so sharply from the merely affluent. Richard Attias, a Moroccan-born French businessman who got his start in computer hardware and is now working to create a New York–based equivalent of the World Economic Forum, describes it this way: "It used to be that the big ate the small; now the fast eat the slow." Sull, the London Business School professor, thinks it is hard for established companies—the big—to be fast, at least in a way that is effective. The problem, his research suggests, isn't that companies don't realize the world has changed. They do. But instead of changing their behavior, Sull has found that the most typical corporate reaction is "active inertia"—businesses do what they always did, only more energetically than before. Their vested corporate interest in the existing order is so great, they have a hard time giving up today's certain profits in the hope of earning a bigger windfall—or avoiding a significant loss—tomorrow.

Sull's favorite example of active inertia is Firestone. The company's founder, Harvey Firestone, was adept at responding to revolution. Firestone began producing tires in Akron, Ohio, in 1900. He saw the potential in Henry Ford's pioneering mass production of automobiles, and in 1906 Firestone was chosen by Ford to supply the tires for the Model T. But in 1988, Firestone was acquired by Bridgestone, a Japanese competitor, for a fraction of its market capitalization a decade and a half earlier. Firestone, like so many strong legacy companies, was undone by the emergence of a new, disruptive technology—the radial tire—that had been introduced to the U.S. market. When Firestone tried to play catch-up, manufacturing radial tires in plants designed to produce the old bias-ply tire, disaster struck. Eventually, Firestone was forced to recall millions of tires and, in congressional hearings, was found at blame for thirty-four deaths.

"Firestone's historical excellence and disastrous response to global competition and technological innovation posed a paradox for industry observers," Sull wrote. "Why had the industry's best-managed company turned in the worst performance in a weak field? Closer analysis reveals that Firestone failed not despite, but because of, its historical success."

Firestone had been built to prosper in the stable postwar United States. According to Sull: "An ossified success formula is just fine, as long as the context remains stable." But in a period of revolutionary change—which is what many industries, countries, and the world economy as a whole are experiencing today—"ossified success formulas" aren't enough, and the outsiders who are good at responding to revolution can outflank the establishment.

Firestone's fate, as explained by Sull, is a cautionary tale of what Jennings, from his frontier market vantage points, warned the cozy Auckland elites might happen to them: "Basically, we are living in a world that is more competitive than any other era, where change is faster and less predictable, and where long-established orders—whether they are economic, political, or industrial—are being challenged and supplanted. In this world, the difference between 'success' and 'failure' is greatly magnified. This applies to specific labor market skills, businesses, industries, and entire countries."

And Firestone, with its active inertia, sounds a lot like Wall Street in 2007 and 2008. Many—even most—of the leaders of the country's big financial companies knew their businesses were built on a bubble. But the structure of their companies and of their industry made it impossible to pull back.

In early July 2007, on a visit to Tokyo, Chuck Prince, then CEO of Citigroup, gave an interview to journalist Michiyo Nakamoto. Credit markets had not yet frozen, but there were enough signs of trouble to prompt Nakamoto to ask Prince about the turmoil in the U.S. subprime mortgage market and difficulties financing some private equity deals. Prince believed the ocean of cheap, globalization-fed money Citi was then still sloshing around in would eventually dry up: "A disruptive event now needs to be much more disruptive than it used to be. . . . At some point, the disruptive event will be so significant that instead of liquidity filling in, the liquidity will go the other way."

Today, those remarks read like a prescient description of the overnight collapse in lending triggered by Lehman's bankruptcy just over a year later. But even though Prince thought a "disruptive event" was inevitable, he also believed we hadn't reached "that point" yet. In the meantime, it was his job to keep on doing business as usual: "When the music stops, in terms of liquidity, things will be complicated. But as long as the music is playing, you've got to get up and dance. We're still dancing."

Corporate PR would today cite that line as a cautionary illustration of why bland jargon is the most prudent idiom for business leaders. Prince's vivid phrase not only made it onto the front page the next day, it has become one of the catchphrases of the crisis: a Google search on it more than two years later turned up nearly one and a half million references. One of the days on which it was evoked most energetically was November 4, 2007, when Prince resigned and his dancing comment became shorthand for Citigroup's larger failure to anticipate the crisis under his leadership.

Prince deserved his pink slip: during his tenure in the corner office, Citi increased its exposure to the subprime market, grew its credit default swap business (including the number of swaps it kept on its own books), and stashed billions of dollars in risky off-balance-sheet vehicles. But he wasn't wrong about dancing to the music. When the music stops, the loser is the one left without a chair, but the rules of modern capitalism don't allow the big players to sit down prematurely, either.

Peter Weinberg is a Wall Street patrician—his paternal grandfather was a seminal early partner of Goldman Sachs and his mother is a Houghton, the great WASP family that founded Corning, Inc. Weinberg sat out the last years of this bubble thanks to what he admits to be lucky circumstance. He'd teamed up with legendary Wall Street deal maker Joe Perella in 2006 to found a boutique advisory firm, and they spent the next twenty-four months focused on raising money and assembling a team. But Weinberg, a seasoned investment banker who rose to run Goldman's London office before striking out on his own, believes it is almost impossible for the CEOs he has spent a career advising to stop their ears to the boom-time music.

"I've been through probably six crises now in my thirty years in the business, and it's the pendulum of capitalism," Weinberg told me in June 2009, sitting in a conference room in his firm's modernist offices in the GM Building on Fifth Avenue. "It's very, very hard to lean against the wind in a bubble. Very, very hard. And very few people can really do it. . . . What if one of the heads of the large Wall Street firms stood up and said, 'You know what? We're going to cut down our leverage from 30 to 1 to 15 to 1. And we're not going to participate in a lot of the opportunities in the market.' I'm not sure that chief executive would have kept his job. . . . It is very hard to separate yourself from the herd as a leader of a large financial institution."

This is an even more familiar story in the entertainment, media, and technology businesses. Consider the music industry. Venerable Warner Music, battered by the Web, is today owned by Len Blavatnik, another Russian veteran of that country's economic upheaval who, like Milner, hopes his skills can be applied to disruptive technological change in the West. And in the technology industry, the cycles of transformative change are so fast that even successful revolutionaries can swiftly be outflanked.

That has already happened to Microsoft. The big question today is whether it will happen to Google. Like Sull's managers—who see the coming threat, but are able to respond to it only by doing more of the same—the Googlers understand what is happening. In 2010, Urs Hölzle, one of Google's first ten employees and the company's first engineering vice president, wrote a memo that company insiders called the Urs Quake. In it he warned that Google was falling behind Facebook in social networking and needed to catch up immediately.

Google's chiefs listened and they launched an effort to do so, called Emerald Sea, after an 1878 painting by Albert Bierstadt. The painting, which the Googlers working on the project had re-created and displayed in front of the elevators near their desks, depicts a wrecked ship being buffeted by an enormous wave. Google, they believed, was the ship, and the social networking revolution was the wave: Google would either learn to ride it—or drown. Even for Google, a company whose insurgent founders are still in their thirties, responding to revolution is hard.

One reason Google may have a chance is that the business leaders of Silicon Valley, like those in the emerging markets, made their first fortunes by responding to revolution. For them, constant change is the status quo. Indeed, responding to revolution is so central to Silicon Valley culture that the most successful entrepreneurs have developed a culture of continuous revolution.

Caroline O'Connor and Perry Klebahn, at Stanford's design school, call this the ability to "pivot." Groupon, which began as a platform for collective political action; PayPal, which started as a way of "beaming" money between mobile phones, and then pivoted to become eBay's banking network; and Twitter, which was a later iteration of a failed podcasting start-up, are all, according to O'Connor and Klebahn, examples of successful pivots.

Another illustration they cite is WorkerExpress. Joe Mellin and Pablo Fuentes launched that company as a way for home owners to schedule hourly construction workers using text messaging. When the idea didn't take off, Mellin and Fuentes studied the research they had done before starting WorkerExpress and realized it would be smarter to target their efforts at large contractors who needed temporary help on job sites. Their pivot worked and even in the teeth of the post-2008 construction bust they built a successful Web-platform company.

One of the examples of a pivot most cited by technorati is the story of Flickr, the photo hosting and sharing site. Flickr's genesis was in 2002, when its founders, Caterina Fake and Stewart Butterfield, created a multi-player online game called Game Neverending. Fake and Butterfield could see two revolutions happening in the technology world—the rise of social media and the rise of games. They hoped to cash in by putting them together. But Game Neverending failed and Ludicorp, the Vancouver company Fake and Butterfield established to create it, was running out of money. They had noticed, though, that one of the game's features, a photo-sharing add-on they'd developed in just eight weeks, was popular. So Fake and Butterfield tried again, this time using the photo-sharing technology to create a stand-alone Web site. It worked. Flickr was launched in February 2004. In March 2005, just thirteen months later, Yahoo! acquired it for a reported $35 million. At the beginning of 2012, the site reported that it was hosting more than seven billion images, about one for each person on the planet.

The pivot is about recognizing when you are on the wrong track and changing course—and that, too, is central to Soros's ability to respond to revolution.

Chanos, who leased office space from Soros's Quantum Fund in mid-town New York between 1988 and 1991, agrees. "One thing that I've both wrestled with and admired that Soros conquered many years ago is the ability to go from long to short, the ability to turn on a dime when confronted with the evidence. Emotionally that is really hard."

"My conceptual framework, which basically emphasizes the importance of misconceptions, makes me extremely critical of my own decisions," Soros told me. "I reexamine them all the time and recognize when I am on the wrong track. . . . I know that I'm bound to be wrong and therefore am more likely to correct my mistakes."

"It's an almost aggressive pessimism about his own ideas, that he is going to be the first person to find out what's wrong with his theory, rather than what's right with his theory," his son Jonathan told me.

Pivoting is so hard for traditional Western companies that Jennings predicts they will be overtaken by bolder, more agile emerging market champions. "The businesses and institutions underpinning the economies currently going through economic transformation will not only be catching up with the West, but eventually taking over leadership," he said. "At that point, it will be their business models and institutions that may have to be reexported."

Already, the premium on responding to revolution has created tremendous upheaval in corporate America. A 2010 study by Deloitte, the tax and consulting firm, measures something it calls the "topple rate," the speed at which big U.S. companies lose their leadership positions. Between 1965 and 2009, the topple rate more than doubled. Even in the C-suite, it turns out, life is more precarious than ever. "The group of winners is churning at an increasing and rapid rate," the report found. "Nearly every advantage, once gained, is shown to be temporary."

The winners of the entrepreneurial sweepstakes of the technology revolution like to think they are mostly smarter and harder working and more determined than everyone else. Tony Hsieh offered me a gentle version of this view. "I could start off anywhere in America with a hundred dollars and by the end of the year I would be a millionaire," he said. "I really think I could. That is just how I am."

Some of that is surely true. But part of winning from moments of revolutionary change is the lucky combination of having the right skills, the right character, and the right position in society at the right time.

Timing is equally important in the Silicon Valley gold rush. Consider Jonathan Kaplan, creator of the Flip video camera. Kaplan isn't a scientist or an engineer. But from the time he graduated from college in 1990 he knew he wanted to be an entrepreneur; early on, he decided the technology industry and San Francisco were where his odds were the greatest. He spent a decade barely getting to first base, mostly with software start-ups that were good, but not great. Then, in 2005, a friend told him technology had advanced so much it was possible to make a video camera as small and easy to use as most regular cameras were at the time. From that powerful insight, the Flip camera was born. It was such a success that Cisco acquired the company for $590 million in 2009.

The Cisco deal turned out to be as well timed as Kaplan's original epiphany—two years later, video technology had advanced so much further that smartphones had become video cameras, and Cisco closed down Flip, taking a huge corporate write-down.

Kaplan, a multimillionaire, had left his job at Cisco two months earlier. But that, Kaplan insisted, shouldn't detract from the inspirational power of his initial ability to respond to revolution.

"There are a lot of young entrepreneurs who look at Flip as a huge success, and they should continue to," Kaplan told the *New York Times*. "The demise of Flip has nothing to do with how great a product it is. Companies have to make decisions that sometimes people like you and I don't always understand."

Sheryl Sandberg, the world's most successful female executive, is another example of the power of being in the right place at the right time. Sheryl is brilliant—she was one of Larry Summers's smartest students—and one of the best operating executives around. But the skill that made her fortune is the ability to understand where the action is. She made the perfect, unconventional choice—twice.

The first was in 2001. She had just finished a stint as Larry Summers's chief of staff at the U.S. Treasury—a high-profile job that gave her, with her MBA and a résumé that already included McKinsey and the World Bank—a plethora of options in corporate America, particularly Wall Street. Instead, Sandberg chose to work for Google, a company the economists and politicos in her Washington universe had barely heard of. In 2008, she made another inspired, iconoclastic decision. Google was flourishing, but Sandberg had a job offer from the new kid on the block, Mark Zuckerberg, who wanted her to come in and be the adult who transformed Facebook into a real company. Again, Sandberg, by then one of the most high-profile women in Silicon Valley, had a number of safer, more prestigious choices. She picked Facebook, whose 2012 IPO made her among the richest self-made woman in the world.

If you are fastidious about taxonomy, you'd probably have to describe Sandberg as an outstanding member of the managerial aristocracy—she is a hugely talented executive, but she isn't an inventor in her own right or the founder of her own firm. But her instinct for picking the right job at the right time is so finely honed that it surely qualifies as responding to revolution. As Warren Buffett put it in his 2006 letter to shareholders, quoting "a wise friend," " 'If you want to get a reputation as a good businessman, be sure to get into a good business.' "

In his study of the Nobel scientists, Robert Merton discovered a similar talent for choosing the right work—a skill that was as important as the ability to do the work itself. "Almost to a man, they lay great emphasis on the importance of problem finding, not only problem solving," Merton wrote in 1968. "They uniformly express the strong conviction that what matters most in their work is developing a sense of taste, of judgment, in seizing upon problems that are of fundamental importance." In an echo of Buffett's wise friend, Merton quoted one Nobel laureate who explained, "I learned that it was just as difficult to do an unimportant experiment, often more difficult, than an important one."

The power of choosing the right work is equally pronounced for members of what Graeme Wood, writing in the *Atlantic*, called the lucky job choice club: being an early employee at a company that prospers dramatically. These aren't the entrepreneurs who have a talent for responding to revolution. They are the people lucky—and maybe savvy—enough to be among the first hires of those paradigm-changing entrepreneurs.

When the IPO comes, this group—the first few dozen employees of Microsoft, or Google, or Groupon—is also catapulted into the super-elite. Two California psychologists, Stephen Goldbart and Joan DiFuria, were so concerned by the psychological impact of joining the lucky job club that, in 1997, during the first Internet boom, they gave a name to its baleful outcome—"sudden wealth syndrome"—and set up an institute to treat folks afflicted by it.

When you make your fortune by responding to revolution, the one rule is that there isn't One Rule. Getting out at exactly the right time may be the smartest business decision Jonathan Kaplan made. But at other times and places, the difference between the millionaires and the billionaires is the difference between those who cashed in early and those who held their nerve.

In 1993, when he had already made $100,000—an unimaginable windfall by Soviet standards—Viktor Vekselberg had a partner who decided it would be prudent to cash in his chips and step away from the table. "I had one friend—let's not criticize him, it was his personal choice—who said, 'What vouchers! What privatization! I don't need that,'" Vekselberg told me. He withdrew his share of the group's profits so far—about $100,000, Vekselberg recalls—while his erstwhile partners went on to become billionaires. Having worked together for twelve-hour days at the beginning of their capitalist metamorphosis, he and Vekselberg haven't been in touch for years. "We don't have much in common anymore," Vekselberg said.

On September 23, 1932, six weeks before the election that would begin his service as one of America's most consequential presidents, Franklin Delano Roosevelt addressed the Commonwealth Club of San Francisco.

The speech he delivered is a model of rhetoric—U.S. political scientists in 1999 judged it to be one of the best addresses of the twentieth century—and it made the intellectual case for what would become the New Deal. From a distance of eight decades, what is striking about the address is its characterization of the robber barons. FDR paints them as business titans, geniuses at responding to revolution who ushered America into the industrial age.

> It was the middle of the nineteenth century that a new force was released and a new dream created. The force was what is called the industrial revolution, the advance of steam and machinery and the rise of the forerunners of the modern industrial plant. The dream was the dream of an economic machine, able to raise the standard of living for everyone; to bring luxury within the reach of the humblest; to annihilate distance by steam power and later by electricity, and to release everyone from the drudgery of the heaviest manual toil.

Bringing this dream to life required the robber barons: "To be made real, it required use of the talents of men of tremendous will, and tremendous ambition, since by no other force could the problems of financing and engineering and new developments be brought to a consummation," the president explained.

But FDR was also firmly of the view that the interests of these talented "men of tremendous will and tremendous ambition" didn't perfectly coincide with those of society as a whole:

> So manifest were the advantages of the machine age, however, that the United States fearlessly, cheerfully, and, I think, rightly, accepted the bitter with the sweet. It was thought that no price was too high to pay for the advantages which we could draw from a finished industrial system. The history of the last half century is accordingly in large measure a history of a group of financial titans, whose methods were

not scrutinized with too much care, and who were honored in proportion as they produced the results, irrespective of the means they used. The financiers who pushed the railroads to the Pacific were always ruthless, often wasteful, and frequently corrupt; but they did build railroads, and we have them today. It has been estimated that the American investor paid for the American railway system more than three times over in the process; but despite this fact the net advantage was to the United States.

From today's polarized perspective, what is striking is how FDR gave the business titans their due for bringing the industrial revolution to America, yet at the same time insisted that their self-interest differed from that of the nation as a whole. We live—or at least until the 2008 financial crisis, we lived—in the age of triumphant capitalism, in which the titan is, as Pitch Johnson told the Moscow MBA students, "the hero of our time."

But the reality is more nuanced. The heroic businessman who brilliantly surfs the wave of revolution is driven by the imperative to build his business. That usually creates a lot of value for the rest of us—the railroads of Roosevelt's speech—but profit, rather than nation building, is the titan's North Star. Being good at responding to revolution doesn't necessarily mean focusing on those businesses that are most important for the nation's long-term growth.

The buzzword in Russia today is "modernization." That is because, despite the country's shift to a market economy and its relatively strong economic growth over the past decade, Russia's leaders have started to worry that they have built a version of capitalism appropriate to the twentieth century rather than to the twenty-first. Where, they wonder, is Russia's Bangalore, not to mention its Silicon Valley?

This absence is particularly galling for Russians because they take great pride in their national scientific and technological prowess—and not unjustifiably so. America laments its lack of engineers, but in the Soviet Union engineering, math, and physics were the most valued degrees. And the country as a whole wasn't bad at putting that knowledge to work; after all, the Soviets made it to outer space before the Americans did, and they built a nuclear arsenal bigger than the American one.

That meant that when communism collapsed, a lot of smart observers thought Russia's liberated scientists would lead a new wave of innovation or, at the very least, offer a stiff challenge to India as an outsourcing center. To understand why that hasn't happened, at least not in a big way, consider the story of Serguei Beloussov. When the Soviet Union collapsed, he was perfectly poised in a position between insider and outsider. He was from an academic family in St. Petersburg, but he had made it to the Moscow Institute of Physics and Technology, the country's premier math and technology school. Like many of the oligarchs, he began experimenting with entrepreneurial ventures while he was still in college, organizing national tours for his university's judo club, among other things, mostly for pocket money.

Beloussov has done well. Today, he owns two software companies, with a global workforce of one thousand. His best-known product is software that allows Windows programs to run on Macs. But Beloussov isn't an oligarch. And that is because he wasn't as good as they were at responding to revolution.

"In Russia, all the property belonged to the state and the most money was made by people who were involved in privatization," Beloussov, wearing dark jeans and a long-sleeved red T-shirt advertising Parallels, one of his companies, told me.

"Business is about money and that is where the money was. Then, ten years ago, the big scarcity in Russia was brick-and-mortar businesses and many of my engineers would come to me and say, 'I want to open a chain of drugstores' or 'I want to build homes.' Then, five years ago, many businessmen decided to work for the government." Only now, he thinks, is it starting to make real sense to work in technology.

Beloussov has no illusions about his own decision to focus on building actual computers and then computer software from the very start. Sipping his nine p.m. espresso in a crowded Starbucks in downtown Moscow, he told me, "I was young and stupid"—he was twenty-two at the time. "If I had invested my first money in privatization, that would have been much more profitable."

Contrast Beloussov's decisions with those of another smart technologist who saw a market opportunity in the late 1980s in the Soviet Union to write computer software: metals and oil magnate Viktor Vekselberg, today worth $12.4 billion.

Vekselberg made his first small fortune in 1988—when Gorbachev's USSR took its first tentative step into capitalism with the cooperative movement—by writing and selling his own computer software program. Within three months he had earned enough, he told me, "to buy an apartment, a car, and a dacha."

He and his five partners next devised a more complicated deal involving salvaging copper wire from scrap heaps in western Siberia (familiar to them because their Moscow institute did a lot of work for the oil fields there), then exporting the copper and using the revenue to import IBM computers, which his group loaded with their own software and sold to Russian companies. The business was hugely lucrative—Vekselberg said he and his partners made a hundred dollars for every single dollar invested—and within a year they had made $1 million. "That sounds funny today," he mused, "but in those days it was huge money."

If this were a Silicon Valley story, Vekselberg and his partners would probably have gone on to become serial software entrepreneurs. If this were a story about India, they would probably have moved on to technology outsourcing. If they were Chinese, they might have used that first million to build a factory. But this was Russia, and Vekselberg was turning out to be one of the country's most adept businessmen, so he saw and jumped on the biggest opportunity: privatization. "People didn't know what to do with privatization vouchers, so we bought up vouchers and used them to participate in privatization auctions. That is how we bought our first real assets, beginning with aluminum factories, and from there on we built our real business."

Beloussov says it isn't his nature to look back, but that his partner "still regrets that we didn't participate in privatization. But it was just impossible for us to understand conceptually."

Today, the Kremlin has given Vekselberg the job of building a Russian Silicon Valley. But Beloussov warns that if the price of oil stays too high, that won't be possible. Most of Russia's technologists have figured out the value of responding to revolution: "Too high a price for oil is bad for an innovation economy," he said. "If the price is too high"—he later told me the ceiling he estimates is around one hundred dollars per barrel—"all the engineers will want to work at the banks and at Gazprom."

Created in 1953 in honor of George C. Marshall, architect of the postwar plan that aided the reconstruction of Europe, the Marshall Scholarship is a glittering academic prize available to American postgraduates to study in the UK. Awarded on the basis of "high ability," the honor is all about brainpower. In the spring of 1990, one of the Americans singled out for that distinction was Reid Hoffman, a California native who graduated from Stanford that year. Hoffman was a quintessential Marshall scholar: he'd earned his bachelor of science in symbolic systems and cognitive science, a hard-core double major, and he'd won the Lloyd W. Dinkelspiel Award, a yearly honor recognizing two students who've made "an exceptional contribution" to undergraduate education. Hoffman arrived in Oxford proud of the prize, excited about what he could learn at that university's renowned philosophy department, and committed to a life of the mind. "When I graduated from Stanford, my plan was to become a professor and a public intellectual," he said. "That is not about quoting Kant. It's about holding up a lens to society and asking, 'Who are we?' and 'Who should we be, as individuals and a society?'"

But twenty years later, Hoffman, who went on to become one of Silicon Valley's most successful entrepreneurs and investors, told me that the worst risk he ever took was that decision to go to Oxford. It was what you might call a risk of omission, or, as Hoffman put it, "the risk I didn't know I was taking."

Going to Oxford on a two-year Marshall Scholarship didn't seem to be a gamble at the time—quite the opposite. "I was focused on my CV," Hoffman said. "Everyone will appreciate I went to Oxford and was a Marshall scholar and these sorts of things."

Here's the rub. While he was at Oxford pursuing his intellectual passion and building his CV, like the good superstar in training he clearly was, Hoffman realized that the world was changing and the old rules no longer applied. "Being in Oxford was in a sense taking a massive risk by taking me out of Silicon Valley," he said. "That was when the online revolution was starting. And being present—being in the network when things are happening, where the opportunities are, is really critical."

Hoffman was lucky. His undergraduate years in the Stanford cognitive science department and having a stepmother who worked in Silicon Valley's venture capital industry meant that even amid Oxford's dreamy spires he was able to figure out that a revolution was taking place more than five thousand miles away. That revelation struck him with such force that today Hoffman still muses over whether, once he realized the action was elsewhere, it was the right decision to stay at Oxford and finish his degree rather than hightail it back to the Valley and its revolutionary vanguard: "I think I made the right choice in one sense and the wrong choice in another."

Once he had his degree, though, Hoffman was determined not to miss out. As a Marshall scholar he was poised to enter the managerial aristocracy and almost certainly become, given his analytical talents, a superstar. But Hoffman wanted more. He wanted to be part of the revolution he saw happening. To do so, he realized, he didn't need a first job with a blue-chip company, he needed to move back to Silicon Valley and get in on the action.

"I actually took myself off the track that lots of my friends have done," Hoffman told me. "You know, become partners at McKinsey and these kinds of things."

But stepping off what Hoffman calls "the career escalator" didn't mean slacking off. Once he returned to the West Coast, Hoffman pursued revolution with the same straight-A fervor he had demonstrated in the more structured worlds of Stanford and Oxford. He moved back home with his grandparents and madly tapped into his network. He called old friends. He even got his stepmother to call old friends on his behalf—a nontrivial leg up, since she was a venture capitalist and had once worked with Brook Byers, one of the name partners in Kleiner, Perkins, Caufield and Byers, the VC firm that is to the Valley what Goldman Sachs is to Wall Street.

Going back home intensified Hoffman's belief that a revolution was happening and that he was at risk of missing it. "'I wish I was here a couple of years ago, when it was really kicking off,'" Hoffman recalls thinking. "'Wow, other people are already doing this. This thing's moving. I'm way behind.'" Hoffman's response, he said, was to decide that "I need to run fast. And the need to run fast is a good impulse to have."

As it turned out, the revolution wasn't quite over. By 1997, with just four years of technology experience under his belt, Hoffman, still running fast, decided to found his own company, Socialnet.com, an online dating site. Socialnet eventually closed down four years later without making much of a mark, but as Hoffman waded into the start-up world, two friends, Peter Thiel and Max Levchin, invited him to join the founding board of directors of their new company, PayPal. In January 2000, Hoffman went to work there full-time, a decision that made him a multimillionaire just two years later when eBay acquired the company.

But the revolution still wasn't over yet, and Hoffman wasn't finished running. "After the eBay/PayPal deal in 2002, I had a plan to take a year off and do some travel," he recalled. "To clear my head and plot the year ahead, I first took a two-week vacation to Australia. While there, I reflected on the moment, and I concluded I needed to return to Silicon Valley and start a consumer Internet company as soon as possible. There was a window of opportunity I could not afford to miss. For one, the market conditions were ripe. There was lots of innovation still to be done on the consumer Web, yet many entrepreneurs—possible competitors—and investors were on the sidelines, scarred from the dot-com bust. They wouldn't be on the sidelines forever. Also, my network was strong coming off the PayPal win, and I could relatively quickly organize the resources to get a new company launched."

That new company was LinkedIn, which went public in 2011, making Hoffman, its cofounder and executive chairman, a billionaire. As a recovering academic, Hoffman has thought hard about the economic forces that have shaped his success. He isn't just a practitioner of responding to revolution—he is one of its theorists. In a book published in 2012, Hoffman argues that the long-term effects of globalization and the technology revolution "are actually underhyped." The result, he believes, is that Detroit—once a symbol of progress, today a symbol of despair—is everywhere. "Once-great companies are falling both more frequently and more quickly than in times past. . . . The forces of competition and change that brought down Detroit are global and local. They threaten every business, every industry, every city."

Hoffman understands that the revolutionary waves he surfs so expertly have created a more polarized society, with both winners and losers. "The gap is growing between those who know the new career rules and have the new skills of a global economy, and those who clutch to old ways of thinking and rely on commoditized skills," he writes. But even as he paints a macro picture of a volatile world with clear winners and losers, Hoffman holds out the hope that each of us can be one of the winners. His book, called *The Start-Up of You*, is a cheerful business advice primer whose premise is that all of us should mimic the strategies of billionaire innovators like himself. "You were born an entrepreneur," Hoffman encourages readers in the opening passage. That doesn't mean, he is quick to stipulate, we should all start our own companies. But he does urge us to think of our own careers as start-ups and manage them with the same agility that the masters of responding to revolution do.

Hoffman, charmingly, doesn't think of himself as a superstar in a nation of supporting players—by following his advice, he wants all of us to have our shot. He may, at forty-four, already be a billionaire and a veteran of two successful start-ups (plus one failed one), but he thinks a 272-page book is enough to teach the rest of us "the mind-sets and skill sets you need to adapt to the future." Indeed, if all of us learn how to respond to revolution, he says—"to manage the start-up of you," that is—society more generally will flourish: "More world problems will be solved—and solved faster—if people practice the values laid out in the pages ahead."

Hoffman is smart, likable, and compassionate. It is no accident he founded LinkedIn: he is known as Silicon Valley's nice-guy billionaire, someone so affable he has figured out how to take the sleaze out of networking. He wants to make the world a better place and he is well aware of the downsides of the revolutionary age we live in. But what's also striking is Hoffman's confidence, from his privileged perch, that all of us will be able to thrive in these revolutionary times if only we develop the right mind-sets and skill sets.

That may well be the case. But, as experts in revolution, and the beneficiaries of them, the plutocrats sometimes miss the fact that for people in the middle and at the bottom, times of dramatic change are as likely to bring painful dislocation as they are to bring dazzling opportunity.

When the Texas-based Randall Stephenson, CEO of AT&T, visited the Council on Foreign Relations in its elegant town house on the Upper East Side of New York, to describe the mobility revolution and its immense commercial potential, one of the council's members asked him a question that underscored the difference between these two outcomes.

The questioner was Farooq Kathwari, the CEO of furniture manufacturer and retailer Ethan Allen. Kathwari is one of Citigroup's dopamine-rich risk takers: he arrived in New York from Kashmir with thirty-seven dollars in his pocket and got his start in the retail trade selling goods sent to him from home by his grandfather.

Here's what he asked Stephenson: "Over the last ten years, with the help of technology and other things, we today are doing about the same business with 50 percent less people. We're talking of jobs. I would just like to get your perspectives on this great technology. How is it going to overall affect the job markets in the next five years?"

Not to worry, Stephenson said: "While technology allows companies like yours to do more with less, I don't think that necessarily means that there is less employment opportunities available. It's just a redeployment of those employment opportunities. And those employees you have, my expectation was, with your productivity, their standard of living has actually gotten better."

Unfortunately, at least in the short term, that benign scenario isn't turning out to be true. The technology revolution is certainly making both Ethan Allen and AT&T more productive, and delivering windfalls to the bosses able to navigate that change. (Stephenson's compensation in 2010 was $27.3 million.) But both companies have been shedding workers. AT&T has fifty thousand fewer workers today than it did before the financial crisis.

Kathwari has made a point of continuing to manufacture in the United States—70 percent of Ethan Allen's products are made in North America. But to remain competitive—"Most of our competitors manufacture outside the U.S.," he told me—Kathwari has turned to technology. His seven North American plants have taken the place of twenty; over the past eight years, Kathwari's workforce has shrunk by about half.

"The big question is what it does to the people, because it creates unemployment," Kathwari told me. "If you look at it from an individual business perspective, you are saying, Great! Technology is key to survival from an individual company point of view. But in the long run we can only be successful if the country is working. Business leaders should be concerned."

Even for those workers who do find new jobs, the consequences of being fired are brutal. Three economists analyzing the 1982 recession have found that U.S. workers take an average 30 percent pay cut when they find a new job after being laid off. Even after twenty years, their earnings were still 20 percent lower than those of peers who kept their jobs in the recession. In emerging markets, the cost of change can be even higher: in the 1990s, the decade when the Russian oligarchs became billionaires, the incomes, health, and birth rates of ordinary Russians plummeted. India's economic rise has coincided with an epidemic of suicides among its rural farmers. The same is true of inland China, which has been left out of the coast's economic renaissance.

Our democratic impulse is to imagine that economic forces affect us all equally and that there exists a set of "management skills"—the equivalent of knowing how to read or to add—that serve all of us equally well. But the tougher reality is that economic transformation—the waves of revolution we are living through—has a very uneven impact. As Nobel laureate Michael Spence put it, "Your education isn't fungible the way an investment portfolio is." Soros can respond to revolution by cutting his losses and making a different bet; finding a new profession at forty-five, after your old one has been rendered redundant, isn't so simple.

We are living through a tale not of two cities but of two economies. Hoffman makes the essential point that the winners of the old economic order are among those whose lives and careers are being disrupted. "For the last sixty or so years, the job market for educated workers worked like an escalator. After graduating from college, you landed an entry-level job at the bottom of the escalator at an IBM or a GE or a Goldman Sachs. . . . There was a sense that if you were basically competent, put forth a good effort, and weren't unlucky, the strong winds at your back would eventually shoot you to a good high level. For the most part this was a justified expectation." Hoffman is right about both those expectations and the disappointment of the upper middle class stuck on a jammed career escalator. But what about the telecom or furniture factory workers Kathwari is worried about? Even if they see the revolution coming, do they have the room in their father's home and the contact book of a venture capitalist stepmom to help them respond to it?

Even Hoffman, who wants to be a sunny self-help guru, is too much of a scholar and an empath not to see that. "Remember: If you don't find risk, risk will find you," he warns in one of his book's scarier passages. "In the past, when you thought about stable employers, you thought IBM, HP, General Motors—all stalwart companies that have been around a long time and employ hundreds of thousands of people. . . . Imagine what it must have been like for someone who thought he was a lifer at HP; his skills, experience, and network were all inextricably linked to his nine-to-five employer. And then: BOOM. He's unemployed."

RENT-SEEKING

They steal and steal and steal. They are stealing absolutely
everything and it is impossible to stop them. But let them steal
and take their property. They will become owners and decent
administrators of this property.

> —*Anatoly Chubais, the architect of Russian privatization,
> in conversation with Sergei Kovalyev, a former dissident
> and Russian politician*

Eating increases the appetite.

> —*Russian proverb, quoted by Kovalyev in response to Chubais*

Raghuram Rajan is a professor at the University of Chicago, the intellectual home of free market economics. He is also a former chief
economist of the International Monetary Fund, another institution
not known for its hostility to global capitalism. A tall, slim forty-nine-year-
old, Rajan favors the pressed button-down shirts and short, neat hair of an
investment banker, rather than the stereotypical rumpled tweeds of a college teacher. In 2008 he returned to his native India to address the subcontinent's most prestigious business association, the Bombay Chamber of
Commerce and Industry, which, founded in 1836, was largely responsible
for the first railway built in India and whose members' wealth could buy

about a third of India's annual economic output. But Rajan was there to caution his country's rising capitalists, rather than to rally them.

India, he said, risked becoming "an unequal oligarchy, or worse, perhaps far sooner than we think." One piece of evidence Rajan cited was a spreadsheet compiled by Jayant Sinha, an old classmate of his from the Indian Institute of Technology, the country's MIT and alma mater to many of its software entrepreneurs. Sinha had calculated the number of billionaires per trillion dollars of GDP in a number of countries around the world. Russia, with eighty-seven billionaires and a national GDP of $1.3 trillion, had the highest billionaire-to-GDP ratio. India, Rajan said, was number two, with fifty-five billionaires and $1.1 trillion of GDP.

Rajan assured his audience that he had nothing against billionaires per se: "We should certainly welcome it if businessmen make money legitimately." But he argued that India's high billionaire-to-GDP ratio was "alarming" because most of the country's super-rich weren't software pioneers or inventive manufacturers. Instead, "too many people have gotten too rich based on their proximity to the government. . . . Land, natural resources, and government contracts or licenses are the predominant sources of the wealth of our billionaires and all of these factors come from the government.

"If Russia is an oligarchy," Rajan warned the assembled magnates, "how long can we resist calling India one?"

In the wake of the financial crisis, some critics have warned that America, too, risks becoming an oligarchy. Simon Johnson, another former chief economist of the IMF, has compared the bankers of the world's superpower to emerging market oligarchs, arguing that they similarly have succeeded in diverting national resources—notably the bailout trillions—to themselves. The financiers, he says, have pulled off a "quiet coup."

Johnson and Rajan have a shared concern: in an age of super-wealth, we need to be constantly alert to efforts by the elite to get rich by using their political muscle to increase their share of the preexisting pie, rather than by adding value to the economy and thus increasing the size of the pie overall. As the gap between the super-rich and everyone else has grown, enrichment through reallocation—which economists call "rent-seeking"—has become a hot political issue. It is one thing for Steve Jobs, whose products are so often objects of adoration, or even Bill Gates, whose products are so often instruments of torture, to accumulate billions. It is quite another for multimillion-dollar compensation to be paid to bankers whose institutions were bailed out by taxpayer trillions, or private equity fund managers who pay 15 percent tax on most of their earnings, or for the CEOs of multinational companies to take home higher paychecks than their billion-dollar firms pay in tax in the United States.

That's why today rent-seeking is a favorite theme for the left. But as a field of formal study, rent-seeking was most energetically elaborated by economists on the right: it is, after all, the product of state control and distribution of wealth, something the right has been in the business of trying to decrease. And as inequality rises in twenty-first-century America, some on the right have returned to the idea that the central economic ill is rent-seeking. Speaking about "The American Idea" at the Heritage Foundation in the fall of 2011, Paul Ryan, the wonkish Wisconsin congressman, argued that, rather than raise taxes on individuals, we should "lower the amount of government spending the wealthy now receive." The "true sources of inequity in our country," he continued, are "corporate welfare that enriches the powerful, and empty promises that betray the powerless." The real class warfare that threatens us, he said, is "a class of bureaucrats and connected crony capitalists trying to rise above the rest of us, call the shots, rig the rules, and preserve their place atop society."

Here's another paradox: some of the most egregious examples of rent-seeking in recent decades have been the unintended consequence of liberal reforms designed to loosen the state's grip on the economy. These range from the transformative privatizations in formerly centrally planned economies to the deregulation of the financial sectors of the Anglo-American economies.

Rent-seeking also takes the more classic form of powerful groups using their influence to bend the rules of the economic game in their own favor. That is easiest to do, of course, when you control the state—which is why, for instance, Nicaragua's authoritarian Somoza family and Mir Osman Ali Khan, the last hereditary prince of the Indian state of Hyderabad, both appear on lists of the richest families of the twentieth century. Finally, innovators can be rent-seekers if they become so successful their companies become monopolist. That was true of the railroad barons in the late nineteenth century and Microsoft in the late twentieth century, and surely will be of some twenty-first-century entrepreneur.

SALE OF THE CENTURY

October is the best month to visit Kiev. The leaves of the horse chestnut trees that line the Khreshchatyk, the wide boulevard that is the Ukrainian capital's central artery, range from dark green to bright yellow, the average high temperature is a crisp sixty-three degrees, and the central European sun isn't yet obscured by the clouds of November.

But on October 24, 2005, attention was turned indoors, to an undistinguished room inside the State Property Fund, a grim Soviet-era building in the exclusive Perchersky neighborhood. On this autumn day, industrialists from as far afield as India and Luxembourg, the international press, some 150 demonstrators, and the nation's television cameras, broadcasting live, converged on the State Property Fund to participate in an event of unlikely drama: the auction of Kryvorizhstal, Ukraine's largest steel mill.

The starting price was $2 billion. In a three-way fight between Mittal Steel, based in Europe and owned by the Indian Mittal dynasty; Luxembourg's Arcelor, working in concert with eastern Ukrainian oligarchs; and the LLC Smart Group, a Dnipropetrovsk-based consortium of Russians and Ukrainians, the number quickly soared to more than double that amount.

"Once more, I am reminding you that on the table is the package of shares for the Kryvorizhstal company," the auctioneer, wearing an ordinary business suit, reminded the bidders and live television audience forty minutes into the proceedings. "Participant number three [Mittal Steel] bids a price of 24,200 million hryvnias [$4.8 billion]. Three! Sold to participant number three."

Recently ousted prime minister Yulia Tymoshenko, wearing her characteristic coronet of wheat-colored braids and displaying her equally characteristic sense of theater, was the first to congratulate Lakshmi Mittal, the family's second-generation steel man and its reigning patriarch. "It was like a football game!" she said triumphantly.

The oligarchs, she told me when we met later (and after she had been reinstalled as prime minister), "hate me—they don't understand me because . . . they cannot buy me or scare me." She was both right and wrong. In 2011, after Viktor Yanukovych, whose candidacy was backed by several eastern Ukrainian oligarchs, was elected president, he imprisoned Ms. Tymoshenko, in a politically motivated case redolent of Mikhail Khodorkovsky. She still isn't scared, though, and was defiant both in the dock and in statements from jail.

The auction was certainly a moment of high political drama for Ukrainians. The democratic Orange Revolution, which Ms. Tymoshenko helped lead, had swept to power ten months earlier partly thanks to public revulsion at the 2004 privatization of Kryvorizhstal, for just $800 million, to a consortium that included the then president's son-in-law. The 2005 reprivatization, at a price that was six times higher, was both a fulfillment of one of the Orange Revolution's central promises and a vindication of one of its chief complaints.

But the Kryvorizhstal auction is also the central drama in an even bigger story. Of all the state-owned assets in the entire former Soviet Union sold to private owners since 1991, when the USSR collapsed, the one with the very highest price tag is Kryvorizhstal. That is an astonishing fact. In the two decades since the end of Soviet communism, the successor states have privatized oil companies that control around one hundred billion barrels of crude oil reserves, a mine that produced 25 percent of the world's nickel, a major diamond producer, and a vast aluminum industry. But it is a Stalin-era steel mill in a grim and anonymous city in southern Ukraine that, if cost is any measure of value, turns out to have been the crown jewel in the former Soviet Union's natural resource and industrial patrimony.

That, of course, is absurd. Which is why the real story of Kryvorizhstal isn't the successful multibillion-dollar sale of a Ukrainian steel mill to an Indian magnate, it is how it dramatizes the vast giveaway of the rest of the assets of the former Soviet Union. That shift from state to private ownership is probably the single largest transfer of assets in human history. When it comes to the creation of twenty-first-century billionaires, the USSR's sale of the century is also the most powerful driver, more important than Silicon Valley's technology revolution or the flourishing of finance on Wall Street and in the City of London. Just consider: of the 1,226 billionaires on the *Forbes* 2012 rich list, 111 were oligarchs from the former Soviet Union, 90 were technologists, and 77 were financiers. The number of billionaires relative to the size of the economy and the gap between the billionaires and everyone else are even more striking: The fortunes of Russia's billionaires could buy roughly a fifth of the country's annual economic output. Compare that with the United States, whose 424 billionaires could buy just over 10 percent of their country's annual economic output, or South Korea, whose 20 billionaires could afford just 4 percent of their country's yearly economic output. *Forbes* declared that in 2012, Moscow was the world's "top city" for billionaires, boasting 78 of them, compared with just 58 in New York, and nearly double London's 39. Indeed, economic historians have found that Russia's oligarchs have done so well for themselves that inequality today is higher than it was under the tsars.

The fire sale of the assets of the former Soviet Union stands out because it marked such a sharp shift from nearly total state ownership, because the loot that was privatized was so valuable, and because the transition was so swift. But it was also part of a wider global trend. If you ever doubt that ideas matter, consider the astonishing, bloodless victory of liberal economic thinking and its concrete impact around the world in the last two decades of the twentieth century. The two great behemoths of state ownership—the former Soviet Union and China—shifted vast assets into private hands. Mixed economies in the developing world like India, Mexico, and Brazil sold off state companies and natural resources. Western capitalist countries, led by Britain, sold off companies that had once been considered natural monopolies and spun off the provision of many services that had once been thought best performed by the state.

Everywhere, the goal was to get the government out. But the irony of the victory of the liberal economic idea is that putting it into practice delivered the greatest rent-seeking windfall in economic history—the state, after all, was in charge of privatization. Influencing that one-off division of the spoils was one of the surest ways to join today's global super-elite.

WHO WAS THE RICHEST MAN IN HISTORY?

In fact, according to calculations by Branko Milanovic, the richest man who ever lived isn't a Russian oligarch, but he does owe much of his fortune to the great wave of liberalization that swept the world when Soviet communism collapsed.

Comparing income across history is hard. The conversion tools we use to make comparisons across geographies today—currency exchange rates or the more subtle measure of purchasing power parity—are ineffective when the goods we consume—horses vs. private jets or personal scribes vs. iPads—are so different. Milanovic gets around this mismatch by turning to Adam Smith. His yardstick of wealth was how much of our compatriots' work we can buy: "A person must be rich or poor according to the quantity of labor which he can command." Among today's billionaires, Milanovic's calculations favor the rich man in a poor country—he can employ more of his less well-paid compatriots. If anything, it is also a measure that overstates the wealth of the ancients—after all, no matter how rich you were in Rome or Egypt, what today are ordinary middle-class services like telephones or airplane travel were in those days luxuries that were literally unimaginable. What Milanovic's approach may understate is the power gap between ancient oligarchs and everyone else: many owned slaves or serfs, whom they were free to beat or kill, and some could raise their own armies, which rivaled the power of the relatively weak state.

Marcus Crassus, who lives on today as a cartoon villain in video games based on Spartacus's slave revolt, which he helped crush, was famous in his own time as the wealthiest man in Rome. He was nicknamed "Dives" or "the Rich" and successfully defended himself when charged with the capital crime of corrupting a vestal virgin by explaining he was after the maiden's money, not her virtue; his fellow Romans thought that account rang true to character. Plutarch estimated Crassus's fortune at 170 million sesterces; Pliny the Elder put it a little higher, at 200 million. That second estimate was roughly the size of the entire government treasury of the Roman empire. Gauged by Milanovic's metric, Crassus's fortune translated into an annual return that was equal to the average yearly income of thirty-two thousand Romans.

That's a lot, but Crassus was handily outearned by the first generation of plutocrats, the robber barons of the Gilded Age. Andrew Carnegie's wealth was at its apex in 1901, when he purchased U.S. Steel. His share in the company was worth $225 million, which yielded an annual income the same as that of 48,000 average Americans. John D. Rockefeller did even better: his peak fortune of $1.4 billion in 1937 yielded an annual income equal to that of 116,000 Americans.

But all three are trumped by the man at the head of the 2012 *Forbes* global rich list, Mexican tycoon Carlos Slim. *Forbes* put Slim's fortune that year at $69 billion, enough to earn an income equivalent to the average annual salary of more than 400,000 Mexicans. Here's another way to see Slim's relative economic weight in Mexico: His fortune could buy 6 percent of Mexico's annual economic output. At his peak wealth, Rockefeller could buy less than 2 percent of the U.S. annual output. Bill Gates, America's top dog in the twenty-first century, could afford less than 0.5 percent of the country's yearly economic output. If you make a telephone call, smoke a cigarette, go to the bank, take a flight, or ride a bike in Mexico, you probably pay a few pesos to Slim. His presence is so ubiquitous that one restaurant in the capital quips on its menu that it is the only place in Mexico not owned by Slim.

Like the Russian oligarchs—as it happens, Milanovic thinks the second-richest person of all time was oil baron Mikhail Khodorkovsky, who he calculates could buy the labor of a quarter of a million Russians in 2003, the year before Khodorkovsky was arrested—Slim owes his leap from millionaire to billionaire to the wave of economic liberalization that swept the world, particularly the previously state-dominated emerging market economies, in the nineties. In Slim's case, the windfall was telecom privatization.

That sale was orchestrated by Carlos Salinas, a Harvard-educated technocrat determined to reform a stagnant Mexican economy whose growth was constrained in part by the dominance of inefficient, state-controlled companies. Like the liberals who spearheaded Russia's great sell-off, Salinas was a true believer in market reforms. And he believed in Slim, whom he had befriended in the eighties. That was a rough decade—the 1982 nationalization of the country's banks and the plummeting price of oil had provoked capital flight and weakened economic growth—but Slim, building on his family's retailing fortune and his own balance-sheet brilliance, held his nerve and bought assets on the cheap, expanding into cigarette production and insurance. Salinas liked Slim's commitment to the country, his ability to see opportunity at a time of peril, and his entrepreneurial verve. The pair were dubbed "Carlos and Charlie's" after a cheap and cheerful local restaurant chain.

Slim was a vocal supporter of his friend's reform effort, speaking in favor of the plan in both public and private and lobbying politicians and the media to back it, too. When Telmex, the country's telecom monopoly went on the block, he pounced. Unlike so many of the post-Soviet privatizations, Telmex was auctioned off for real money—$1.76 billion, for a more than 20 percent controlling stake, which was widely considered reasonable at the time. (Even at that healthy price, one of the losing bidders, and an erstwhile close friend of Slim's, Roberto Hernández, has suggested the auction was rigged. Both Slim and Salinas have repeatedly denied that charge.)

Telmex's privatizers were right to argue that the state monopoly had done a dreadful job serving Mexicans. Before Telmex was sold off, the average wait for a telephone line was a year, and only one-quarter of Mexican homes had a phone. But the sale was also a rent-seeker's dream. That's partly because, to dress up Telmex on the auction block and make the privatization a political success in the short term, the winner was offered a six-year extension of the company's national phone monopoly and the only national cell phone license.

These formidable advantages were enhanced by a remarkably weak regulatory setup. The sale itself was conducted by the finance ministry, rather than the telecommunications ministry, and a telecom regulator was created only three years after the Telmex privatization. Once it was up and running, the regulator was severely outgunned; its annual budget was just a couple of days' revenue of the Slim telephone businesses. Even when regulators do rule against Telmex, as a study by Mexican and American political scientists Isabel Guerrero, Luis-Felipe López-Calva, and Michael Walton has found, the company is very effective at using *amparos*, a Mexican court injunction that allows government rulings to be blocked, to delay unfavorable decisions. When Salinas's party, the PRI, gave way to Vicente Fox, Mexico's first president elected by the opposition party in decades, Slim's cozy relationship with the state endured—Fox named a former Telmex employee, Pedro Cerisola, as minister of communications and transport.

The result has been lucrative market dominance for the Slim telecom empire, which controls about 80 percent of all fixed lines, and about 70 percent of all cell phones. One consequence of that near-monopoly control is low investment in innovation—Mexico's is among the lowest in the OECD. Indian companies filed five telecom patents in 2001 and thirteen in 2005; Mexican firms didn't file any between 1991 and 2005. Another is high price. Within the OECD, Mexican businesses pay the highest rates for a basket of cell lines and landlines; Mexican individuals pay the second-highest rate. As a result, in 2007 half of Mexicans had a landline telephone and 60 percent had a cell phone. That is a great improvement on 1990, but a poor performance compared with a country like Turkey, which has roughly the same per capita GDP as Mexico but a phone penetration of 75 percent.

Slim is the biggest beneficiary of Mexico's liberalization, but he isn't its only one. In 1991, shortly after Salinas launched his reform drive, there were two Mexicans on the *Forbes* billionaire list. In 1994, at the end of the Salinas presidency, there were twenty-four. Like Slim, Mexico's other billionaires were enriched not only by the initial sell-off of state assets, but also by an ongoing ability to influence the rules of the economic game. The political scientists who rated Slim's success at getting telecom judgments that helped Telmex did a broader calculation of the legal effectiveness of the country's plutocrats. They found that billionaires were three times more likely than other plaintiffs to win rulings in their favor and triumphed over state regulators an average of three out of four times when their disputes went to court.

The rise of the Mexican and former Soviet privatization billionaires is an easy target, because the broader impact of liberalization on their countries' economies has been mediocre. Mexico grew by an average of 3.5 percent a year in the 1990s and under 2 percent a year in the first decade of this century. Russia, after a sharp decline following the collapse of communism, has grown by an annual average of over 4 percent since 2000. Those are good numbers, but they pale in comparison with the performance of emerging market tigers like China, where average annual growth over the past decade has been 9 percent; India, which averaged 7 percent; or Brazil, which grew at an average rate of over 3 percent.

But as Rajan warned his audience at the Bombay Chamber of Commerce, even in India, with its stellar economic growth and democratic political system, rent-seeking is turning out to be a very effective way to join the super-elite.

RENT-SEEKING AND THE END OF THE LICENSE RAJ

It wasn't supposed to turn out this way. Manmohan Singh, another idealistic technocrat who became prime minister in 2004, had brought the global market reform revolution to India in 1991 when he was finance minister. The animating idea was to liberate the country from the License Raj, a protectionist system that sheltered state-dominated firms and the privately owned national champions who were in on the game. The old system was a good deal for government officials and for the private firms granted access to the License Raj, but it was a poor setup for everyone else. India's GDP increased at a sleepy average of around 3 percent in the decades between independence and 1991—known, with self-deprecating irony, as "the Hindu rate of growth"—and India's consumers, who were poor to begin with, had their purchasing power further eroded by being limited to more costly and lower-quality domestic goods.

Like Soviet communism, which had been a partial ideological inspiration for "third-way" India—when he trained as an economist in the 1970s, one of Singh's projects, like that of all Indian economists of his generation, was learning how to create a five-year national central plan—the License Raj was a rent-seeking dystopia. Singh's reforms were meant to end that systemic corruption and create an economy where the way to get rich was by producing more, better, and cheaper goods and services.

By many measures, the reforms were a dazzling success. The Indian economy grew an average of 7 percent in the past two decades, and average annual per capita income nearly quadrupled between 1991 and 2011. But on the road to the market, Indians have had one unwelcome surprise. Ending the License Raj hasn't ended rent-seeking. In fact, government connections are probably more lucrative today than they were in the old system.

As in other liberalizing emerging markets, India's reforms have been a hugely effective mechanism for billionaire creation. India had just one billionaire in 1991, on the eve of Singh's reforms. In 2012, there were forty-eight. With a fortune of $22.3 billion, Mukesh Ambani was the richest Indian in 2012. He had just under a third of the wealth of Slim and, because India is so vast, a fraction of his control of the national economy. As a group, though, India's plutocrats—the forty-eight billionaires—in 2012 had a combined net worth equal to more than 14 percent of their country's GDP. That's equal to the economic footprint of America's 424 billionaires.

The rent-seeking side of Indian capitalism became a dramatic part of the national conversation in 2010, when tapes tax investigators had made of more than 140 conversations of Niira Radia, a glamorous Delhi lobbyist, were leaked to the media. In the hundreds of hours of talk between Radia, businessmen, journalists, and politicians, ministries are described as ATM machines and the ruling party is called "our shop." She is explicit about how lucrative mobile phone licenses were allocated: "When it came to spectrum, they went to [Andimuthu] Raja [the telecommunications minister] and paid him a bribe and got spectrum allocated," she tells a rival businessman.

One measure of the impact was an Indian version of the popular protests that swept the world in 2011, from Tahrir Square to Zuccotti Park. The subcontinent's 99 percent coalesced around Anna Hazare, a veteran activist whose anticorruption hunger strike rallied the country's hitherto quiescent urban middle class and may lead to the creation of a stronger anticorruption investigative body.

One of Hazare's top lieutenants is Dr. Kiran Bedi. Bedi is a national legend in her own right. She was the first Indian woman police officer— officials asked her to consider another career when she applied to join the force in 1972—and rose to be the head of its investigative division. She once doused herself in water from a street fountain before running into a burning building to lead her team in the rescue of its seventeen occupants. She is equally famous for having Indira Gandhi's car towed for parking illegally—a beloved signal that no one was above the law. When I met Dr. Bedi in Mumbai in 2011, she was a sixty-one-year-old grandmother with glasses and her black hair trimmed in a brisk boyish haircut. Bedi is small— she claims five feet, three inches—and was once lifted from the ground by a student protester she was policing. She was dressed in a vibrant turquoise shalwar kameez that matched her energetic manner.

"India has been overwhelmed by corruption scams," Dr. Bedi told me. "While it has been apparent that India is shining, India has also been declining in many ways in that there has been rampant exposure of corruption.

"It was a relationship of illicit wealth between the people in power and the people who had money," Dr. Bedi said. "The rich could get richer by buying to be rich. They could afford to buy better contracts and those contracts which are expensive and monopolistic—the mining rights, the key infrastructure rights . . . They broke the balance of a level playing field for the younger and the newcomers, so therefore I think that was the imbalance which happened in the economy or in the distribution of the economy."

Nor is it just the activists who have come to fear that alongside India's remarkable economic surge the rot has been spreading, too.

"Corruption is endemic," Rajiv Lall, the chief executive officer of the Infrastructure Development Finance Company, a partly state-owned financial institution, and the official who invited Rajan to give his Bombay Chamber of Commerce lecture, told me. "I don't think anybody here is pretending that there's no corruption in the country. And corruption can take on a new dimension, especially in this time of great transformation."

"The Gini coefficient [an economic measure of income inequality] always rises whenever growth takes off," Arun Maira, a former industrialist and now a member of the country's influential planning commission, told me. "When you open more opportunity, like more free markets and the opportunity for people to do their own thing, those who already have some capital, or they have some education, or they have access to people in power so that they could help get access to the new opportunities more easily, they will first grow themselves, their own wealth. So you will get the people with something becoming richer faster than those who don't have access to education, to some capital, and to the system."

As Mr. Maira pointed out, one of the most powerful advantages of the 1 percent is "access to people in power." Corrupt business deals are the most extreme use—and abuse—of those relationships. But there is a more subtle reason the game is most effectively played by those who are already winning it.

"The tendency is that people who have access to power and access to governments, etc., tend to get a better deal actually," said Kris Gopalakrishnan, the cochair of Infosys, the pioneering Indian technology company. "The policies, the roots are framed because they are people who give inputs to those policies. Because you don't ask everybody when policies get formed. You ask the key people I need to talk to."

To understand what it is like to operate in a society where both opportunity and corruption are flourishing, I spoke to a young, up-and-coming Mumbai businessman. Raj, who is in his midthirties, agreed to be frank in exchange for my promise not to use his name (the details of his life are precise; the name is disguised). In America, where he went to business school, Raj would be a member of the 1 percent. In India, where he was born, Raj is part of the 0.1 percent, but he is no billionaire.

After getting his MBA at Duke, Raj went to work for one of the major consulting companies in New York; he still owns a one-bedroom apartment in the Flatiron district, which he bought partly as an investment and partly to maintain a connection with the city he loves. Two years ago, however, he moved to his company's newly opened office in his hometown, Mumbai, and he plans to make the rest of his career in India. Raj believes the Indian economy will grow at least 7 percent a year for the next decade, creating a world of possibilities unimaginable in the slower-developing West. One example: in addition to his day job and his duties as the father of six-year-old and six-month-old daughters (his American-born wife works part-time at another multinational), Raj has founded his own company, which manufactures molded-plastic injection parts.

"You could be a billionaire if you moved to India, too," he tells me. "All you need is the luck to meet the right government official and a willingness to risk going to jail."

Raj is thriving both in his day job as a consultant and in his weekend shift at the factory. The consultancy is booming because "Indian firms are now going global." One of his clients, for instance, whom Raj describes as a "midlevel player" with a net worth of around $500 million, is considering the acquisition of a company with operations in Mexico and Europe. "This globalization is new for Indian companies at this level, and it will be the big trend for the next five years," he said.

Raj's plastics business, which initially failed to take off but now is expanding at about 100 percent a year, is thriving for a different reason. "It took me a long time to figure out who to bribe in government to get a government contract," Raj said. I asked if he minded paying backhanders. Not especially, he said, but he wished it had been easier and quicker to identify and befriend the right decision maker in the civil service.

RED OLIGARCHS

On March 5, 2012, the three thousand members of the National People's Congress gathered in Beijing for their annual ten-day meeting. The National People's Congress is nominally the highest governmental body in China. In practice, real power resides with the twenty-five-member Politburo and its Standing Committee. The National People's Congress partly serves as a political Potemkin village, a rubber-stamp legislature whose role is to create a pretense of popular representation in what is an authoritarian system, just as the "elections," with their 99 percent majorities, did in the Soviet era.

But the National People's Congress isn't purely ornamental. The NPC's March meeting is held every year alongside the annual Chinese People's Political Consultative Conference. Together, the two events are known as the *lianghui*—or two meetings—and they form the most important event on the Chinese political calendar. The lianghui let the world know which political faction is ascendant within the Communist Party—at the 2012 meetings Bo Xilai, the flamboyant party secretary of Chongqing and a powerful Politburo member, was publicly demoted, in a sign that the statist group, of which he was the most prominent member, was in decline— and which direction economic policy is likely to take. They are a forum at which political trial balloons can safely be floated and the private factional battles that are at the heart of China's real politics can subtly be rehearsed before a wider audience.

Most important, in a country that brutally abolished hereditary social distinctions when Mao's Communists came to power, the National People's Congress is the closest China comes to a modern-day Debrett's list—if you want to know who's who in China, there's no better place to start than the delegate list. That's why a Bloomberg story based on a study published on the eve of the 2012 congress by the Hurun Report, the best source of intelligence on China's rich, was so striking.

According to Hurun, the seventy richest members of the NPC made more money in 2011 than the total combined net worth of all the members of all three branches of U.S. government—the president and his cabinet, both houses of Congress, and the justices of the Supreme Court. The top seventy members of the NPC added $11.5 billion to their combined net worth in 2011, bringing their total to $89.8 billion. That 2011 gain of the top seventy Chinese legislators is more than 50 percent greater than the total net worth of all 660 members of the three federal branches of U.S. government, whose 2011 net worth was $7.5 billion. The contrast is equally striking when you compare the very richest members of the NPC with their U.S. equivalents. The wealthiest 2 percent of the NPC—the top sixty members—had an average net worth of $1.44 billion in 2011. The top 2 percent of U.S. legislators—eleven Congress members—had an average wealth of $323 million. Zong Qinghou, China's beverage magnate with an estimated wealth of nearly $10 billion and one of the five richest men in China depending on the year, is a deputy of the NPC. Other business tycoons in the group include Lu Guanqiu, the chairman of the Wanxiang Group, China's leading auto parts maker, and Wang Jianlin, a real estate developer.

These calculations by the Hurun Report were striking partly because, at a moment when American public opinion was becoming uncharacteristically agitated about the nexus of political power and money, they showed that when it came to creating billionaire politicians the Americans are pikers compared to the Chinese. More broadly, they are also a reminder that, for all its success in raising 300 million of its 1.3 billion citizens out of poverty since the introduction of market reforms in the late 1980s, Beijing has also created one of the world's most conducive economies for rent-seeking. "There are skeletons behind every entrepreneur in China," Rupert Hoogewerf, publisher of the Hurun Report, told a reporter.

We don't often equate the rise of China with the rise of the red oligarchs. That's partly because, unlike most economies that are friendly to rent-seeking, China has been so phenomenally successful: rent-seeking and the sustained high growth that China has experienced don't often go together. It is also because, in contrast with the countries of the former Warsaw Pact, which transferred the property of the communist state into private hands with a big-bang sell-off, China's market reforms have been slower and its avenues for rent-seeking have been more varied and more opaque than a quick privatization drive led from the top.

Finally, China's billionaires are among the world's most discreet. China's rising bourgeoisie loves conspicuous consumption: gold is so popular you can buy it at ATMs, all the West's great luxury brands are enjoying robust growth in China, and the market for the highest-end possessions—old wine and fine art in particular—is driven significantly by Chinese demand. In 2011, according to a study by the European Fine Art Foundation, China as a whole accounted for almost a third of the global art market revenue, outshopping the United States for the first time. But at the very, very top, China's billionaires understand that notoriety is dangerous. The Russians invite British politicians to party on their yachts in the Mediterranean and buy sports teams in New York and London; the Indians vie to build the biggest mansion and to do the sexiest deal with a famous Western partner; the Latin Americans buy penthouses in Manhattan and stakes in U.S. media companies. While the Chinese state has been flexing its muscles in the Western political economy, Chinese billionaires, of whom there are ninety-five—the third-largest cohort in the world—are less visible. That is because they know that the Chinese regime—still, after all, a one-party communist state—is highly ambivalent about its plutocrats. Hence the party's official policy of pursuing "harmonious growth" and Premier Wen Jiabao's insistence, on the eve of the lianghui, that "we should not only make the cake of social wealth as big as possible, but also distribute the cake in a fair way and let everyone enjoy the fruits of reform and opening up." "Four legs good, two legs better" is the politically dangerous contradiction at the heart of China today. One way to appease the restive four legs is to imprison the occasional Chinese plutocrat, which is why you probably can't name a single one.

But if you have the self-discipline to fly below the radar, China is a rent-seekers' paradise. That is because over the past few decades the Middle Kingdom has offered three lucrative routes to rent-seeking, and many of its billionaires have taken advantage of all of them. The Chinese hate comparisons with Russia's capitalist transition—when my book on Russia's sale of the century was translated into Chinese, the first question Chinese journalists always asked me was "How were the Russian market reforms a failure compared to the Chinese approach?"—but many of their plutocrats have been the beneficiaries of a slower and more opaque version of the same transition from total state ownership to some private property. Tellingly, both the Chinese and the Russians refer to the murky first fortunes of their liberalization-era plutocrats as their "original sins."

Second, China has what you might call robber baron plutocrats: the rent-seeking billionaires who develop a network of government connections and use them to reap windfall fortunes at a moment of rapid economic growth—in China's case, the shift from a poor, rural economy to an urban and industrial one. America doesn't think too highly of its robber barons, but these, like the privatization plutocrats, are not the worst kind to have. Both use personal connections to unfairly benefit from a massive transition, and both capture value that a fair and effective state would have diverted to the common good. But both are also the beneficiaries, and very often the drivers, of an economic transition that transforms the economic prospects of the country as a whole. That's why, over the past three decades, China's average per capita income has risen from $200 to $5,400, and 50 percent of its people now live in cities, where the average income is over three times higher than in the countryside. The rent-seeking beneficiaries of these big shifts in the United States in the nineteenth century and in China over the past three decades were part of a change that had broadly shared benefits.

Third, and most important, rent-seeking in China isn't just the result of a fast and turbulent economic transformation—though that is, of course, taking place. Making money through government connections isn't a temporary, one-off thing in the People's Republic, or a "corrupt" instance of rule breaking. In a state-capitalist system like China's, making money by being close to the state isn't an exception to the rules or a violation of them—it is how the system really works.

"What moves this structure is not a market economy and its laws of supply and demand, but a carefully balanced social mechanism built around the particular interests of the revolutionary families who constitute the political elite," explain Carl Walter and Fraser Howie in their award-winning book on the Chinese economy, *Red Capitalism*. "China is a family-run business.

"Failure to grasp the impact of unbridled Western-style capitalism on its elite families in a society and culture lacking in legal or ethical counterbalances is to miss the reality of today's China. Greed is the driving force behind the protectionist walls of the state-owned economy inside the system and money is the language."

Unlike their Russian comrades, China's red oligarchs didn't get rich in a one-off privatization of the country's natural resources. China hasn't had a mass privatization moment, and it lacks Russia's vast oil and metal wealth. Instead, China's rent-seekers prospered through privileged access to the two essential economic goods the state does control: land and capital. A preponderance of China's plutocrats, including Wu Yajun, the country's wealthiest woman—and, of course, one of the delegates to the 2012 National People's Congress—have made their fortunes in real estate. Because land use is still closely controlled by the state, that is a business which inevitably involves close ties with the government. And almost all businesses need credit. For all China's success in nurturing private business, more than 90 percent of loans in the country are still made by state-controlled banks. To borrow, you need a favorable relationship with the state and its mandarins, something the bosses of state-owned enterprises, who are simultaneously business executives and senior government officials, have automatically. As Walter and

Howie, who have worked in Chinese finance for decades, explain: "What would the chairman of China's largest bank do if the chairman of Petro-China asked for a loan? He would say: 'Thank you very much, how much, and for how long?'"

The subtle hand of the Chinese government in appointing its rising class of plutocrats—according to Hurun, there were 271 billionaires in China in 2011, and the cutoff to make the list of the one thousand wealthiest Chinese was $310 million—is perhaps most apparent in the emergence of red dynasties, whose scions are known as the "princelings." These are the sons and daughters of today's Chinese leadership, and often the grandchildren of the leaders of the Maoist revolution. They form an important political faction in the Chinese Communist Party, and many of them are plutocrats. Li Peng was China's premier from 1987 to 1998. Today, his family are utility tycoons. His daughter Li Xiaolin, who has been called "China's Power Queen," serves as chair and CEO of China Power International Development, and his son Li Xiaopeng managed Huaneng Power International, the country's largest independent power generator, before entering politics in 2008. Zhu Yunlai, son of Zhu Rongji, another former premier, who was in office from 1998 until 2003, is a senior executive at CICC, the Chinese investment bank, which counts the illustrious private equity firms KKR and TPG among its shareholders. In rent-seeking societies, the plutocrats are appointed by the state. Who better to appoint than your own children?

Another sign of the political nature of wealth in China is Beijing's ability to defrock its oligarchs. That reversal of fortune is often dramatic—a strong predictor of China's future jailbirds is its current rich list. In 2002, Zhou Zhengyi, who made his fortune in Shanghai real estate, was identified as the eleventh richest man in China, with a fortune of $320 million; in 2003, he was imprisoned on corruption charges. In 2008, Huang Guangyu, the Beijing-based founder of the GOME retail chain, was named the second-richest, by *Forbes*. In 2010, he, too, was jailed for corruption. The list goes on. The point isn't that China's plutocrats are squeaky clean and are being unjustly imprisoned—like all businesspeople in a rent-seeking society they have their original sins. But where all property involves, if not theft, then at least some rule bending and palm greasing, everyone is vulnerable. As *The Economist* noted in 2003, Zhou's dealings were far from exceptional: "If they wanted to, China's authorities could probably find grounds for accusing most of the country's richest people of bending (if not breaking) the rules. But China's legal culture thrives on the principle of 'killing the chicken to scare the monkeys.' Mr. Zhou . . . was a conspicuous potential chicken."

The dramatic denouement of the March 2012 NPC is that now the biggest monkey is directly in the state's sights, too. Bo Xilai, the charismatic former chief of the thirty-four-million-strong Yangtze River megalopolis of Chongqing, was one of the leading elite critics of China's rising inequality: on the eve of the NPC he told reporters in Beijing that the country's Gini coefficient had exceeded 0.46 (it is 0.45 in the United States) and warned: "If only a few people are rich, then we'll slide into capitalism. We've failed. If a new capitalist class is created then we'll really have turned into a wrong road." But at the same time, Bo was a princeling—his father was Bo Yibo, one of the Eight Immortals of the Communist Party—and the patriarch of a clan with wealth as well as political power. His son Bo Guagua reportedly drove up in a red Ferrari to pick up a daughter of then U.S. ambassador Jon Huntsman for a date. (Guagua denies driving the Ferrari; the Huntsman daughter says she can't remember the make of the car.) Guagua was educated at Harrow, the British public school with an annual tuition of $50,000; Oxford, where he helped organize the Silk Road Ball; and Harvard. Bo's wife, Gu Kailai, is a lawyer who ran a lucrative international law firm, Kailai, and an advisory firm called Horus Consultancy and Investment. Since Bo Xilai's fall from grace, the family's documented fortune is now pegged at $136 million and the figure seems to rise every day.

In early March 2012, Bo was one of China's rising leaders—he was seen as a strong candidate for membership in the Standing Committee of the Politburo, the nine-person body that rules China. Over the next five weeks, in the most dramatic political fight in the country since Tiananmen Square, Bo went from princeling to pariah, first losing his job and then facing investigation for "suspected serious violations of discipline." Gu, his wife, has been charged with murder. The fall of Bo Xilai is partly a tale of red capitalism intrigue and skulduggery—the attack on the Bo clan began with the mysterious hotel death of a British national who worked with Gu and alleged efforts to block investigation of it. But it is also being read as a fight between the red oligarchs, personified by Bo, and the reformers, who are fighting for a more transparent and competitive system. As Stephen Roach, the former chairman of Morgan Stanley Asia who now teaches at Yale, told me, "The emphasis once again is shifting much more back to the reformers. . . . [Bo Xilai's sacking is] very powerful evidence in favor of returning to this pro-reform, pro-private-enterprise, pro-market-based direction that China has been on for the last thirty-two years, barring a few pretty obvious bumps in the road from time to time."

Professor Roach is right. Bo Xilai was China's most visible advocate of state capitalism, a system rife with opportunities for rent-seeking. His downfall has been part of a wider drive to make the Chinese economy more fair and open, most notably Premier Wen Jiabao's striking attack on state banks, an important source of wealth for the red oligarchs. As Wen told an audience of business leaders in remarks broadcast on China National Radio, "Let me be frank. Our banks earn profit too easily. Why? Because a small number of large banks have a monopoly. . . . To break the monopoly, we must allow private capital to flow into the finance sector."

But as in the other emerging markets, and indeed in the West, too, understanding China's great political struggle as a fight between venal red rent-seekers and virtuous market reformers doesn't tell the entire story. Some of the most successful princelings are the children of some of China's most effective market reformers, and even the entrepreneurs whose fortunes are largely based on creating real value needed a helping hand from the state to survive and thrive. To paraphrase Proudhon, in a country like China, where money and government are so intimately intertwined, all fortunes required a little rent-seeking.

RENT-SEEKING ON WALL STREET AND IN THE CITY

On January 22, 2007, Mike Bloomberg, the mayor of New York, and Chuck Schumer, the senior senator for the state, released a study they had commissioned from McKinsey, the world's leading management consultants. The report, titled "Sustaining New York's and the US' Global Financial Services Leadership," warned of impending financial crisis and offered detailed guidance on how to avert it.

Less than seven months later, the greatest financial crisis since the Great Depression did indeed begin, when BNP Paribas, the French bank, froze withdrawals from three of its funds, a step we would see in hindsight as the opening shot in the economic Armageddon of 2008.

But this is not the story of two Cassandras and their unheeded cry that Wall Street's bubble was about to burst. Instead, the Bloomberg/Schumer report focused on a very different danger: the risk that London, or perhaps Hong Kong or Dubai, might soon eclipse New York as the world's financial capital. Were that to happen, Schumer and Bloomberg warned in an op-ed published in the *Wall Street Journal* on November 1, 2006, foreshadowing the full report, "this would be devastating for both our city and nation."

To avert such disaster, Schumer and Bloomberg counseled urgent action. The first problem to fix was the overly harsh regulation of Wall Street. As they wrote in their op-ed, "While our regulatory bodies are often competing to be the toughest cop on the street, the British regulatory body seems to be more collaborative and solutions-oriented." The full McKinsey report, made public two months later, elaborated on this danger: "When asked to compare New York and London on regulatory attractiveness and responsiveness, both CEOs and other senior executives viewed New York as having a worse regulatory environment than London by a statistically significant margin."

A specific risk posed by America's overly strict financial regulators, McKinsey warned, was that their approach was driving the highly desirable derivatives business abroad. "Europe—and London in particular—is already ahead of the U.S. and New York in OTC [over the counter—which is to say difficult for regulators to monitor] derivatives, which drive broader trading flows and help foster the kind of continuous innovation that contributes heavily to financial services leadership," the McKinsey report cautioned. "'The U.S. is running the risk of being marginalized' in derivatives, to quote one business leader, because of its business climate, not its location. The more amenable and collaborative regulatory environment in London in particular makes businesses more comfortable about creating new derivative products and structures there than in the U.S."

Moreover, the report sounded an alarm about the future. America's overly zealous regulators were on the verge of another colossal mistake: they were planning to raise capital requirements for U.S. banks, a measure McKinsey warned was unnecessary and would weaken the country's financial champions in the fierce global competition for business. "U.S. banking regulators have proposed changes that would result in U.S. banks holding higher capital levels than their non-U.S. peers, which could put them at a competitive disadvantage," the study said. These tougher new requirements were unnecessary, in McKinsey's view. Instead, the report advocated a more sophisticated approach that took into account the economic environment. "This application also ignores some of the changes in capital requirements that occur as a result of economic cycles," the report argued. "In a strong economic environment, for instance, capital requirements in a risk-based system should actually decline."

Read with the benefit of hindsight, the Bloomberg/Schumer/McKinsey report is a parody of hubris. The overall concern with overly harsh U.S. regulators, a year before regulatory laxity permitted the worst financial crisis in three generations, is clearly absurd. The specific fears are even more specious. Alarm about a U.S. regulatory environment that was unduly restrictive of derivatives—those were the very financial instruments at the heart of the crisis. Worry that new capital requirements would be unnecessarily onerous—when it turns out that higher capital requirements were precisely what the banking system needed. Had Michael Moore set out to write a satire about the shortsighted greed of U.S. financial and political elites, he could not have invented better examples.

The arguments in the report are so wrong that it is easy to mock Mc-Kinsey, the author, and Bloomberg and Schumer, the sponsors. But what is really striking is how bipartisan and transatlantic the consensus within the Anglo-American financial and political elite was on the ideas in the study. Bloomberg is an independent; Schumer is a Democrat. Eliot Spitzer, the erstwhile sheriff of Wall Street as New York's attorney general and then governor of New York State, joined Bloomberg and Schumer at the press conference announcing their report and broadly supported its conclusions. Two days before Bloomberg and Schumer took to the op-ed pages of the *Wall Street Journal* to raise the curtain on their report, another bipartisan pair, Glenn Hubbard, the dean of Columbia Business School, former Bush adviser, and future Mitt Romney adviser, and John Thornton, the active Democratic donor and former president of Goldman Sachs, announced that they, too, had organized a study on costly regulation and whether it was causing the U.S. capital markets to lose ground to foreign rivals.

Hank Paulson, the Republican Treasury secretary and former chairman and CEO of Goldman Sachs, traveled to New York a few weeks after these twin editorials to give a speech to the Economic Club of New York on "The Competitiveness of U.S. Capital Markets" in which he praised the Bloomberg/Schumer op-ed as being "right on target." To make his point that Americans were in danger of overregulation, Paulson approvingly quoted a Democratic predecessor as secretary of the Treasury and fellow former Goldman Sachs chairman, Bob Rubin: "In a recent speech, former Treasury secretary Bob Rubin said this about regulation: 'Our society seems to have an increased tendency to want to eliminate or minimize risk, instead of making cost/benefit judgments on risk reduction in order to achieve optimal balances.'"

A final U.S. contribution from the department of irony. A few weeks after the Schumer/Bloomberg op-ed had been published, one captain of finance wrote a letter to the editor to support their fight against "overregula-tion." He was John Thain, then the CEO of the New York Stock Exchange. Two years later, Thain, by then CEO of Merrill Lynch, was forced to sell the nearly hundred-year-old firm to Bank of America at a fire sale price be-cause of a financial crisis caused in great measure by inadequate regulation.

Across the ocean, the elite consensus was equally strong. A few days after the McKinsey study was released in New York, Sir Howard Davies, the director of the London School of Economics, former head of Britain's top regulator, the Financial Services Authority, and former deputy gover-nor of the Bank of England, opined, from the snowy slopes of Davos, that Bloomberg had "set a cat among the snow eagles this week." The New York mayor, Sir Howard argued, was absolutely right: the American capital mar-kets "are losing market share relentlessly against London." The English peer's fear was that in order to level the global playing field, the United States would try to impose its overly onerous regulatory approach on the rest of the world: "The Americans, as we know, are famously generous people, and they are even prepared to export their regulations, free of charge to the rest of the world."

From Sir Howard's perspective, the danger as viewed from Davos in 2007 was that the Republican administration of George W. Bush would seek to force the rest of the world to adopt America's unnecessarily tough regulation of its financial sector. But Sir Howard held out the hope that Britain's Labour government and its famously brainy economic duo of Prime Minister Gordon Brown and his Harvard- and Oxford-trained ad-viser, Edward Balls, would defend Great Britain's superior "light-touch" regulatory approach against the Yanks. Sir Howard's column is titled "Balls Must Save Us from U.S. Regulatory Creep." Of Davos, he reports: "Gordon Brown patrolled the conference corridors, ready to explain that the London markets, like the NHS [the National Health Service], are safe in his hands. In this territory, he has a good story to tell." (Incidentally for Sir Howard, the future embarrassment of having written this opinion piece would turn out to be a lesser example of the personal dangers of buying into the worldview of the global plutocracy. On March 3, 2011, he resigned as director of the LSE because of the embarrassment he had caused the school by accepting a £1.5 million donation from Saif Gadhafi, son of the dictator, and agreeing to a £2.2 million deal to train Libyan civil servants. Sir Howard had also been a paid adviser to Libya's sovereign wealth fund.)

Once you get beyond how jarringly wrong all of these bold-faced names were, and how uniform, bipartisan, and international their consensus, you notice the epistemological wrong turn at the center of their mistake. The premise of this entire 2006–2007 conversation about the regulation of U.S. financial markets was that you learn whether your rules are working by asking the banks upon which they are imposed. Here's how McKinsey described its methodology: "To bring a fresh perspective to this topic, a McKinsey team personally interviewed more than 50 financial services industry CEOs and business leaders. The team also captured the views of more than 30 other leading financial services CEOs through a survey and those of more than 275 additional global financial services senior executives through a separate on-line survey." There's a nod toward other points of view—"to balance this business perspective with that of other constituencies, the team interviewed numerous representatives of leading investor, labor, and consumer groups"—but it is a token effort compared to the meticulous attention focused on the bankers. And, like asking children whether they are satisfied with their bedtime, or surveying workers to find out whether they are paid enough, the results of the McKinsey investigation were entirely predictable.

The paradox, of course, is that these captains of finance were not only wrong about what was best for America—they were wrong about their own self-interest, too. I happened to interview John Thain on September 16, 2008, the day after he sold Merrill Lynch. On the Street, the deal itself was widely viewed as a masterstroke, particularly compared to Dick Fuld's failure to find a buyer for Lehman Brothers a few weeks earlier. But Thain was anything but triumphant. We met in the Wall Street office whose $1.2 million redecoration would soon become infamous. I was blithely unaware of the million-dollar splendor of the furnishings, but I could see that Thain, who was normally precisely turned out and glowing with health, looked tired and discombobulated. "I totally understand why Dick Fuld couldn't do it," Thain told me when I asked him why he had been able to sell his bank but Fuld had not.

"This was a hard thing for me to do, and I've been here for eight months. . . . It is heart-wrenching. I totally understand why it was impossible for him. The emotional difficulty of selling your company is very great. It is really hard."

The self-interested, and ultimately self-destructive, herd mentality on Wall Street and in the City of London shaped policy around the world, but it didn't prevail everywhere. One exception was Canada. Canadian regulators required their banks to hold more capital and permitted less leverage than their peers in London and New York. The result was no bailout of the Canadian financial sector and a recession (and budget deficit) that were much softer than in the United States. To this day, the Bank of Canada divides the world into "crisis economies," which means those whose banks failed, and everyone else, like Canada.

Ottawa chose a different course because the government had a profoundly different attitude about its duties toward the system as a whole and its relationship with its bankers. As minister of finance in the 1990s, Paul Martin laid the foundations for this approach. Martin is no hoi polloi class warrior—he's a self-made multimillionaire. But, he told me, his priority in finance was: "I knew there was going to be a banking crisis at some point and so did everyone else who has read any history. I just wanted to be damn sure that when a crisis occurred it wouldn't occur in Canada, and that if it did occur internationally, Canada's banks wouldn't be badly sideswiped by the contagion."

Don Drummond, who later became the chief economist at TD Bank, was a senior official at the finance ministry in the 1990s. "The perspective of government on the financial sector is: 'We are the regulator—our job is to tell you what to do, not to help you grow,'" he told me. "The government has always felt its job was to say no." Thanks to this mind-set, Martin and his team had the self-confidence to opt out of what became the international contest to create the most attractive haven for global capital. Canada raised its capital requirements as they were lowered in other parts of the world.

"I think one of the things that happened was the great competition between New York and London pushed the two into more of a light touch in terms of regulation," Martin recalled. "I remember talking to [the regulator] and we agreed that we were not prepared to take that approach. Light-touch regulation in an industry that was so dependent on liquidity didn't make any sense."

One Bay Street financier summed it up more saltily: "Canadian regulators didn't have penis envy."

With hindsight, that decision seems brilliant. At the time, though, to many it seemed, well, limp. One measure of how strongly the tide of world opinion was running against the Canucks is that the International Monetary Fund, meant to be the stern guardian of the global economy, chided Canada for not doing enough to promote securitization in its mortgage market—one of the American financial innovations that contributed to the crisis. Even communist China accused the Canadians of being too cautious about capitalism. Jim Flaherty, Canada's finance minister, told me that on a visit to Beijing in 2007, "they were suggesting that maybe Canadian banks were too timid."

Canada's bright young things were sympathetic to this critique. One newspaper columnist liked to write about "the tale of two Royals," comparing the stodgy Royal Bank of Canada to its buccaneering, world-beating Edinburgh cousin, the Royal Bank of Scotland. (The British government had to nationalize RBS in 2008 and spent billions to cover its loses; RBC in 2012 was one of the top twenty banks in the world, with a market capitalization of $74 billion.) A Canadian finance executive who spent the 1990s in Toronto, then moved to Asia, and now lives in London sheepishly recalls thinking: "Come on, guys, get in the game! The world's changing."

The regulatory race to the bottom between New York and London—and the plutocracy's eager and misguided complicity in that contest—is an important cause of the 2008 financial crisis. But it is also a crucial episode in another story: the rise of the super-elite. Much of the story of the rise of the 1 percent, and especially of the 0.1 percent, is the story of the rise of finance. And less regulation, more complexity, and more risk are important reasons why finance has become a bigger part of so many developed Western economies, particularly the United States and the United Kingdom, and why financiers' income has overtaken that of almost everyone else.

That connection with regulation, or its absence, is also why the rise of finance is partly a story about rent-seeking. The government bailouts of banks and bankers in 2008 enraged populists on both the right and the left—the super-elite got a rescue that was denied everyone else. But the link between the state and the financial super-class is much deeper than providing a trillion-dollar safety net. Like Carlos Slim's Telmex, and the beneficiaries of Russia's loans-for-shares privatization, the bankers on Wall Street, in the City of London, and in Frankfurt owe much of their wealth to helpful decisions by their regulators and legislators.

In Goldin and Katz's Harvard-based study of the impact of gender on life choices, they learned a lot about the different life choices and life outcomes for men and women. To their surprise, though, the most gaping disparity they found had nothing to do with gender. It was, instead, the gap between the bankers and everyone else.

"The highest earnings by occupation are garnered by those in finance, for which the earnings premium relative to all other occupations is an astounding . . . 195 percent," they concluded. In other words, Harvard-educated bankers make nearly twice as much as their classmates who choose different jobs.

The higher incomes in finance seemed to provoke an equally dramatic shift in the career choices of Harvard grads. Just 22 percent of the men in the class of 1970 took jobs in finance and management. Twenty years later, 38 percent of the men of the class of 1990 went into finance and management—more than the numbers who chose law and medicine combined. Women shifted their choices even more sharply. Just 12 percent of the women in the class of 1970 took jobs in finance and management. Two decades later the number had nearly doubled, up to 23 percent.

That marks a profound cultural transformation. A few years ago, I interviewed a longtime friend of Paul Volcker, the legendary chairman of the Fed. Both Volcker and this friend studied economics at Harvard. I asked the friend, an academic, why neither of the pair had gone to Wall Street. "That was a third-rate choice," he told me. "When we were at Harvard, the most prestigious job was academia; next was government service. Only the weakest students went into finance. Things have certainly changed."

What's most striking about these numbers, and this cultural shift that has come with it, is the extent to which they suggest that the rise of the super-elite is largely the rise of finance.

Wider studies of the 0.1 percent tell the same story. One of the most comprehensive analyses of who is in that top slice found that, in 2005, 18 percent of the plutocrats were in finance. As the Harvard data suggested, that number has grown sharply in recent decades, up from 11 percent in 1979. The only occupation that accounts for a bigger share of the income at the very top is the CEO class. Moreover, within the generally prospering community of the 0.1 percent, the incomes of bankers are growing the fastest of all.

The numbers in the UK, where the ascendancy of finance in the national economy has been even more pronounced, paint the same picture. A recent study found that 60 percent of the increased share in income of the top 10 percent went to bankers—meaning that nearly two-thirds of the enrichment of the earners at the top was driven by the City of London. As in the United States, the gains are skewed to the very tip of the pyramid: among the financiers who are part of Britain's top 1 percent, the top 5 percent (or 0.05 percent of workers overall) take 23 percent of the total wages of that gilded slice of the population. The dominance of top dogs in finance is even stronger than that of the 0.05 percent in other jobs.

One reason the preeminence of the financiers within the global super-elite matters is that it highlights how crucial financial deregulation has been to the emergence of the plutocracy. That story has been told most convincingly in a historical study published in 2011 by economists Thomas Philippon and Ariell Reshef.

I first heard of the paper when a draft version of it was presented at the central bankers' conference in Basel, a prestigious annual wonk fest for the world's central bankers and the academic economists who are their intellectual groupies. Held just six months after the peak of the financial crisis, the 2009 Basel meeting was tenser and more focused on the problems of the present day than usual. On his way home from the meeting, a G7 central banker, who had worked on Wall Street before going into public service, e-mailed me a link to Figure 1 in the Philippon and Reshef paper, with a short comment: "This says it all."

That U-shaped chart plots the evolution of wages and skills in finance over the course of the twentieth century. Here's how the two economists describe their findings:

From 1909 to 1933 the financial sector was a high-education, high-wage industry. The share of skilled workers was 17 percent points higher than the private sector; these workers were paid more than 50 percent more than in the rest of the private sector, on average. A dramatic shift occurred during the 1930s: the financial sector starts losing its high human capital and high-wage status. Most of the decline occurs by 1950, but continues slowly until 1980. By that time, the relative wage in the financial sector is approximately the same as in the rest of the economy. From 1980 onwards another dramatic shift occurs: the financial sector becomes a high-skill, high-wage industry again. In a striking reversal, its relative wage and skill intensity goes back almost exactly to their levels of the 1930s.

Bankers were the backbone of the super-elite in the first part of the century; then, starting with the Great Depression, their incomes leveled off, continuing in that period between World War II and 1970 when banking was a stable, boring business, like a utility. Then, from 1980, finance got more complicated and income again soared, eventually reaching the level of 1933. What is especially interesting about this data, which Philippon and Reshef were the first to put together, is how closely it follows the rise, fall, and then rise again of income inequality in the United States. Philippon and Reshef find that the rise of finance accounts for 26 percent of the increase in the gap between the top 10 percent and everyone else over the past four decades. This is partly because finance became a magnet for highly educated Americans. But in a trend Goldin and Katz also document, and which seems to have been intuitively understood in Harvard Yard twenty years ago, the same skills and experience deliver a super-return when deployed on Wall Street as compared to anywhere else in the economy. Philippon and Reshef call this the "finance wage premium" and estimate it at 30 percent to 40 percent.

The second important piece of the puzzle is figuring out why the behavior of bankers followed this U-shape. Why was banking far less popular and prestigious than law and medicine for the Harvard men of 1970, while the class of 1990 flocked to Wall Street? The economists measure the impact of various changes, including globalization, the technological revolution, and financial innovations like the creation of mathematically complex credit derivatives. All of them have some impact, but they find that the change with the single greatest explanatory power is deregulation, which they calculate has driven nearly a quarter of the increase in incomes in finance and 40 percent of the increase in the education of workers in that sector. Volcker and his smartest classmates chose to become professors and civil servants. Today, many of Harvard's smartest economists choose Wall Street.

Emerging market oligarchs who owe their initial fortunes to sweetheart privatizations are perhaps the most obvious beneficiaries of rent-seeking. But through financial deregulation, Western governments, especially in Washington and London, played an even greater role in the rise of the global super-elite. As with the sale of state assets in developing economies, the role of deregulation in creating a plutocracy turns classic thinking about rent-seeking upside down. Deregulation was part of a global liberalization drive whose goal was to pull the state out of the economy and let market forces rule. But one of its consequences was to give the state a direct role in choosing winners and losers—in this case, giving financial engineers a leg up.

Christopher Meyer, a management consultant at the Monitor Group, recently wrote a book about emerging market businesses and how they will reshape the global economy. Rent-seeking is obviously a big part of his story. But when I asked him which country's businesspeople were the world's champion rent-seekers, his answer surprised me: "In the financial industry, the United States has the most co-opted regulatory apparatus." He went on to explain: "They are so innovative. They are driven to do it, and they're doing a great job of what they're paid to do. I don't think this comes out of evil. I think this comes out of what we call runaway effects. The more you get incented to do it, the more you do it. And because so much of our incentive system is financial, then that's what we got. We're getting what we pay for, literally. And so Wall Street's done a fabulous job of making the world safe for Wall Street."

One telltale sign the state is deciding who gets rich is how much time and money plutocrats spend on selecting their government and influencing its decisions. As before, the answer is hardly contrarian. But when IMF economists Deniz Igan, Prachi Mishra, and Thierry Tressel set out to document how powerful the influence of Wall Street was on Washington, their conclusion, framed in sober academic language, was as incendiary as any agitprop from the Tea Party or OWS. The killer fact was their finding that between 2000 and 2006 laws increasing regulation of the finance and real estate sectors had just a 5 percent chance of passing. Laws that deregulated were three times more likely to pass.

One Russian oligarch told me that a pleasant surprise for him during the privatizations of the 1990s was that you didn't have to bribe many of the country's most senior technocrats. "Well, of course, I wrote the law myself, and I took special care with it," Konstantin Kagalovsky told me, still, a couple of years later, delighted at the power of ideas. That was also true in the first decade of this century in Washington: Igan and Mishra found, predictably, that more conservative politicians, who were ideologically broadly in favor of less regulation, were more likely to back legislation that loosened the rules.

But direct intervention played a key role, too. Igan and Mishra found that the finance and real estate sectors spent $2.2 billion lobbying Washington between 1999 and 2006, reaching a peak of $720 million in the 2005–2006 period. In keeping with the sector's relatively increasing weight within the super-elite overall, its lobbying spending grew faster than that of business generally, and accounted for more than 15 percent of all lobbying spending in D.C. by 2006. Good news for Wall Street's government relations officers—their money worked: "Lobbying expenditures by the affected financial firms were significantly associated with how politicians voted on the key bills."

What's especially important about this study is that it documents the relationship between Wall Street and Washington before the 2008 financial crisis and subsequent multitrillion-dollar bailout. That rescue is what prompted populist anger on both right and left and claims, as Sarah Palin put it in an op-ed in the *Wall Street Journal*, that Washington had occupied Wall Street. But the real government capture actually happened in the three decades before 2008, with the long, steady, bipartisan rollout of financial deregulation.

Dani Kaufmann grew up in Chile. He was studying at Hebrew University when Pinochet seized power in a coup in 1973, and elected not to return, ending up instead at Harvard, where he eventually earned a PhD in economics. His next stop was the World Bank, where he worked on Africa and then, after the collapse of the Soviet Union, the transition to capitalism in what used to be the Warsaw Pact states. By the time Kaufmann returned to World Bank headquarters in Washington, he knew that his life's project would be to study corruption and its opposite, good governance, two themes he knew well from his work in Africa and the former Soviet Union, and viscerally from his Latin American roots.

But as Kaufmann looked further into rent-seeking around the world, the ways that it slowed economic development, and how it could be stopped, he discovered something that surprised him. The naked forms of corruption that development organizations and NGOs agonized over most—bribes demanded by government officials with coercive power, like policemen, or required for ordinary state services, like teaching, or even despots extracting their nation's wealth and sending it to numbered Swiss bank accounts—were only part of the story.

About $1 trillion, by Kaufmann's estimate, was paid in outright bribes around the world every year. But orders of magnitude more money was being made thanks to what he dubbed "legal corruption": "The cost to society of bribing a bureaucrat to obtain a permit to operate a small firm pales in comparison with, say, a telecommunications conglomerate that corrupts a politician to shape the rules of the game granting it monopolistic rights, or an investment bank influencing the regulatory and oversight regime governing it."

As he developed the idea, Kaufmann started to try to measure it. One idea he had was to ask global business leaders themselves, as identified by the World Economic Forum, to rate levels of both explicit corruption, such as bribery, and legal corruption, like campaign contributions and lobbying, in 104 countries. The results confirmed his hunch, especially when it came to the United States. Predictably, the United States was ranked one of the least nakedly corrupt countries in the survey, coming in at twenty-five, just below Canada and well above countries like Italy, Spain, and South Korea. But when it came to legal corruption, the business leaders put the United

States at fifty-three, squarely in the middle of the global pack, and worryingly close to countries like Russia, in position seventy-four, and India, at seventy.

Suggestively, the countries where the surge in income at the very top has been most marked—the United States, the United Kingdom, and fast-growing emerging markets like Russia, India, and China—also rank relatively high in Kaufmann's legal corruption table. That connection is most marked when you compare the high-inequality countries with nations with comparable levels of GDP but less inequality. In most such pairs—Norway or the Netherlands compared to the United States or United Kingdom, for instance; or Estonia compared to Russia—less legal corruption goes along with a smaller gap between the 1 percent and everyone else.

No one openly champions "legal corruption" as a good way to run a country, but one reason it is harder to denounce than it seems is that many of the reforms that enable legal corruption were actually intended to make economies more transparent, more fair, and more effective. That is true of the privatization drives that sometimes devolved into giveaways, and it is true of deregulation efforts in areas like finance or telecommunications. Liberalization doesn't have to be legally corrupt, but because it is often about opening vast new economic opportunities, it can easily become so, especially if governance is weak.

That's why what looks, from the outside, as if it must be a nakedly corrupt decision—for instance, the Telmex privatization or Russia's loans for shares—is at least sometimes the work of reasonably honest and genuinely well-intentioned market reformers. That was true, astonishingly, of Russian reforms at the outset and it is certainly true of financial deregulation.

But legal corruption gets more complicated and more compromising once you start dividing the spoils. Eventually the material gap between the true-believing technocrats and the businessmen their reforms enrich becomes an obstacle and a temptation for even the most upright civil servant. The widening financial divide becomes even harder to tolerate as the reformers realize that the wealth their programs transferred has made the beneficiaries not only rich, but politically powerful, too. It was this heart-breaking epiphany that corrupted many of the Russian reformers and persuaded them to try to make themselves into oligarchs. Those who didn't often regretted it. The Western-educated wife of a former Soviet leader who took significant personal risks to enact his reform plan told me, as her husband was leaving office, "I could have charged $100,000 for one-hour meetings with my husband. Now I wish I had." Her plan, she hastened to add, would of course have been to donate all the money to her charitable foundation.

In Western countries with significant legal corruption, that financial gulf creates a revolving door between the regulators and the regulated. One study of the SEC found that, between 2006 and 2010, 219 former SEC employees had filed almost eight hundred disclosure statements for representing their new clients' dealings with the agency, their former employer. Nearly half of these disclosures were filed by people who had worked at the sharp end of the SEC's relationship with business, in its enforcement division.

It is easy to understand the appeal of switching from gamekeeper to poacher—in 1980, the top regulators earned one-tenth the incomes of the leaders of the businesses they policed; by 2005 the ratio had jumped to one-sixtieth. Moreover, if the revolving door were locked, the gamekeepers might be even weaker. Given the income gap, how many members of the Harvard class of 2012 will choose government service, especially if there is no opportunity to switch to a more lucrative private sector role later on? And at a time of increasing economic complexity, what chance does government have of keeping up with business if the best and the brightest go to the private sector?

Finally, the age of globalization has brought one more twist to the story of rent-seeking and how it has helped to create the super-elite: like so much else, rent-seeking has now gone global. That's not entirely a new story— multinationals have long paid bribes to secure contracts abroad, and some of the most lucrative examples of historic rent-seeking have involved overseas concessions, like the East India Company's right to trade in India granted by the British Crown, or the Hudson's Bay Company's rights to the Canadian fur trade.

But the international ripple effect of rent-seeking is today even more extensive. A fortune created by rent-seeking in one country can have a powerful effect thousands of miles away. Britain's football clubs and, increasingly, its newspapers are being bought up by emerging markets oligarchs, particularly Russians. Between 2008 and 2011 the second-largest shareholder in the *New York Times* was Carlos Slim.

Even rent-seeking plutocrats who've made their fortunes the old-fashioned way—by being authoritarian despots—have been cheerfully courted by the global plutocracy. That was the case with Saif Gadhafi, who, just two years before protesters bloodily overthrew his father's four-decade-long dictatorship, was courted by a private equity tycoon over Saturday lunch in his magnificent home on Park Avenue and gave speeches at Davos and at the Council on Foreign Relations. The London School of Economics accepted a £1.5 million gift from the Gadhafi family and awarded Saif a degree; the Monitor Group, one of the most respected and internationally minded consultancies, became a paid adviser to the regime for a yearly fee that reached a peak of $3 million.

Legal corruption is going global, too. The threat that business, particularly finance, might move to another country was one of the most powerful arguments in favor of deregulation, especially before 2008. Witness, for example, the 2007 McKinsey/Bloomberg/Schumer report prepared by McKinsey for Michael Bloomberg on the threat that other, less onerously regulated financial centers, particularly London, posed to New York's pole position as the world's preeminent financial capital. One of the key recommendations was that the United States shift to the British "light touch" regulatory philosophy.

As rent-seeking wealth spills across borders from the country where it was granted to other parts of the world, as rent-seeking plutocrats do deals with one another, and as economic rules go global, the question Professor Rajan asked of the Bombay Chamber of Commerce may need to be adjusted. He asked his Indian audience if their country was at risk of political capture by rent-seeking national oligarchs. An equal, and probably greater, danger is the rise of an international rent-seeking global oligarchy.

———◆———

SIX

PLUTOCRATS AND THE REST OF US

If you really wanted to examine percentage-wise who was hurt the most on their income, it was Wall Street brokers.

—Alan Greenspan, shortly after his appointment as chairman of Gerald Ford's Council of Economic Advisers in 1974, explaining the impact of inflation

He was remembering now why he didn't like the rich: their self-pity. Persecution was the common ground of their conversation, like sport or the weather for everyone else.

—Robert Harris, *The Fear Index*

A stranger to human nature, who saw the indifference of men about the misery of their inferiors and the regret and indignation which they feel for the misfortunes and sufferings of those above them, would be apt to imagine that pain must be more agonizing and the convulsions of death more terrible to persons of higher rank than to those of meaner stations.

—Adam Smith, *The Theory of Moral Sentiments*

DELIVERING HAPPINESS

If you ever have to work at a call center, make sure it is Zappos. The online retailer has built a business around the idea of, as founder Tony Hsieh put it in his bestselling advice book cum autobiography, *Delivering Happiness*, the unlikely premise that buying and selling stuff over the phone can be an emotionally nurturing experience for both parties. In pursuit of that goal, Zappos has created a corporate culture so widely admired that the on-line shoe seller now has a business sideline teaching others how to operate the Zappos way—for $5,000 and two days of your time, you and your top team can be trained on how to bring the Zappos culture back to your own cubicles.

A cheaper option is to take one of the free company tours Zappos offers to anyone who wants one, including complimentary pickup and return on a bus driven by one of the characteristically upbeat members of what they call "the Zappos family." When I stepped outside my hotel on the Las Vegas strip and got on board on a blisteringly hot day in August 2010, a vacation-ing family of three from Virginia were already seated. They had been re-cruited to make the visit the day before while hiking in one of the canyons outside the city. There they met an evangelical Zappos employee—there is no other kind—who urged them to visit.

On the outside, Zappos's headquarters in Henderson, Nevada, a suburb of Las Vegas, is a typically nondescript, low-rise building in a corporate park surrounded by desert and freeways. But inside you can start to see what all the fuss is about. Visitors are greeted by a popcorn machine, hula hoops, a take-what-you-like bookshelf, and badges with an array of colorful markers and the instruction "Pimp your name tag." The mood is part self-improvement seminar—the bookshelf is heavy on the works of Jim Collins and Clay Christensen—part wacky college dorm, and part low-rent version of luxe Silicon Valley firms like Google and Facebook. Zappos, too, has free food and a concierge desk for employees, but neither is quite up to the swish standards of the Valley.

When we meet for lunch at a steakhouse a five-minute drive away (this is one of those neighborhoods without sidewalks), Hsieh tells me he moved Zappos from San Francisco to Las Vegas because the city has "a call center population" and a twenty-four/seven culture. That's a nice way of saying this is a place where you can find the lower-skilled, lower-paid workers you need for customer service. Within that universe, though, Zappos really does deliver on its promise of being "free from boring work environments, go-nowhere jobs, and typical corporate America!"

Our tour guide—he proudly informs us that you need to know two hundred things about Zappos to be a certified host—says, "I was working at a call center that was kind of the opposite of this—kind of a sweatshop" before joining two and a half years earlier. A year and a half earlier he'd recruited his better half: "I was having great days and my wife wasn't, so I got her a job here."

Part of the appeal is that Zappos—core value number three: create fun and a little weirdness—encourages its employees to let their freak flags fly: when you walk past the cubicles of the recruiting team, they blast you with music and wave barbells in time, brightly colored mullet wigs and feather boas are a favored work accessory, and the otherwise grim rows of cubicles and windowless meeting rooms are enlivened with homemade decor that includes bright balloons, streamers, and Chinese dragons.

A lot of life at Zappos is about "WOW"—core value number one: deliver Wow through service—and that delight starts with making employees feel privileged to work at Zappos. In my two days in Henderson I was told a dozen times that "you have a better chance of getting into Harvard than getting a job here." On a "WOW!" wall—writing on the walls is, of course, positively encouraged—someone had written, "I am WOW'ed that people want to tour my job." There is a "Royalty Room," complete with throne and crowns, because "when you see yourself as royalty, you will treat yourself and other people better."

Members of the Zappos family are taught to deliver WOW by going "above and beyond the average level of service to create an emotional impact on the receiver and give them a positive story they can take with them the rest of their lives." Everyone at Zappos has a personal tale of WOW—our tour guide's is sending flowers to a caller because her daughter had been in a car accident—and performing these small acts of kindness seems to be as delightful for the giver as it is for the receiver.

"I'm completely happy answering the phones—and that sounds insane," Michael Evon, a forty-year-old mother of two with braces, blond hair, and blue eyes, told me. "They really let me accommodate the customer. There are a lot of exceptions made and it gives you a great feeling—you are able to help someone."

Sometimes, that help is just having a good, long chat. Zappos employees pride themselves on marathon conversations with shoppers—an astonishing and humanizing goal in a line of work where getting off the phone as quickly as possible is usually the goal. Evon's longest is six hours—a little short of the record seven and a half hours—with a customer who called to return a pair of shoes and ending up buying a bathing suit and bonding. "She was fifty and I just happened to be the same astrological sign as the guy she's dating," Evon said. "It was things I love—fashion, travel, and psychology."

Evon's best WOW was straight out of a Jodi Picoult novel: the mother of an autistic girl called because the shoes she had purchased for her daughter didn't fit. But simply returning the shoes and replacing them with a more comfortable pair would be a problem because the autistic girl would be upset to be parted from the ill-fitting pair. A compassionate Evon let the customer keep the old shoes and sent her the right-size pair at no extra cost. Courtney, the mother, sent Evon a grateful e-mail, which she proudly shared with me: "She was very sympathetic of my situation and I was very grateful and appreciative of the service and attention she showed me. . . . With customer service agents like that, I will definitely continue to shop with Zappos. . . . Oh, and the replacements fit GREAT!! Thank you Michael and thank you Zappos!"

The Zappos family makes a point of flattening the corporate hierarchy.

The company's ruling troika are described as "our monkeys" on the corporate Web site (the third most powerful executive, Fred Mossler, has no title at all), everyone pitches in answering the phones during peak holiday periods, and there is no dress code. On the day I visited, top bosses, including Hsieh, had posed in a dunk tank, allowing themselves to be dumped in a pool in the parking lot to raise money for charity. There are no corner offices at Zappos. The executives sit in the same rows of cubicles as everyone else; Hsieh and his then CFO, Alfred Lin, had decorated their row of desks with streamers and stuffed animals chosen to evoke a jungle theme.

For wage slaves from elsewhere, Zappos exerts a powerful appeal. "I'm moving here. I'm done," said Greg, the Virginia father, who works as a paralegal in Washington, D.C., and was in Las Vegas for a law conference. "I love that—the CFO just has a desk on the floor."

"Yeah, it's like that at your firm, isn't it," Joanne, his wife, said sarcastically.

Hsieh and his team have performed a miracle humanizing what can be one of the most alienating jobs in the service economy. If you are a Zappos customer—I, too, have had my WOW with the magical provision of a hard-to-find pair of running shoes—you are a beneficiary of the happy workers their approach inspires.

But if you look closely enough inside Zappos, you can see another story, too. That is the tale of the 1 percent and the 99 percent and how sharply their lives and life prospects differ—even if they sit at the same row of cubicles and eat in the same cafeteria.

Inside the Zappos family, the 99 percent are inordinately proud of working at a place that is harder to get into than Harvard. But while Evon attended local community college without getting a degree, Zappos's effective founders actually went to Harvard—Hsieh and Lin met as undergraduates at Quincy House, where the former was struck by the latter's vast appetite for pizza. Slacking off was never an option—both are the children of Tiger Mother immigrants from Taiwan.

Lin recalls that his parents told him and his brother, who went on to trade derivatives for Credit Suisse, that they would be "temporarily poor" in their first years in the United States. The boys both attended Stuyvesant High School, one of New York City's top, application-only public schools, where they were such enthusiastic members of the math club they now contribute to its support. Lin studied applied math at Harvard and went on to start a PhD at Stanford, until he was rescued from the academic grind by Hsieh, who cajoled him into joining him at his first company, LinkExchange. They sold it to Microsoft two years later for $265 million.

Hsieh likes to depict himself as something of a rebel against the Tiger upbringing. In his autobiography he proudly describes evading violin practice by playing a tape of himself to convince his alert mother he was hard at it. But Hsieh was enough of a scholar to study computer programming at Harvard and get a first job at Oracle, before deciding, less than a year out of college, that the real opportunity was in starting his own business and being part of the Internet revolution.

Not yet forty, Hsieh and Lin are already multimillionaires—Amazon bought Zappos in 2009 for $1.2 billion in stock—for whom life has become a series of appealing choices. When I was in Henderson, Lin had just accepted an offer from Michael Moritz, the legendary Silicon Valley venture capitalist, to return to the West Coast and join his firm. Hsieh was about to go on a cross-country bus tour to promote his book.

Evon's shift starts at six a.m.—being a few minutes late is a firing offense—and her workweek includes Saturdays and Sundays. She isn't complaining: "It's okay. When you are hired here they say if you take this position we need you when we need you." Unemployment was nearly 15 percent in Nevada and her husband was working as a real estate agent in a market where house prices had fallen by a third over the past two years. One of the perks at Zappos is free lunch, and many of the parents who work there, at a call center starting salary of $11.50 an hour, told me they made a point of eating their main meal at work to spare their family grocery budget.

At Zappos, where everyone wears jeans and no one has an office, the chasm between the top and the bottom is as sharp as it gets. This paradox of an egalitarian culture coexisting with extreme economic and social inequality is a crucial and often overlooked part of the relationship between the super-elite and everyone else.

Most of today's "working rich" plutocrats didn't start out hugely privileged. And many of them operate in worlds—Silicon Valley and also the trading floors of Wall Street and its service firms such as Bloomberg, where one of the biggest corporate faux pas is to demand an office—in which the cultural dividing lines between the tribunes and the hoi polloi are intentionally blurred. But, of course, even if the billionaire is in a T-shirt and drives his own car, his universe is very different from that of a call center worker. Below is an exploration of what the plutocrats think of the rest of us.

THE BILLIONAIRE IN BLUE JEANS

Pittsburgh was one of the smelters of America's Gilded Age. As the industrial revolution took hold there, Andrew Carnegie was struck by the contrast between "the palace of the millionaire and the cottage of the laborer." Human beings had never before lived in such strikingly different material circumstances, he believed, and the result was "rigid castes" living in "mutual ignorance" and "mutual distrust" of one another.

The twenty-seven-story Mumbai mansion of the Ambani family, rumored to have cost a billion dollars, is just seven miles away from Dharavi, one of the world's most famous slums, and the gap between these two ways of life is even wider than anything Carnegie could find in the Golden Triangle. So, for that matter, is the difference between Bill Gates's futuristically wired 66,000-square-foot mansion overlooking Lake Washington, which is nicknamed Xanadu 2.0 and whose library bears an inscription from *The Great Gatsby*, and the homes of the poor of Washington State, where unemployment in 2012 was slightly above the national average.

Even so, the correct etiquette in today's plutocracy, particularly among its most admired tribe, the technorati of the U.S. West Coast, is to downplay the personal impact of vast wealth. In April 2010, when MIT students asked him how it felt to be the richest person in the world, Bill Gates suggested it wasn't a very big deal. "Well, the marginal return for extra dollars does drop off," Gates said. "I haven't found any burgers at any price that are better than McDonald's." He admitted there were some great perks, like flying on a private jet, but said that after a "few million or something, it's all about how you're going to give it back."

If you traveled to Mountain View to visit Eric Schmidt when he was CEO of Google, you would have found him in a narrow office barely big enough to hold three people. The equations on the whiteboard may well have been scribbled by one of the engineers who works next door and is welcome to use the chief's office whenever he's not in. And while it is okay to have a private jet in the Valley, employing a chauffeur is frowned upon. "Whereas in other cultures, you can drive your Rolls-Royce around and just sort of look rich and have a really good time, in technology it's not socially okay to have a driver who drives you to work every day," Schmidt told me. "I don't know why, but you'll notice nobody does it."

This egalitarian style can clash with the Valley's reality of extreme income polarization. "Many tech companies solved this problem by having the lowest-paid workers not actually be employees. They're contracted out," Schmidt explained. "We can treat them differently, because we don't really hire them. The person who's cleaning the bathroom is not exactly the same sort of person. Which I find sort of offensive, but it is the way it's done."

When he was CEO of Bain Capital and building his current net worth of about $200 million, Mitt Romney drove a Chevrolet Caprice station wagon with red vinyl seats and a beaten-up fender. Carlos Slim's trademark look is slightly scruffy casual wear, and he loves to tell journalists he doesn't own any homes outside his native Mexico. But even when he dresses down, a billionaire inhabits a world apart. A little more than a decade ago, I asked Mikhail Khodorkovsky, at that moment the richest man in Russia (and, as it happens, also someone who favored casual clothes and lived in a modest house), what he thought of the rest of us. "If a man is not an oligarch, something is not right with him," Khodorkovsky told me. "Everyone had the same starting conditions, everyone could have done it." (Khodorkovsky's subsequent experiences—his company was appropriated by the state in 2004 and he is currently in prison for fraud and embezzlement—have tempered this Darwinian outlook: in jail cell correspondence he admitted that he had "treated business exclusively as a game" and "did not care much about social responsibility.")

This worldview is straight out of the pages of Ayn Rand, but Khodorkovsky told me his uncompromising position was based not on literature but on life experience. During the 1998 Russian financial crisis some of his non-oligarch minions had made mistakes that had cost Khodorkovsky hundreds of millions. With hindsight, he blamed himself—they weren't oligarchs, therefore something was wrong with them, therefore they shouldn't have been trusted to make such big decisions.

Remember the line about Björn Borg, of whom Ilie Nastase said, "We're playing tennis, he's playing something else"? The extreme self-confidence you hear in Khodorkovsky's comment is partly the product of believing you have an extreme aptitude for making money, one that is probably largely independent of time and circumstance.

The robber barons felt that way, too. "That this talent for organization and management is rare among men is proved by the fact that it invariably secures enormous rewards for its possessor, no matter where or under what laws or conditions," Carnegie wrote. "The experienced in affairs always rate the man whose services can be obtained as partner as not only the first consideration, but such as render the question of his capital scarcely worth considering: for such men soon create capital; in the hands of those without the special talent required, capital soon takes wings."

If you have that special talent, you have a special regard for others who possess it, too. Khodorkovsky trusted only fellow oligarchs. Steve Schwarzman thinks they are likely to make good presidents. "We ended up making twenty-four times our money" from a joint investment, Schwarzman told Bloomberg TV when asked why he had decided to host a fund-raiser for Mitt Romney's presidential bid at his triplex home at the storied apartment building at 740 Park Avenue. "In finance, that's the way to make friends."

The flip side of that high opinion of fellow plutocrats can be a lack of sympathy, shading sometimes into disdain, for everyone else. For the super-elite, a sense of meritocratic achievement can inspire self-regard, and that self-regard—especially when compounded by their isolation among like-minded peers—can lead to obliviousness and indifference to the suffering of others.

Eric Schmidt, the chairman of Google, admitted to a journalist in December 2011 that no one in his world thought much about Occupy Wall Street and the discontent of the 99 percent. "We live in a bubble," he said. "And I don't mean a tech bubble or a valuation bubble. I mean a bubble as in our own little world. . . . Companies can't hire people fast enough. Young people can work hard and make a fortune. Homes hold their value." What is striking about those remarks is that the unemployment rate in Santa Clara County, where Google's Mountain View campus is located, was 8.6 percent, slightly higher than the national average. And some of the most violent and controversial Occupy demonstrations were in Oakland, a forty-five-minute drive from Schmidt's office.

Matt Rosoff, a business journalist based in San Francisco, argues that even in Silicon Valley, the epicenter of the West's second gilded age, Schmidt's perspective reflects the particular experience of the 1 percent. "I recently talked to an IT engineer at a midsize financial services company downtown and he complained that his budget is being slashed every year, as he's expected to do more with less," Rosoff wrote on his *Business Insider* blog. "He's over forty and sees no chance of getting hired at one of these sexy start-ups run by 20-somethings and funded by VCs who are younger than him. So maybe Eric Schmidt and the people he talks to really don't discuss the Occupy movement. But that's not a Silicon Valley thing—that's just the circles he travels in."

The plutocratic bubble isn't just about being insulated by the company of fellow super-elites, although that is part of it. It is also created by the way you are treated by everyone else.

One financier, speaking about his friend who is one of the top five hedge fund managers in the world, said, "He's a good man—or as good as you can be when you are surrounded by sycophants." A few days after

Dominique Strauss-Kahn's arrest on accusations of assaulting a hotel maid in New York, I happened to share a car with a U.S. technology executive. The American technologist thought he understood the IMF chief's psychology. The thing was, he told me, when you ascend to a certain level of the super-elite, you come to inhabit a world in which all of your needs are catered to. That, he said, can lead to a dangerous sense of entitlement. As an illustration, he told me that on a recent holiday he had stayed in a Four Seasons hotel. The service was exceptional—at one point, as he was sitting by the pool and dropped the spoon he was using to eat his melon, a waiter instantly appeared with a choice of three differently sized replacement spoons. The Silicon Valley executive said that readjusting to ordinary life had been hard: he had become impatient and rude when confronted by the slightest delay or discomfort. "When you are used to being catered to twenty-four/seven, you start to feel the world should be built around you and your needs. You lose all sense of perspective," he told me. "I think that is probably what happened to Strauss-Kahn." His point was that the impact of privilege was unconscious. A few minutes earlier, he had provided another, unintended example. We had struggled for a few minutes to find the car and driver that had been arranged to take him (I was cadging a ride) from the airport to our conference. He had fumed about the wait, berating himself for breaking with his usual practice of having his Mountain View–based assistant be on call no matter what the hour (it was morning at Heathrow Airport) to ensure smooth transfers.

A recent family of academic studies suggests that my acquaintance may have been on to something when he pointed to the coarsening effect of privilege. Paul Piff, a psychologist at UC Berkeley, and four other researchers devised seven different experiments to test the impact of affluence on how we treat others. "Is society's nobility in fact its most its most noble actors?" the researchers ask. Their answer is a resounding no: "Relative to lower-class individuals, individuals from upper-class backgrounds behaved more unethically." Their explanation for the behavior of these ignoble nobles was an echo of the Silicon Valley executive's Heathrow observation: "We reason that increased resources and independence from others cause people to prioritize self-interest over others' welfare and perceive greed as positive and beneficial, which in turn gives rise to increased unethical behavior." One of the experiments studied San Francisco intersections. The team found that the drivers of new, expensive cars were twice as likely to cut off other vehicles or pedestrians as the drivers of old, cheap cars. In another test, experimental subjects with higher real-world incomes were more likely to deceive a hypothetical job applicant in order to persuade him or her to accept a lower salary—an accomplishment that earned the manager in the experiment a bonus. Even imagining you were rich changed the way experimental subjects behaved. In another study, participants were prompted to think of themselves as either very rich or very poor, and were then invited to take candy from a jar that afterward would be given to children in a nearby lab. The subjects who had imagined they were very rich took more candy.

THE AMERICAN MIDDLE CLASS NEEDS TO TAKE A PAY CUT

Or consider the view of some Western members of the plutocracy concerning the strains imposed on the American middle class by globalization. In a dinner speech in New York on a gloomy evening in the autumn of 2011, one Greenwich-based hedge fund manager observed that "the low-skilled American worker is the most overpaid worker in the world." He seemed genuinely worried about the high unemployment and falling wages that were the likely consequences of that circumstance (if you doubt this claim of hedge fund compassion, perhaps the fact that he grew up in Scandinavia will help persuade you), but he said business couldn't fail to take it into account.

The U.S.-based CEO of one of the world's largest fund managers told me that his firm's investment committee often discussed the question of who wins and who loses in today's economy. In a recent internal debate, he said, one of his senior colleagues had argued that the hollowing out of the American middle class didn't really matter. "His point was that if the transformation of the world economy lifts four people in China and India out of poverty and into the middle class, and meanwhile one American drops out of the middle class, that's not such a bad trade," the CEO recalled.

I heard a similar sentiment from the Taiwanese-born, thirtysomething CFO of a U.S. technology company. A gentle, unpretentious man who went from public school to Harvard, he's nonetheless not terribly sympathetic to the complaints of the American middle class. "We demand a higher paycheck than the rest of the world," he told me. "So, if you're going to demand ten times the paycheck, you need to deliver ten times the value. It sounds harsh, but maybe people in the middle class need to decide to take a pay cut."

And even those plutocrats who are sympathetic to the plight of the U.S. middle class feel compelled to contribute to it. One private equity investor invited me to lunch at Michael's, the restaurant that is practically a canteen for the New York media set, to talk about income inequality. When we moved on to other subjects, he told me about a recent deal his firm had done to acquire an Indian outsourcing company. A fringe benefit was that he could now use it to outsource his own company's research. The result was better work, more motivated employees, and lower costs. "We were paying University of Connecticut BAs $120,000 a year to do dead-end jobs," he told me. "Now we pay Indian PhDs $60,000 and they are thrilled to work for us."

You wouldn't hear comments like these in many middle-class U.S. households. What's striking, though, is how similar these views are to the perspectives of plutocrats in the emerging markets.

"You know, historically, economic activities tend to migrate because people who don't have it have a lot more urge to have it, they're willing to work harder for less money, and that's part of life," B. N. Kalyani, the chairman of Bharat Forge, India's largest exporter of motor parts, told me. "You had your golden period; now, hopefully, we'll have ours."

Kris Gopalakrishnan, the cochair of Infosys, told me bluntly that the per capita consumption of the Western middle class would have to decline as the developed and developing worlds "meet somewhere in the middle."

My Golf Caddy Caused the Financial Crisis

When I asked one of Wall Street's most successful investment bank CEOs if he felt guilty for his firm's role in creating the financial crisis, he told me with evident sincerity that he did not. The real culprit, he explained, was his feckless cousin, who owned three cars and a home he could not afford. One of America's top hedge fund managers made a near identical case to me, though this time the offenders were his in-laws and their subprime mortgage. And a private equity baron who divides his time between New York and Palm Beach pinned blame for the collapse on a favorite golf caddy in Arizona, who had bought three condos as investment properties at the height of the bubble.

It is this not-our-fault mentality that accounts for the plutocrats' profound sense of victimization in the Obama era. You might expect that American elites—and particularly those in the financial sector—would be feeling pretty good, and more than a little grateful, right now. Thanks to a $700 billion TARP bailout and trillions of dollars lent nearly free of charge by the Federal Reserve (a policy Soros himself told me was a "hidden gift" to the banks), Wall Street has surged back to precrisis levels of compensation even as Main Street continues to struggle.

But instead, many of the giants of American finance have come to, in the words of a mystified administration economist, "hate" the president and to believe he is fundamentally opposed to them and their well-being. In a much quoted newsletter to investors in the summer of 2010, hedge fund manager—and 2008 Obama fund-raiser—Dan Loeb fumed, "So long as our leaders tell us that we must trust them to regulate and redistribute our way back to prosperity, we will not break out of this economic quagmire." Two other former Obama backers on Wall Street—both claim to have been on Rahm Emanuel's speed dial list—recently told me that the president is "antibusiness"; one went so far as to worry that Obama is "a socialist."

In some cases, this sense of siege is almost literal. In the summer of

2010, for example, Blackstone's Schwarzman caused an uproar when he said an Obama proposal to raise taxes on private equity firm compensation—by treating carried interest as ordinary income—was "like when Hitler invaded Poland in 1939."

However histrionic his metaphors, Schwarzman (who later apologized for the remark) is a Republican, so his antipathy for the current administration is no surprise. What is perhaps more surprising is the degree to which even former Obama supporters in the financial industry have turned against the president and his party. A private equity manager who is a passionate Democrat and served in the Clinton administration proudly recounted to me his bitter exchange with a Democratic leader in Congress, who was involved in the tax reform effort. "Screw you," he told the lawmaker. "Even if you change the legislation the government won't get a single penny more from me in taxes. I'll put my money into my foundation and spend it on good causes. My money isn't going to be wasted in your deficit sinkhole."

Indeed, within the private equity fraternity, which would be hardest hit by a change in the tax treatment of carried interest, this is very much the majority view. When I met him in his boathouse on Martha's Vineyard, the cofounder of a private equity firm warned that raising the taxes on his industry would "kill" investment in this country and drive the money overseas. He also said it was morally unjust because private equity professionals like himself put their own money at risk and so did not deserve to have their profits taxed like regular income. Finally, he argued that raising the tax would actually be fine for him—he was near retirement and had already made his billion—but would be "unfair" to his junior partners. They earned $500,000 or so a year and accepted such moderate compensation only in the hope of huge, and lightly taxed, payouts after a decade or two of work. This white-haired grandfather had voted for Obama in 2008, though he was backing Jon Huntsman in 2011. Like so many of his peers, he came from a humble background—his father was a Pennsylvania steelworker.

The fight over carried interest is fascinating because it offers such clear insight into the power of self-interest to shape ideology. On a human level it is hard not to have at least a little sympathy for the fierce defenders of the current system—after all, a 20 percentage point tax hike is hard to stomach no matter how rich you are—but intellectually their position is close to indefensible. One piece of evidence came in a November 2011 speech Mike Bloomberg delivered in Washington. Bloomberg is, of course, himself both a plutocrat and one of the country's most prominent financial entrepreneurs. As New York's mayor, he has defended Wall Street with the hometown zeal of a Detroit politician supporting the carmakers or a prairie leader backing farmers.

Nonetheless, here was Bloomberg on carried interest: "Since fair is fair, tax loopholes in the financial industry that are outdated should be closed, too, such as taxing carried interest at ordinary income rates. And I say this even though many of the people who would be affected are my constituents—so I assume I will get some phone calls later this afternoon."

GALT'S GULCH

Carried interest is a very specific issue that touches a very specific group of people. The rise of Occupy Wall Street has brought a broader critique of the 1 percent to the fore, and in doing so has spurred some of the plutocrats to mount a more general self-defense.

On October 11, 2011, Occupy Wall Street protesters marched past the Upper East Side homes of some of New York's wealthiest residents, including John Paulson, the hedge fund manager who earned billions betting against subprime mortgages. Paulson & Co. issued a statement pointing out: "The top 1 percent of New Yorkers pay over 40 percent of all income taxes, providing huge benefits to everyone in our city and state. . . . Paulson & Company and its employees have paid hundreds of millions of dollars in New York City and New York State taxes in recent years and have created over 100 high-paying jobs in New York City since its formation." In response, Occupy Wall Street protesters left a mock tax refund check outside Paulson's house.

Jamie Dimon, the highest-paid Wall Street CEO, earning $23 million in

2010, is another unapologetic defender of the 1 percent. "Acting like everyone who's been successful is bad and because you're rich you're bad—I don't understand it," Dimon said when asked about public hostility toward bankers at an investors' conference in New York in December 2011. "Sometimes there's a bad apple, yet we denigrate the whole."

Peter Schiff, CEO of a Connecticut-based broker-dealer and unsuccessful candidate in the 2010 Republican primary for a Senate seat in that state, took the message straight to Zuccotti Park, walking through the square with a video camera and a handwritten sign that announced: "I am the 1%."

I heard similar sentiments at a public interview I conducted with GE's Jeff Immelt that month. During the question-and-answer session a white-haired gentleman sitting almost exactly in the middle of the room rose to speak. He admitted that his comments would be "not a question, it's almost a statement." It was one he assumed Immelt had sympathy with, but that "you can't make given the position you sit in." He went on to warn: "Our problem frankly is, as long as the president remains antiwealth, antibusiness, antienergy, anti–private aviation, he will never get the business community behind him. . . . The rhetoric is so poisonous . . . and the problem and the complication is 40 or 50 percent of the country are on the dole that support him."

The speaker was Leon Cooperman, a sixty-nine-year-old self-made billionaire. Son of a South Bronx plumber, Cooperman made it to Columbia Business School, then Goldman Sachs, then founded his own hedge fund. A few weeks after he made his statement to Immelt, Cooperman expanded on his views in an open letter to President Barack Obama, which instantly became the talk of Wall Street. In it, Cooperman complained the 1 percent were being unfairly caricatured: "Capitalists are not the scourge that they are too often made out to be"; the wealthy are not "a monolithic, selfish and unfeeling lot who must be subjugated by the force of the state." Instead, Cooperman urged the president and his supporters to remember that they needed the rich: "As a group, we employ many millions of taxpaying people, pay their salaries, provide them with health care coverage, start new companies, found new industries, create new products, fill store shelves at

Christmas, and keep the wheels of commerce and progress (and indeed of government, by generating the income whose taxation funds it) moving."

Foster Friess, the Wyoming mutual fund investor who shot to national prominence as the backer of the main super PAC supporting Republican primary candidate Rick Santorum, made the same point when I spoke to him in February 2012.

"People don't realize how wealthy people self-tax," Friess told me when I asked him whether, given the country's economic troubles, it was fair to ask the rich to pay a bigger share. "You know, there's a fellow who was the CEO of Target. In Phoenix, he's created a museum of music. He put in around $200 million of his own money. I have another friend who gave $400 million to a health facility in Nebraska or South Dakota, or someplace like that. You look at Bill Gates, just gave $750 million, I think, to fight AIDS."

Friess's point is that the common good is better served when the wealthy "self-tax" by supporting charities of their own selection, rather than paying taxes to fund government spending.

"I think we should get rid of taxes as much as we can," Friess told me. "Because you get to decide how you spend your money, rather than the government. I mean, if you have a certain cause, an art museum, or a symphony, and you want to support it, it would be nice if you had the choice to support it. Where we're headed, you'll be taxed, your money taken away, and the government will support it.

"It's a question—do you believe that the government should be taking your money and spending it for you, or do you want to spend it for you?" Friess explained.

As for the idea that an economic age, like our own, that is conducive to creating vast fortunes should also be one in which taxes are high—Friess considers that absurd. "If you look at what Steve Jobs has done for us, what Bill Gates has done for society, the government ought to pay them. Why do they collect money from Gates and Jobs for what they've contributed? It's ridiculous."

Indeed, Friess is unpersuaded by the entire 99 percent paradigm. In his view, it is the Americans at the bottom of the income distribution who are getting the free ride. "I'm just so amazed at this concept that President Obama says, 'I'm not gonna let half the American people that pay no taxes bear the unfair burden of the other half, who are not paying their fair share.' It's pretty comical, when you think about it," he told me. "About 46 percent of the American public pay no income taxes."

Friess believes we all rely on the 1 percent, and should respect them accordingly. "It's that top 1 percent that probably contributes more to making the world a better place than the 99 percent. I've never seen any poor people do what Bill Gates has done. I've never seen poor people hire many people," he told me. "So I think we ought to honor and uplift the 1 percent, the ones who have created value."

Friess is very conservative, but among the plutocrats, his views about the oppression of the rich are not unusual. In a rare interview with the *Chicago Tribune* in the spring of 2012, Ken Griffin, a Chicago-based billionaire hedge fund manager, complained that plutocrats don't have enough of a voice in American politics and that political engagement is an onerous burden it is their duty to bear.

"I think [the ultrawealthy] actually have an insufficient influence," Griffin, who donated more than $1 million to Republican political causes in the 2012 election cycle, told the *Chicago Tribune*. Over time, the Griffins have given roughly $1.5 million to the conservative causes supported by David and Charles Koch. "Those who have enjoyed the benefits of our system more than ever now owe a duty to protect the system that has created the greatest nation on this planet."

Griffin also complained about the necessity of lobbying: "I spend way too much of my time thinking about politics these days because government is way too involved in financial markets these days." That dependence on government regulation, Griffin worries, is limiting the free speech of the rich. "This is the first time class warfare has really been embraced as a political tool. Because we are looking at an administration that has embraced class warfare as being politically expedient, I do worry about the publicity that comes with being willing to both with my dollars and, more importantly, with my voice, to stand for what I believe in. As government gets bigger every single day, how does my willingness to stand up for what I believe is right become eclipsed by my dependency on institutions that are ultimately controlled by the government? Remember, I live in financial services, and every bank in the United States is really under the thumb of the government in a way it's never been before."

Like so many of today's working rich, Griffin, who was a billionaire before his fortieth birthday, thinks of himself as a self-made man: "I started my career with myself, two employees, and a one-room office. Nothing was given to me per se, except for a great education—my college degree [at Harvard]—and a country that allows somebody to just go for it." Griffin is proud his firm, like all hedge funds, didn't need government money to survive the crisis, and he doesn't see himself as a beneficiary of the bailout that rescued the financial sector more broadly.

One day in November 2011, Dennis Gartman, a former commodities analyst and foreign exchange and bond trader, devoted his daily investment note to a rousing defense of the 1 percent:

> We celebrate income disparity and we applaud the growing margins between the bottom 20 percent of American society and the upper 20 percent for it is evidence of what has made America a great country. It is the chance to have a huge income . . . to make something of one's self; to begin a business and become a millionaire legally and on one's own that separates the U.S. from most other nations of the world. Do we feel bad for the growing gap between the rich and the poor in the U.S.? Of course not; we celebrate it, for we were poor once and we are reasonably wealthy now. We did it on our own, by the sheer dint of will, tenacity, street smarts and the like. That is why immigrants come to the U.S.: to join the disparate income earners at the upper levels of society and to leave poverty behind. Income inequality? Give us a break. God bless income disparity and those who have succeeded, and shame upon the OWS crowd who take us to task for our success and

wallow in their own failure. Income disparity? Feh! What we despise is government that imposes rules that prohibit or make it difficult to make even more money; to employ even more people; to give even more sums to the charities of our choice.

Much of this pique stems from simple self-interest. In addition to the proposed tax hikes, the financial reforms that Obama signed into law in the summer of 2010 have made regulations on American finance more stringent. But, the rage in the C-suites is driven not merely by greed but by an affront to the plutocrats' amour propre, a wounded incredulity that anyone could think of them as villains rather than heroes. Aren't they, after all, the ones whose financial and technological innovations represent the future of the American economy? Aren't they doing, as Lloyd Blankfein quipped, "God's work"?

You might say that the American plutocracy is experiencing its John Galt moment. Libertarians (and run-of-the-mill high school nerds) will recall that Galt is the plutocratic hero of Ayn Rand's 1957 novel, *Atlas Shrugged*. Tired of being dragged down by the parasitic, envious, and less talented lower classes, Galt and his fellow capitalists revolt, retreating to "Galt's Gulch," a refuge in the Rocky Mountains. There, they pass their days in secluded splendor, while the rest of the world, bereft of their genius and hard work, collapses.

That was, of course, a fiction, and one with as much bodice ripping as economics. But versions of Galt's Gulch are starting to show up in more sober venues. James Duggan, a founding principal of a Chicago firm of tax and estate planning lawyers, believes "wealth is fleeing the country." Some of the self-exiled rich are, Mr. Duggan argues, "conscientious objectors": "There are those who are simply going offshore to make a statement. Their level of discontent with the current circumstances in our country, coupled with attacks on the wealthy, has created a distinct sense of rebellion among many wealthy citizens. While they may love the country, they are objecting to the current trends and responding by moving themselves or their assets, or both, away from the cause of the problem."

On December 8, 2011, two days after Barack Obama made income inequality the theme of a speech in Osawatomie, Kansas, Ed Yardeni, an economist and investment adviser, devoted his influential daily post to a 1 percent fantasy of extraterrestrial immigration: "We may need an escape plan if Europe blows up and if President Barack Obama spends the next eleven months campaigning rather than presiding. Just in the nick of time, NASA yesterday announced that its Kepler space telescope has found a new planet, Kepler-22b. It is the most Earth-like yet. . . . Those of us who favor fiscal discipline, small governments and low taxes might consider moving there and starting over."

Meanwhile, a few modern-day plutocrats are actually trying to build a real Galt's Gulch here on earth. This is the project of the Seasteading Institute, which is hoping to construct man-made islands in the international waters of the ocean, beyond the legal reach of any national government. These oases, where the rich would be free to prosper unrestrained by the grasping of the 99 percent, are the brainchild of Milton Friedman's grandson and are being funded in part by Silicon Valley billionaire and libertarian Peter Thiel.

Not all plutocrats want to escape to a Seastead. Paul Martin and Ernesto Zedillo are members in good standing of the global elite. Martin is a former Canadian prime minister, finance minister, deficit hawk, and, in his life before politics, a multimillionaire businessman. Zedillo is a former Mexican president, holds a doctorate in economics, directs Yale University's Center for the Study of Globalization, and serves on the boards of the blue chips Procter & Gamble and Alcoa. Yet when I interviewed the two of them in a wide-ranging public conversation in Waterloo, Canada, they sounded an awful lot like the kids camped out in Zuccotti Park.

"I have yet to talk to anybody who doesn't say that they aren't reflecting a disquiet that they themselves feel," Martin said. "I think really the powerful thing is that Occupy Wall Street has hit a chord that really is touching the middle class—the middle class in Canada, the middle class in the United States, the middle class right around the world—and I think that makes it actually very, very powerful."

Zedillo thought OWS should widen its sights: "I could argue as an economist it's not only about Wall Street. They should have an Occupy G20."

Martin and Zedillo would be welcome at any corporate dining room on Wall Street, or at any financier's dinner party on the Upper East Side, but it was striking how strongly their views of Occupy Wall Street differed from the conventional wisdom among American business elites, especially financiers.

That dissonance was not lost on Martin. He started out diplomatically—"I think that most people have basically given them [the protesters] a fair amount of credit"—but then couldn't resist, adding, "I don't want to pick on U.S. bankers, but the reaction, the one that really got me, was the banker who basically said, 'You know, these are just a bunch of welfare bums. What we've got to do is cut welfare.' A New York banker saying we've got to cut welfare is staggering to me. Why doesn't he just look in the mirror? I think that actually what's happened is that the inability of some people to defend their position has become so manifest that it's actually added to the power of Occupy Wall Street."

Some plutocrats are worried about the eventual political consequences of the intellectual divide between their class and everyone else. Mohamed El-Erian, the Pimco CEO, is a model member of the super-elite. But he is also a man whose father grew up in rural Egypt, and he has studied nations where the gaps between the rich and the poor have had violent resolutions. "For successful people to say the nasty end of the income distribution doesn't apply to me is shortsighted," he told me. "I don't know how you opt out of the world economy, but some people think we should try to do that. And in some unequal societies, confiscation can become a policy tool."

El-Erian told me that in June 2010. In the fall of 2011, after the launch of the Occupy Wall Street movement, he went further. "No nation can tolerate for long excessive shifts in income and wealth inequalities as they tear at the fabric of society," he wrote to me in an e-mail. "Think of this simple analogy—that of an increasingly fancy house in a poor and deteriorating neighborhood. The well-being of the house cannot be divorced from that of the neighborhood as a whole."

El-Erian worried that his fellow plutocrats weren't paying enough attention to the foreclosures down the block, though: "Some elites live astonishingly sheltered lives."

THE CENTER CANNOT HOLD

Mark Carney is not most people's idea of a radical. In Ottawa, where he has lived for the past eight years, the trim forty-seven-year-old is known as an uxorious husband and hands-on dad to his four daughters. The Canadian capital is hardly a party town, but even there he has a reputation as a homebody for whom an exciting night out is a school concert. At Harvard, he played hockey (he is Canadian, after all), but he never rose beyond backup goalie. He spent more time in the library than on ice, earning a magna in economics. At Oxford, where he got his PhD, this son of a high school principal and a schoolteacher is remembered by his classmates for his studiousness: Carney always sat in the front row at lectures many of the other students didn't even bother to attend. From there, he went to Goldman Sachs, spending thirteen years at the firm's offices in London and New York and Toronto. When Carney decided to go home, his first job was as a highly competent but self-effacing civil servant in the Bank of Canada before joining the finance ministry in 2004. And today, as governor of the Bank of Canada, he devotes most of his time to pondering such wonkish matters as how to measure global liquidity and the need for countercyclical regulation.

But in the fall of 2011, Carney became a protagonist in a central battle between the plutocracy and the rest of us—a crucial fight over the regulatory power of the state. The showdown took place on a Friday afternoon in September in Washington, D.C. It was the weekend of the biannual meeting of the IMF and World Bank, a gathering of the world's central bankers and finance ministers that takes place in the U.S. capital every fall and spring. The meetings have been on the calendar since these Bretton Woods institutions were first formed, and gradually a number of private sector conclaves have come to be held on their fringes.

In 2011, one of those fringe meetings was organized by the Financial Services Forum, a bankers' association. Its chairman, Goldman Sachs chief Lloyd Blankfein, invited Carney to address the group of about thirty bankers. They were particularly interested to talk to the Canadian not only because of his strong performance in the financial crisis—Canada was the only G7 country that didn't need to bail out its banks—but also because Carney was tipped to become the next head of the Financial Stability Board, a body of international regulators that comes closest to being the world's banking boss. The FSB's big job at the moment is refining and implementing new international bank capital rules. These regulations, known as Basel III, have taken on particular importance because a lack of capital in many U.S. and European banks was a central cause of the 2008 financial meltdown.

Meetings of bankers are generally pretty dry affairs, and relatively large international gatherings of this sort, whose participants don't know one another well, are usually even more decorous. But this particular conversation soon heated up.

Jamie Dimon, CEO of JPMorgan Chase, told Carney he thought the proposed Basel III rules were "cockamamie nonsense." In fact, the bank chief said, the rules ran counter to the national interest. "I have called it anti-American," Dimon said, according to one participant. "The only reason I am calling it anti-American is because I am American. I also think it's anti-European."

Another participant remembered Dimon's remarks slightly differently. In his recollection, Dimon insisted that Carney's view was "anti-American," a phrase Dimon had floated in a newspaper interview a few weeks earlier and which, he allegedly told the Washington group, had resonated with a lot of people, "so I'm going to keep on using it." At a time when multinationals, including JPMorgan, which earns around a quarter of its revenue outside

North America, are increasingly global concerns, explicitly determined to go wherever the money is, it is noteworthy, to put it kindly, to hear a bank boss depict himself as a beleaguered national champion.

At first, Carney responded calmly: "I hear what you are saying. I don't think it will surprise you that I am taking a different view. These are reasonable responses to the financial crisis."

As Dimon's tirade continued, his fellow bankers nervously tried to lower the temperature. Rick Waugh, the CEO of Scotiabank and a Canadian who has had his own disagreements with Carney, tried to intervene in their increasingly heated exchange.

But Dimon was unstoppable and soon Carney got mad. Visibly angry, the Canadian central banker abruptly left the room.

The other bankers, including Blankfein and Josef Ackermann, then the CEO of Deutsche Bank, looked uncomfortable, though it was Dimon's tone, not his message, that concerned them. Ackermann tried to smooth things over by saying that Carney had left because of a tight schedule. (This was true: Carney was late for a press conference.)

After the meeting Blankfein sent Carney—remember, he is a Goldman alumnus—an e-mail to patch things up. Dimon, who stands by the substance of his remarks, realized the tone and forum had been inappropriate, and phoned Carney on Saturday to apologize. He didn't reach him. Dimon called again when Carney was back home in Ottawa on Monday. This time they spoke and, according to a JPMorgan executive, Dimon said he was sorry. "Jamie knew he messed up," the executive said. "It wasn't the right place and it wasn't the right tone." He told the Canadian he had the utmost respect for him and thought the world of him.

By then, though, the battle had been joined. The day before the Dimon apology, a Sunday, Carney was the first speaker at the annual meeting of the Institute of International Finance, another international banking lobby group. He was introduced cordially by Waugh, a sparring partner back home who nonetheless told the audience, "He's my governor and I'm very proud of that fact."

But neither Waugh's courtesy nor Dimon's bellicosity persuaded Carney to temper his message. "It is hard to see how backsliding would help. If some institutions feel pressure today, it is because they have done too little for too long, rather than because they are being asked to do too much too soon," Carney said.

"Everyone is claiming to be a Boy Scout while accusing others of juvenile delinquency," he said. "However, neither merit badges nor detentions will be self-selected but, rather, determined by impartial peer review and mutual oversight."

Dimon and Carney were fighting about a lot of money: the Basel III requirements would significantly increase JPMorgan's cost of doing business and could cut into its profits. But much more is at stake than JPMorgan's balance sheet. That weekend exchange is a telling moment in the story of the plutocrats' relationship with the state—more significant, even, than high-profile wrangling over taxes on the plutocracy, like carried interest or the charge on large estates.

Here's why. Even the most ardent right-winger agrees the state has the right to levy taxes—the fight is about who pays and how much. The battle between Carney and Dimon gets at a bigger and more contentious issue: Are the interests of the state and its big businesses synonymous? If not, who decides? And if they do clash, does the state have the right—and the might—to curb specific businesses for the collective good?

This dispute has been around for a long time—remember the assertion of General Motors CEO Charlie Wilson, controversial from the moment he uttered it, that what is good for General Motors is good for America? And it is being fought everywhere there is private business. Carlos Slim's relative economic power is so overwhelming that many local observers believe that even if the government of President Felipe Calderón wanted to regulate his businesses more aggressively, it would lack the muscle to do so. In the late 1990s, Russia's oligarchs boasted that they controlled the Kremlin—a state of affairs that helped Vladimir Putin win public support for a repressive reassertion of state power. China's plutocrats don't fight the state because they are the state—and when any of them forget that, they are treated with summary brutality: between 2003 and 2011, at least fourteen Chinese billionaire businessmen were executed.

In the West, particularly in the United States, the rise of the super-elite coincided with a strengthening of the conviction that what was good for business was good for the economy as a whole—and that business was in the best position to judge what worked. As Jed Rakoff, a New York judge and former federal prosecutor who has been pushing the SEC to be more exacting in its policing, reflected in an interview, "In the 1990s, of course, free enterprise, capitalism, and so forth were glorified to a degree. Some of that was political. We had finally won the battle against the Iron Curtain and part of the reason we won was because our economic system was a lot better than theirs. But I think maybe it was an overglorification of capitalism. I don't mean to suggest that I'm personally for socialism. I'm not. But I am personally for some regulation."

That glorification extended to the masters of the universe on Wall Street. Donald Kohn, a former vice chairman of the Federal Reserve and a central banker whom Alan Greenspan called "my first mentor at the Fed," now believes that this equation of the private interest with the public interest has gone too far. In fact, he, like Greenspan, has come to the view that it was a mistake even to think that bankers would be skilled at defending their own interests—that the markets could, as the prevailing theory had it, regulate themselves. At a British parliamentary hearing in May 2011, Kohn testified, "I placed too much confidence in the ability of the private market participants to police themselves."

COGNITIVE CAPTURE

The Fed's excessive faith in the bankers it regulated was caused by a phenomenon Willem Buiter has dubbed "cognitive state capture." Like Carney, Buiter is no wild-eyed flamethrower. A former academic economist who served on the Monetary Policy Committee of the Bank of England, Buiter has himself joined the ranks of the global super-elite: born in Holland and possessor of British and American passports, since 2010 he has been chief economist for Citigroup. But in a paper delivered at the Federal Reserve's annual economic conference in Jackson Hole in August 2008, Buiter argued, "The Fed listens to Wall Street and believes what it hears, or at any rate, the Fed acts as if it believes what Wall Street tells it. Wall Street tells the Fed about its pain, what its pain means for the economy at large, and what the Fed ought to do about it."

Buiter readily admits that during the financial crisis "Wall Street's pain was indeed great—deservedly so in many cases." But he asks, "Why did Wall Street get what it wanted?" His answer is cognitive state capture.

"It is not achieved by special interests buying, blackmailing, or bribing their way toward control of the legislature, the executive, or some important regulator or agency, like the Fed, but instead through those in charge of the relevant state entity internalizing, as if by osmosis, the objectives, interest, and perception of reality of the vested interest they are meant to regulate and supervise in the public interest," Buiter explains. "There is little room for doubt, in my view, that the Fed under Greenspan treated the stability, well-being, and profitability of the financial sector as an objective in its own right."

With hindsight, some of the leaders of the Fed during those years have become openly repentant. As Kohn said at the British parliamentary hearing, "I have learned quite a few lessons, unfortunately for the economy, I guess, in the past few years." He added later, "I deeply regret the pain that was caused to millions of people in the United States and around the world by the financial crisis and its aftermath."

On Wall Street, though, the need for a more assertive state is not obvious. And if Dimon expresses this point of view with particular passion, that may be because he is one of the bankers who has the most right to it: he was, after all, one of the few CEOs who was actually pretty good at self-policing. Under his stewardship, JPMorgan, which is essentially a creature of Dimon's deal-making genius, deftly avoided many of the most toxic assets that wrecked the balance sheets of other Wall Street firms. Dimon's

JPMorgan was strong enough to help Tim Geithner, then head of the New York Fed, in March 2008 by saving Bear Stearns (admittedly at a fire sale price); Dimon even left his own star-studded fifty-second birthday party to make the transaction happen. Dimon insisted from the start that his bank took the TARP bailout money only as a favor to the Treasury, which worried that unless the rescue was collective it would further stigmatize Wall Street's weakest players. In 2009, the *New York Times* described Dimon as President Obama's favorite banker, and his chief of staff at the time, Rahm Emanuel, even promised to speak at a JPMorgan board meeting. (Emanuel changed his mind after his plans were reported and the White House reconsidered such a visible demonstration of coziness with a specific Wall Street firm.)

All of which not only adds to Dimon's natural cockiness (he, too, is another largely self-made plutocrat, who ascended from Queens to Wall Street via Harvard Business School), it fuels his conviction that business will do a better job running the economy if the government, with its burdensome rules, stays out of the way.

Hence, a few months before his dispute with Carney, Dimon enlivened a public question-and-answer session in Atlanta with his own regulator, Fed chairman Ben Bernanke, by warning of the dangers of higher capital requirements. For one thing, Dimon argued, "Most of the bad actors are gone." For another, he cautioned, in an inversion of the Charlie Wilson line, that what was bad for JPMorgan would be bad for the country as a whole. "I have this great fear that someone's going to write a book in ten or twenty years, and the book is going to talk about all the things that we did in the middle of the crisis to actually slow down recovery. . . . Has anyone bothered to study the cumulative effect of all these things [regulations] and do you have a fear like I do that when we look back and look at them all, that they will be a reason it took so long that our banks, our credit, our businesses, and most importantly job creation start going again? Is this holding us back at this point?"

That wasn't the first time Dimon went public with his skepticism of the government's ability to manage the economy. In January 2010, at the hearings of the Financial Crisis Inquiry Commission in Washington, D.C., he said, "My daughter called me from school one day and said, 'Dad, what's a financial crisis?' and without trying to be funny, I said, 'It's the kind of thing that happens every five to seven years.' And she said, 'Then why is everybody so surprised?'"

That couldn't be more different from Mark Carney's worldview. He obliquely dismissed Dimon's daughter anecdote in Berlin nine months later, not referring to Dimon by name but alluding to his remarks and charaterizing the attitude they betrayed as "jaded." Carney asked why the rest of us "should be content with the dreary cycle of upheaval" the unnamed bank CEO had described. In the Washington speech he delivered forty-eight hours after his direct clash with Dimon, Carney challenged what he called Wall Street "fatalism" head-on: "In no other aspect of human endeavor do men and women not strive to learn and to improve. The sad experience of the past few years shows that there is ample scope to improve the efficiency and resilience of the global financial system. By clarity of purpose and resolute implementation, we can do so. The current reform initiatives mark real progress."

Carney also took on another shibboleth of the banking lobby—that new rules would make little difference because they would always be arbitraged away. This is a polite way of saying bankers and their lawyers will always outsmart their regulators. It is a familiar poacher/gamekeeper argument— you can make the same point about terrorists and security regulations— with the added oomph of money and meritocracy. With bankers outearning their regulators by more than 100 to 1 (the ratio of Dimon's salary to Bernanke's), surely the bureaucrats will be hopelessly intellectually outmatched?

The gap appears not just in the pay slips but in resources. One White House official who had earned as much as $5 million a year in the private sector was dismayed to learn he was expected to fly economy class to meetings in Asia, a significant discomfort and one that, at more than fifty, he felt made it hard for him to do his job. On a trip from Washington to New York in the spring of 2011, CFTC (Commodity Futures Trading Commission) officials took the Megabus (thirty dollars per person round-trip), rather than

Amtrak or the Delta shuttle, saving more than a thousand dollars. To avoid the cost of hotels, SEC staffers sometimes try to squeeze in trips to New York, where most of the banks they regulate are based, into a single day. In the movies the underdog on the bus beats the plutocrat on the private jet, but it is hard to see why that should happen in real life with any regularity.

Carney, who earns $500,000 a year, less than one-twentieth the 2011 compensation of Canada's most highly paid Bay Street banker, explained why bankers' outsmarting the system only made regulation even more important: "New and better rules are necessary, but not sufficient. People will always try to find ways around them. Some may succeed, for a while. That is why good supervision is paramount. Rules are only as good as the supervisors who enforce them, and good supervisors look beyond the letter of the rules to their spirit."

Eight months later, Dimon inadvertently bolstered Carney's case. On May 10, 2012, JPMorgan revealed that a trader known as the London Whale had made a bet on credit derivatives that went sour, leading to a loss of at least $2 billion, and which analysts close to the bank believed could rise to $6 billion. Wall Street, led by Dimon, had spent the previous three years warning that Washington's regulatory overreach was stifling the financial system. The London Whale's trades suggested that the real danger was still too much risk. As Congressman Barney Frank put it, "The argument that financial institutions do not need the new rules to help them avoid the irresponsible actions that led to the crisis of 2008 is at least $2 billion harder to make today."

In the fight over capital requirements, the bankers would be delighted if the Fed returned to its Greenspan-era reliance on market self-regulation. But the bigger issue of the relationship between plutocrats and the state can't be reduced to business battling for smaller government. Often, a big, intrusive state is the plutocrat's best friend—true of state capitalist regimes like China and Russia and of industries, like the defense business, that live on state largesse, or of companies, like the U.S. steel industry under George

W. Bush, that have lobbied for and won protectionist legislation. In 2008 and 2009 it was true of Wall Street, too, when the bankers pushed for and got a massive government bailout to save their companies—the biggest state intervention in a national economy, as a percentage of GDP, since Lenin's nationalization. In fact, even the most ardent believer in small government and free enterprise can also think it is the duty of business to cut the best possible deal with the state. As Ken Griffin, the billionaire hedge fund manager who supports conservative super PACs, explained, "CEOs have duties to their shareholders. If the state's willing to hand out gifts, there are many who feel compelled to go get them." So this isn't just a question of big versus small government.

The issue, instead, is whether the interests of business and of the community at large are always the same and, if they aren't, whether the government has the will, the authority, and the brains to defend the latter, even against the protests of the former. That's why Carney wanted to raise capital requirements. As he reminded his Sunday morning Washington audience, "Four years ago, manifest deficiencies in capital adequacy, liquidity buffers, and risk management led to the collapse of some of the most storied names in finance and triggered the worst financial crisis since the Great Depression. The complete loss of confidence in private finance—your membership—could only be arrested by the provision of comprehensive backstops by the richest economies in the world. With about $4 trillion in output and almost twenty-eight million jobs lost in the ensuing recession, the case for reform was clear then and remains so today."

Carney then cited a Bank of Canada calculation that found that "even if Basel III were to reduce slightly the probability of such crises in the future," the economic value of that decreased risk to the G20 countries would be about $13 trillion. In other words, this may hurt your business a little, but it will help the economy as a whole a lot.

Luigi Zingales, a professor at the University of Chicago's Booth School of Business, frames this as the choice between being promarket and being probusiness. Super-elites are often the product of a strong market economy, but, ironically, as their influence grows they can become its opponents.

Here is how Zingales, an ardently patriotic immigrant to America and a passionate defender of the market economy, describes the dynamic: "True capitalism lacks a strong lobby. That assertion might appear strange in light of the billions of dollars firms spend lobbying Congress in America, but that is exactly the point. Most lobbying seeks to tilt the playing field in one direction or another, not to level it. Most lobbying is *pro-business*, in the sense that it promotes the interests of existing businesses, not *pro-market* in the sense of fostering truly free and open competition. Open competition forces established firms to prove their competence again and again; strong successful market players therefore often use their muscle to restrict such competition, and to strengthen their positions. As a result, serious tensions emerge between a pro-market agenda and a pro-business one."

Whose New Class?

In January 1977, America's boardrooms and universities were jolted by an unexpected piece of news. Henry Ford II, chairman and chief executive of the Ford Motor Company and grandson of the original Henry, had resigned from the board of the Ford Foundation.

A former naval officer known for his aggressive and blunt management style—he rejected Lee Iacocca's proposal to put a Honda engine in a Ford car on the grounds that "no car with my name on the hood is going to have a Jap engine inside"—Ford laid out the reasons for his departure in a blistering resignation letter that he released to the press:

The Foundation exists and thrives on the fruits of our economic system. The dividends of competitive enterprise make it all possible. A significant portion of the abundance created by United States business enables the Foundation and like institutions to carry on their work. In effect, the Foundation is a creature of capitalism—a statement that I am sure would be shocking to many professional staff people in the field of philanthropy. It is hard to discern recognition of this fact in anything the Foundation does. It is even more difficult to find an understanding of this in many of the institutions, particularly the universities, that are the beneficiaries of the Foundation's grant programs. . . . I am just suggesting to the Trustees and the staff that the system that makes the Foundation possible very probably is worth preserving. Perhaps it's time for the Trustees and staff to examine the question of our obligations to our economic system; and to consider how the Foundation, as one of the system's most prominent offspring, might act most widely to strengthen and improve its progenitor.

The departure of the Deuce, as Ford was known, had no direct repercussions for the foundation that carried the family name. It had been created by his grandfather and his father, Edsel, in 1936, largely as a tax shelter and a vehicle to ensure continued family control over the car business. That structure worked, but it also meant that by 1977 the founding family had only moral authority over the philanthropy.

In the social and cultural tumult of the 1970s, that didn't count for much. McGeorge Bundy, then president of the Ford Foundation, responded with lofty unconcern to the public rebuke from the family scion: "He has a right to expect people to read his letter carefully, but I don't think one letter from anyone is going to change the foundation's course."

But Ford's departure turned out to be a turning point. That was partly because of the prominence of the man, his company, and his family's philanthropy. At that moment, Ford was the second-highest-paid CEO in America and the Ford Motor Company the country's fourth-largest corporation by sales. In its universe, the Ford Foundation cast an even longer shadow. It was by far the nation's biggest philanthropy; in 1954 it outspent runner-up Rockefeller fourfold and third-place Carnegie ten times over.

Most important, Ford's letter crystallized a fear that had been growing in the minds of many American businesspeople—that they were losing the national battle of ideas. Ford's Greatest Generation had won the Second World War, and when they came home they had helped create two decades of unprecedented, and widely shared, national prosperity. But they now feared that the institutions that created the country's intellectual and ideological weather—its universities, its foundations, and its newsrooms—had turned hostile to business and to capitalism.

Irving Kristol captured what he described as this battle between "the academic and business communities" in a seminal essay he published three months after Ford's *cri de guerre*. "It is a fact that the majority of the large foundations in this country, like most of our major universities, exude a climate of opinion wherein an anti-business bent becomes a perfectly natural inclination."

Judged by today's standards, that is certainly the case. The marginal tax rate on top earners was 70 percent, capital gains were taxed at a maximum rate of 49 percent, and Wall Street, constrained by the separation between investment and retail banking of the Glass-Steagall Act, was still the rather sleepy handmaiden of industry. Like their philanthro-capitalist successors, the foundations of the 1960s and 1970s hoped to leverage their projects into influence on government policy.

But rather than bringing the techniques and skills of the private sector to the social sector, the foundations of that era hoped to transform private charity into state largesse. As Paul Ylvisaker, a Harvard social theorist who became an influential Ford staffer, later explained, the job of the foundation was to promote "programs and policies, such as social security, income maintenance, and educational entitlement, that convert isolated and discretionary acts of private charity into regularized public remedies that flow as a matter of legislated right."

Kristol said business needed to fight back. Different corporations, he wrote, could well have different views of their social responsibility, but they would all surely agree that it included keeping the world safe for capitalism and capitalists: "Most corporations would presumably agree that any such conception ought to include as one of its goals the survival of the corporation itself as a relatively autonomous institution in the private sector. And this, inevitably, involves efforts to shape or reshape the climate of public opinion—a climate that is created by our scholars, our teachers, our intellectuals, our publicists: in short, by the New Class."

Kristol concludes his essay with a modest proposal. To change public opinion, business needed to support those "dissident" elements of the New Class "which do believe in the preservation of a strong private sector." Unless it recruited its own army on the intellectual battlefield, business would surely lose the political and ultimately economic wars, too: "In any naked contest with the New Class, business is a certain loser. Businessmen who cannot even persuade their own children that business is a morally legitimate activity are not going to succeed, on their own, in persuading the world of it. You can only beat an idea with another idea, and the war of ideas and ideologies will be won or lost within the New Class, not against it. Business certainly has a stake in this war—but for the most part seems blithely unaware of it."

Kristol was, of course, one of those dissident members of the New Class—he concludes his essay by urging businessmen to seek out intellectuals like himself "to offer guidance," just as they would hire competent geologists to help find oil—and over the next thirty years he, his fellow conservative intellectuals, and the business leaders who bankrolled them did a remarkable job of building up a network of conservative think tanks, foundations, elite journals, and mass media outlets. But what is really striking isn't the rise of what Hillary Clinton once dubbed the "vast right-wing conspiracy," it is the extent to which the climate that Kristol complained of so bitterly in 1977 is today so much more conducive to his ideas.

Just take a look at the pages of America's leading newspapers. In April and May of 2011, when unemployment was 9 percent and the ten-year rate on U.S. Treasury bills—the American government's cost of borrowing money—hovered around a historically low 3 percent, the five largest papers in the country published 201 stories about the budget deficit and only sixty-three about joblessness. The left won the great culture wars of the 1960s, but the right has succeeded in setting the terms of the economic debate. A good outcome for the 1 percent.

The life choices of Democratic first families tell a similar story. Amy Carter, who came of age in the White House, took part in anti-apartheid protests at the South African embassy in 1985 (for which she was arrested).

She met her husband at an Atlanta bookstore where he was a manager and she was a part-time employee. Chelsea Clinton, the next Democratic daughter, has worked at a hedge fund and as a management consultant. Her husband, a fellow legacy Democrat, worked at Goldman Sachs before they married and went on to set up his own hedge fund.

One reason Kristol's wing of the New Class won is that they were right. Capitalism works, and its triumph became a global fact with the collapse of the Soviet Union.

The demise of communism was, of course, tremendously encouraging for the free market intellectuals of America's New Class, but it had an even more profound impact on the New Class in the emerging markets. The intellectuals in most of those markets have lived through some version of central planning, ranging from the repressive Soviet model to the freer but also inefficient Indian version. You could argue that, as a group, the New Class didn't do too badly under communism—that, after all, was the thesis of Djilas as well as Szelényi and Konrád—but to most people who actually experienced it, that theory doesn't stand up to the routine humiliations of life in a dictatorship. In the emerging economies, the scorecard is even starker. In India and China, the past three decades of freer markets have lifted hundreds of millions of people out of poverty, a feat the previous three decades of left-leaning development economics had singularly failed to accomplish.

The result is the intellectual dominance of the sort of thinking Kristol described as a dissident view in 1970s America. In the 1990s, the brightest intellectuals in the former Warsaw Pact, from Warsaw itself to Tallinn to Moscow, were those figuring out how to transition from communism to capitalism. The smartest Chinese were working on the same question. Today the most famous African intellectual outside that continent is Dambisa Moyo, whose big idea is that foreign aid is self-serving and disempowering.

In the United States, that self-proclaimed capitalist tool *Forbes* magazine is suffering the slow, sad decline that seems to be the fate of most print magazines; meanwhile, it now publishes fifteen international editions, including versions in three former Soviet republics, India, China, and the Middle East. The *Harvard Business Review*, the proudly dry bible of the C-suite, has eleven foreign editions and can be found in most kiosks in the Moscow subway.

The Kristol wing of the New Class is globally ascendant for a more material reason, too. In Kristol's day, left-leaning intellectuals could get comfortable, socially prestigious jobs at the like-minded institutions whose ideological climate Kristol so deplored—elite universities, think tanks, the media. Today, the finances of universities and the mainstream media are in pretty rough shape, particularly by comparison with the bank balances of the plutocrats. (The publisher of the *Financial Times* once remarked to me ruefully that in a very good year the media group's entire profit was equal to one midlevel Wall Street trader's bonus.) Some think tanks are in rude health, but those are very much under the sway of their engaged philanthro-capitalist founders.

Those members of the New Class Kristol most feared—academics in the humanities—are those who today are most hard-pressed. Indeed, getting a doctorate in the humanities, once a ticket to the top tier of the New Class, is today such a wretched business one disappointed academic has created a popular Web site called 100 Reasons NOT to Go to Graduate School. Emory English professor Mark Bauerlein, a former staffer of one of those New Class institutions most demonized by the right, the National Endowment for the Arts, told the *Yale Daily News*: "It just doesn't make sense for people to go to school in the humanities."

Meanwhile, super-elites prosper and their spending on what they like to call "thought leadership" grows, with a predictable impact on the climate of the institutions of the New Class. In her inaugural commencement address, Harvard president Drew Faust observed sadly that the obvious reason so few Harvard graduates were pursuing careers in the humanities and so many were going to Wall Street was, "as bank robber Willie Sutton said, that's where the money is."

Awareness of those changed incentives has wrought a powerful cultural change. In 1969, radical Harvard activists rallied together to force ROTC off campus. But when some Harvard students walked out of former Bush adviser Greg Mankiw's class, the *Harvard Crimson*, training ground for the *New York Times* masthead, condemned the protesters in an editorial titled "Stay in School." A half dozen students staged a walk-in in support of their professor, and were greeted with applause and shouts of "We love Greg Mankiw." Professor Mankiw, himself an adviser to the Romney campaign, noted that today's undergraduates are less concerned with social justice than his cohort had been. "My first reaction was nostalgia," he wrote in an op-ed about the protest. "I went to college in the late 1970s, when the Vietnam War was still fresh and student activism was more common. Today's students tend to be more focused on polishing their resumes than on campaigning for social reform."

Many of Professor Mankiw's students will go to work on Wall Street. But among those who remain in the New Class, the ones most closely connected to the super-elite will be the ones who prosper. The best way to earn a living as an intellectual is as a teacher of the super-elite, or an employee. The only four fields where average professor salaries are in the six figures are law, engineering, business, and computer science.

Most important, academics in fields the plutocracy values can multiply their salaries by working as consultants and speakers to super-elite audiences, often in the emerging markets. As Niall Ferguson told me, during a whirlwind weekend when he had given a speech to a private equity conference hosted by a Turkish plutocrat in Istanbul, followed by a speech in Yalta for Ukrainian plutocrat Victor Pinchuk, the roads out of Cambridge, Massachusetts, get jammed on Thursday afternoons as Harvard Business School professors rush to the airport to get to their international speaking gigs. A bestselling New York nonfiction writer likes to tell his more literary—and less well-off—friends that his secret is to write books businesspeople can read on a transatlantic flight.

Even as they cash their speaking fees from the super-elite, these academics shape the way all of us think about the economy. That is mostly through their work in the classroom and at their computers, but also in their role as "independent" experts in legislative debates. A 2010 study by three of my colleagues at Reuters found that of ninety-six testimonies given by eighty-two academics to the Senate Banking Committee and the House Financial Services Committee between late 2008 and early 2010—a crucial period when lawmakers were debating their response to the financial crisis—roughly one third did not reveal their ties to financial institutions.

WINNER-TAKE-ALL POLITICS

Politicians are sometimes described as another branch of the New Class, and they are even more dependent on the super-elite than are their academic brethren, who, after all, can still rely on the comforts of the tenure system (even if it is growing rather threadbare). This, again, is true of politicians as a group, not just of those on the right. Fund-raising is the biggest part of the story, of course, but the connections are deeper than a disclosure form.

For one thing, an increasing number of politicians are members of the super-elite themselves. Nearly half of all members of Congress—250 in all—were millionaires in 2010, and their median net worth was $913,000, more than nine times the national average. American legislators are getting richer: their net worth increased 15 percent between 2004 and 2010. At least ten lawmakers are full-fledged plutocrats, with fortunes of more than $100 million.

One academic study has suggested that serving in Washington helps these leaders get rich. Professor Alan Ziobrowski of Georgia State and his colleagues found that the stock portfolios of House members beat the market by 6 percent, while senators' investments outperformed by 12 percent. The economists attributed this investing prowess to a "significant information advantage"; helpfully, lawmakers were not subject to insider trading laws until April 4, 2012, when President Obama signed into law a bill forbidding the practice. But a different study by LSE and MIT researchers challenged that conclusion, finding that legislators were actually lousy investors, doing less well than the market average. In either case, though, the financial gap—and the difference in perspective it brings—between U.S. politicians and their constituents is growing.

One thing that isn't in dispute is the material value of a political career after leaving elected office. Politicians can't fully monetize their plutocratic networks until they retire. When they do, they can become multimillion-aires. Between 2000 and 2007 the Clintons earned $111 million, nearly half of it in Bill's speaking fees, many of them paid by global plutocrats like Pinchuk. Tom Daschle, the former Democratic Senate majority leader, spent four years on the payroll of private equity investor Leo Hindery, earning more than $2 million and perks including one now notorious chauffeured car.

LUNCH WITH SECRETARY PAULSON

These connections occasionally create a political scandal—like Daschle's car, or the consulting fees earned by the academic economists who made the mistake of agreeing to be interviewed in the hit 2010 documentary film *Inside Job*—but the real story isn't one of individual corruption. It is, as Buiter argues, about systemic capture.

The vampire squid theory of the super-elite is entertaining and emotionally satisfying. It can be fun to imagine the super-elites who went to Wall Street and their Harvard classmates who became economics professors and those who became U.S. senators participating in a grand conspiracy (hatched ideally, at the Porcellian Club) to rip off the middle class. But the impact of these networks is much less cynical, and much more subtle, though not necessarily of less consequence.

Consider, for instance, the striking impact of income on how likely a U.S. senator is to respond to the views of his or her constituents. Research by politician scientist Larry Bartels showed that senators were 50 percent more likely to react to constituents in the top third of the income distribution than constituents in the middle third. Those at the bottom had almost no chance of being heard. Again, remarkably, Bartels found no measurable difference between Democrats and Republicans.

You could see the power of these networks in a remarkable private lunch Hank Paulson, then the secretary of the U.S. Treasury, attended in New York in July 2008, in the midst of the financial crisis. The lunch was hosted by Eric Mindich, a Goldman Sachs alumnus and founder of the Eton Park hedge fund, at his Third Avenue office. A dozen or so other hedge fund managers, at least five of them also veterans of Goldman Sachs, where Paulson had been CEO until moving to the Treasury in 2006, were there, too. As a Bloomberg journalist discovered three years later, thanks to a Freedom of Information request and dogged reporting, over lunch Paulson outlined his plans to put Fannie Mae and Freddie Mac under conservatorship, bringing the quasi-private firms fully under government control. Seven weeks later, that's what he did.

The men in the room were in a position to benefit materially from this insight into the secretary's plans. One was so acutely aware of the value of this private information he immediately called his lawyer to ask if it would be legal to trade on it; the lawyer said no. It is impossible to tell if the other diners were equally fastidious, but if they weren't they would have made a killing. Fannie and Freddie shares dropped to less than a dollar, a fraction of their former value, when Paulson put the companies into receivership in September, a windfall for anyone who had sold the stock short.

The most astonishing thing about the lunch is that it took place in plain sight. With so many participants—many of them mere acquaintances—Paulson surely would not have expected the gist of the discussion to remain secret for long. Indeed, some experts interviewed about the lunch afterward speculated that Paulson's intention in discussing his plans was to informally warn the broader market of what was coming and thus prevent a disruptive reaction.

Nor is Hank Paulson a neophyte who might be expected to make this sort of public misstep. His appointment as Treasury secretary in 2006 wasn't Paulson's first stint in D.C. In his early twenties, Paulson worked at the

Pentagon, and then in Richard Nixon's White House. Throughout his thirty-year career at Goldman Sachs Paulson was renowned for his political savvy both inside the firm and far beyond its old headquarters at 85 Broad Street, deftly building an influential network of connections as far afield as China. He made his career in the relationship business of investment banking, and within Goldman Sachs, Paulson was known as an expert operator. "When he ran the Chicago office, he managed to get the entire firm to work for him," one Goldman Sachs partner who had worked closely with Paulson told me admiringly.

So how did this smart, experienced leader come to participate in such an ill-judged lunch, the sort of insider meeting that is the stuff of fantasy for the Goldman haters? Zingales, the Republican professor at the university that is the intellectual home of free market economics, subscribes to Buiter's theory of cognitive state capture.

"The proportion of people with training and experience in finance working at the highest levels of every recent presidential administration is extraordinary. Four of the last six secretaries of Treasury fit this description. In fact, all four were directly or indirectly connected to one firm: Goldman Sachs," Zingales writes. "There is nothing intrinsically bad about these developments. In fact, it is only natural that a government in search of the brightest people will end up poaching from the finance world, to which the best and brightest have flocked."

But these hardworking meritocrats are subject to Charlie Wilson's misapprehension. "The problem is that people who have spent their entire lives in finance have an understandable tendency to think that the interests of their industry and the interests of the country always coincide. When Treasury Secretary Henry Paulson went to Congress last fall arguing that the world as we knew it would end if Congress did not approve the $700 billion bailout, he was serious and speaking in good faith. And to an extent he was right: His world—the world he lived and worked in—would have ended had there not been a bailout," Zingales argues. "But Henry Paulson's world is not the world most Americans live in—or even the world in which our economy as a whole exists."

The distortions of a very specific worldview are magnified by the human factor the Eton Park lunch reveals. "Compounding the problem is the fact that people in government tend to rely on their networks of trusted friends to gather information 'from the outside,'" Zingales explains. "If everyone in those networks is drawn from the same milieu, the information and ideas that flow to policy makers will be severely limited."

By way of further illustration, Zingales turns to France, where, thanks to the power of the École Polytechnique as a feeder for the political elite—a meritocratic grip much stronger than that of the Ivy League in the United States—many of the country's leaders were trained as engineers, especially in the field of nuclear engineering. And, sure enough, France's political leaders turn out to have been cognitively captured by the nuclear industry: more than half of the electricity France uses is produced by nuclear power, a higher percentage than in any other country.

The power of cognitive capture is that it is fully internalized. Critics, especially on the left, sometimes like to think of the super-elite in Orwellian terms, as masters of Doublethink who heartlessly pursue their own self-interest in full knowledge that the underclass will suffer as a consequence. The reality is much less nefarious: most super-elites genuinely are convinced that the policies that happen to serve their own interests, or those of their firm, or of their industry, are also right for everyone else.

In the spring of 2010, as the lobbying around the Dodd-Frank financial regulation bill was reaching a fever pitch, I moderated a business panel. One of the participants was a senior executive at JPMorgan who complained in heartfelt terms about how time-consuming and expensive it was for her company to "educate" the lawmakers in Washington.

Duke's Dan Ariely has done research to gauge this very human tendency to come to believe in what suits us. He has found that when something is in our personal best interest, we come to see it not just as "good for me" but as unqualifiedly "good." "It turns out that if I pay you lots of money to see reality in a certain way, you will," he told me. "Imagine I paid you $5 million a year to view mortgage-backed security as a good product. Now, I'm sure you could pretend to like them, but the question is, would you really start believing that they are better products than they really are. That turns out to be the case. People actually can change their deeply held beliefs.

"When you have a financial incentive to see reality in a certain way, you will see it that way, not because you're bad, but because you are human," Professor Ariely said.

And we wear spectacles shaded not only by our self-interest, but also by that of our friends. "We are deeply social animals," Professor Ariely told me. "We see things from the perspective of our friends, not of strangers. One of the things that inequality does is it creates not a single society, but it creates multiple societies. It might be that inequality is creating another layer of separation between the in group and the out group."

John Dashwood's Half Sisters

Jane Austen lived at the dawn of the industrial revolution, before the leisured, landed gentry faced the coming full assault on its position from the rising meritocrats of manufacturing and commerce. But even then, and without the assistance of experimental setups like Ariely's, she was an acute observer of this human tendency to self-justification.

Recall the opening scene of her 1811 novel *Sense and Sensibility*. John Dashwood promises his father on his deathbed to treat his stepmother and three half sisters generously. At the time, he sincerely intends to do so. "'Yes, he would give them three thousand pounds: it would be liberal and handsome! It would be enough to make them completely easy. Three thousand pounds! He could spare so considerable a sum with little inconvenience.' He thought of it all day long, and for many days successively, and he did not repent."

But as the newly minted squire of Norland Park talks it over with his wife in the ensuing weeks, John gradually reduces the intended amount: "Perhaps, then, it would be better for all parties if the sum were diminished by one half.—Five hundred pounds would be a prodigious increase to their fortunes!" Note that the reduction is in the interests of "all parties."

Then John wonders whether an annuity, paid solely to his stepmother, might not be best: "A hundred a year would make them all perfectly comfortable."

Upon further thought, he decides that would be excessive, too. "I believe you are right, my love," he tells his wife. "It will be better that there should be no annuity in the case; whatever I may give them occasionally will be of far greater assistance than a yearly allowance, because they would only enlarge their style of living if they felt sure of a larger income, and would not be sixpence the richer for it at the end of the year. It will certainly be much the best way. A present of fifty pounds, now and then, will prevent their ever being distressed for money, and will, I think, be amply discharging my promise to my father."

By the end, John decides that even this is too much: "He finally resolved, that it would be absolutely unnecessary, if not highly indecorous, to do more for the widow and children of his father, than such kind of neighborly acts as his own wife pointed out."

CONCLUSION

We may have democracy, or we may have wealth concentrated in the hands of the few, but we cannot have both.

—*Louis Brandeis*

The society that puts equality before freedom will end up with neither. The society that puts freedom before equality will end up with a great measure of both.

—*Milton Friedman*

The lagoons off the north Adriatic coast that eventually became Venice were first settled by refugees from more salubrious inland cities fleeing successive invasions by the Huns and sundry Germanic tribes. These marshy islands, plagued by fog in the winters and insects in the summer, made a good hiding spot—not only were they hard to reach, they were so grim and inhospitable there was no point in sacking them.

But by the early fourteenth century, Venice had become the richest city in Europe, three times the size of London and as big as Paris. Venice was an imperial power—the republic financed the Fourth Crusade and established suzerainty over the fertile plains to the north, reaching Lake Garda and the river Adda to the north and west, along the Dalmatian coast deep into what is today Croatia, into the Mediterranean, where it controlled Cyprus, and into the Aegean, where it ruled Crete.

La Serenissima's true power and vocation was commerce. At the republic's zenith, it dispatched thirty-six thousand sailors and thirty-three hundred ships into the world's maritime trade routes. Venice dominated the salt business—the oil of that era—and trade with Byzantium and the Near East. A Venetian merchant, Marco Polo played a central role in introducing China to western Europe, with his pioneering account of his visit to the Middle Kingdom; his father, also a trader, had done business with the Golden Horde of the Tatars. Francesco Petrarca, sitting at a Venetian window overlooking the Basin of St. Mark and writing a letter to a friend in the fourteenth century, was awed by the trading prowess of the Venetians and the commercial ambitions that drove it: "If you'd seen this vessel, you would have said it was not a boat but a mountain swimming on the surface of the sea. . . . It is setting out for the river Don, for this is as far as our ships can sail on the Black Sea, but many of those on board will disembark and journey on, not stopping until they have crossed the Ganges and the Caucasus to India, then on to farthest China and the Eastern ocean. What is the source of this insatiable thirst for wealth that seizes men's minds?"

Venice owed its might and money to the super-elites of that age, and to an economic and political system that nurtured them. At the heart of the Venetian economy was the *commenda*, a basic form of joint-stock company that lasted for a single trading mission. The brilliance of the commenda was that it opened the economy to new entrants. It was a partnership between a "sedentary" investor, who financed the trip, and a traveler, who did the hard and risky work of making the journey. If the sedentary partner paid for the entire mission, he received 75 percent of the profits; if he financed two-thirds of the voyage, he got half. The commenda was a powerful engine of both economic growth and social mobility—historians studying government documents from AD 960, 971, and 982 found that new names accounted for respectively 69 percent, 81 percent, and 65 percent of all the elite citizens cited.

Venice's elite were the chief beneficiaries of the rise of La Serenissima. But like all open economies, theirs was turbulent. We think of social mobility as an entirely good thing, but if you are already on top, mobility can also mean competition from outsider entrepreneurs. Even though this cycle of creative destruction had created the Venetian upper class, in 1315, when their city was at the height of its economic powers, they acted to lock in their privilege. Venice had prospered under a relatively open political system in which a wide swath of the people had a voice in the selection of the republic's ruler, the doge, and successful outsiders could join the ruling class. But in 1315, the establishment, which had been gradually tightening its control over the government, put a formal stop to social mobility with the publication of the Libro D'Oro, or Book of Gold, which was an official registry of the Venetian nobility. If you weren't in it, you couldn't join the ruling oligarchy.

This political shift from a nascent representative democracy to an oligarchy marked such a striking change that the Venetians gave it a name: La Serrata, or the closure. And it wasn't long before the political Serrata became an economic one, too. Under the control of the oligarchs, the Venetian state gradually cut off the commercial opportunities for new entrants. The commenda, the legal innovation that had made Venice (and other Italian city-states) rich, was banned. La Serenissima's reigning elite were acting in their own immediate self-interest—shutting out the entrepreneurial upstarts meant the vested interests could enjoy sole control over the city's lucrative trade routes. But in the longer term, La Serrata was the beginning of the end for the city's oligarchs, as well as for Venetian prosperity more generally. By 1500, the population of Venice was smaller than it had been in 1330. In the seventeenth and eighteenth centuries, as the rest of Europe grew, the city that had once been its richest continued to shrink.

The story of Venice's rise and fall is told by the scholars Daron Acemoglu and James Robinson as an illustration of their thesis that what separates successful states from failed ones is whether their governing institutions are inclusive or extractive. Extractive states, they argue, are controlled by ruling elites whose objective is to extract as much wealth as they can from the rest of society and to maintain their own hold on power.

Inclusive states give everyone a say in how their society is ruled and access to economic opportunity. Inclusive societies often find themselves benefiting from a virtuous circle, in which greater inclusiveness creates more prosperity, which creates an incentive for ever greater inclusiveness. The history of the United States, founded in a revolutionary bid for greater inclusiveness, can be read as one such virtuous circle.

But Acemoglu and Robinson cite the story of La Serrata as evidence that virtuous circles can be broken. Elites who have prospered thanks to inclusive systems can be tempted to pull up the ladder they climbed to the top. There are a lot of reasons to be worried about the rise of the plutocrats—the impact soaring inequality has on civic values, on crime rates, on morality, or even, according to some studies, on health. The big danger, though, is the one represented by La Serrata. As the people at the very top become ever richer, they have an ever greater ability to tilt the rules of the game in their favor. That power can be hard to resist.

One reason La Serrata is such a useful example is that the Venetian oligarchs who closed off their society were the products of a robust, open economy. They didn't start out as oligarchs—they'd made themselves into oligarchs. That's important because as soaring income inequality has become an undeniable political fact, even in societies, such as the United States, that have been squeamish about open discussions of class, a dominant response has been to try to sort the plutocrats into the white hats and the black hats. Steve Jobs is a hero; Lloyd Blankfein is a villain. Big business is bad; small business is good. Private equity is vulture lending; community banks are virtue lending. Wall Street banks are speculators who didn't deserve their bailout; Detroit carmakers are manufacturers who did.

No one likes this approach better than the "good" plutocrats. "There's a lot of anger in society because of what the government did to the benefit of the financial industry, because it was seen as unfair," Eric Schmidt told me. "And you don't find that anger against, for example, Microsoft and Bill Gates, right? Who is seen as a historic, American figure who created a global company. So I think it's very important to distinguish between rich people who get there by taking the economic rents of the country for their own benefit versus the people who, in fact, create a new corporation or a new source of wealth."

There's a lot that's right about this impulse. Dividing the plutocrats into the rent-seekers and the value creators is a good way to judge whether your economy is inclusive or extractive. And creating more opportunities for productive enterprise, and fewer for rent-seeking, is how you create an inclusive economic system. But this approach takes you only so far.

For one thing, there's no magical sorting hat for plutocrats, and without one, figuring out who is adding value and who is rent-seeking is an inexact science. Indeed, even the exercise of trying to separate the virtuous plutocrats from the venal ones, and to treat them differently, is an invitation to precisely the sort of rent-seeking that creates the "wrong" kind of wealth in the first place.

As Emmanuel Saez, the economist who tracks the 1 percent, told me, "It's probably true that some activities are truly creative, like a normal market, while others are more zero-sum game." But deciding which was which was a different story: "I would say it is very hard who is going to make that case. I don't think anyone would be comfortable having the government decide this is a good business and this is a bad business, and the bad business punish it with, say, special taxes. Because then you will have all the lobbying forces, right? . . . It's so hard even for economists to say, 'This is a good business. This is a bad business.' Especially while the thing is happening, it's extremely hard."

More important, the difference between the good guys and the bad guys is smaller than we might like to think. Inclusive and extractive societies are very different, but the economic elites within them are driven by the same imperative to make money and win competitive advantage for themselves and their companies. Trying to slant the rules of the game in your favor isn't an aberration, it is what all businesses seek to do. The difference isn't between having virtuous and villainous businesspeople, it is about whether your society has the right rules and policing able to enforce them.

Consider, by way of example, how Warren Buffett, the most hallowed figure in America's pantheon of officially virtuous billionaires, described his investing philosophy in his 2008 letter to shareholders. "A truly great business must have an enduring 'moat' that protects excellent returns on invested capital," Buffett explained. "Though capitalism's 'creative destruction' is highly beneficial for society, it precludes investment certainty. A moat that must be continuously rebuilt will eventually be no moat at all." Like the Venetians who put themselves in the Book of Gold, Buffett understands that the creative destruction of an open economy is good for the country as a whole; but smart capitalists like him prefer to be defended by uncrossable moats.

Buffett goes on to explain that his preferred moats are being a low-cost producer or possessing a well-known worldwide brand. But favorable government regulation can create a powerful moat, too.

And taking advantage of that government moat is a business decision, not a question of ideology or morality, as we saw in hedge funder and anti-government crusader Ken Griffin's telling comment that CEOs' "duties to their shareholders" justify business leaders' opening their hands to a state "willing to hand out gifts."

Even when the moats are created through pure entrepreneurial brilliance, they don't always serve the greater good. Microsoft went from being one of the world's most admired innovators to the bête noire of technology geeks because it created a very effective and very lucrative moat. That boundary made Bill Gates a billionaire; competition authorities in the United States and Europe decided it was so harmful to the rest of us they forced Microsoft to build a few bridges across it.

All businesspeople would like their own Serrata. And as they become more powerful relative to everyone else, their ability to impose one increases.

One of the goals of the Book of Gold was to pass oligarchic privilege to the next generation. That is the second big threat posed by the surge in income inequality. Today's plutocrats are modern-day robber barons, the beneficiaries of an era of extreme economic change. But as they pass their fortunes down to their children, today's "working rich" plutocrats may give way to a rentier elite more similar to the sons and daughters of privilege of the Roaring Twenties, the plutocrats who were "born rich." That transfer of privilege from one generation to the next is a gradual, cumulative, and very personal process. But as a mechanism for turning an inclusive social and economic order into an exclusive one, it could be as powerful as the more overt Serrata.

What's at work is an economic phenomenon that Alan Krueger, the head of the president's Council of Economic Advisers, has dubbed the Great Gatsby Curve. Based on research by Canadian economist Miles Corak, the Great Gatsby Curve traces a relationship between income inequality and social mobility: as societies grow more unequal, social mobility is choked off. That creates a particular paradox for societies that owe their surge in wealth at the top to entrepreneurial vigor unleashed by having a social starting point with high social mobility—think of Silicon Valley, with its fine public universities and government-funded research, or Venice in the age of the *commenda*. The success of these societies, which manifests itself partly in the emergence of a super-elite, threatens to destroy one of the preconditions for their rise: high social mobility.

Membership in today's Book of Gold is more subtle than being included in a list of the aristocracy, or even inheriting a trust fund. In our increasingly complex economy, the real Book of Gold is a degree from an elite university, and those are increasingly the province of the global super-elite. Indeed, statistics have shown that graduating from college is more closely linked to having wealthy parents than it is to high test scores in high school: class matters more than going to class. This intergenerational form of rent-seeking is the hardest to oppose. It is one thing to berate bankers for lobbying for favorable regulation or Microsoft for using its market dominance to cut out competition. But who can blame the 1 percent for seeking for their children what the 99 percent seeks, too? High social mobility, after all, means some downward mobility at the top. And in a society where that gulf is a widening chasm, that can be particularly hard to stomach.

At Davos in 2012, I spoke about access to the Ivy League and social mobility with Ruth Simmons, then the president of Brown University. She is a widely respected pioneering member of the super-elite—the first African American to lead an Ivy League university—and has been rewarded with an enthusiastic embrace by the plutocrats, including that crowning prize, a seat on the board of Goldman Sachs. (That is more than a status symbol—it paid more than $300,000 a year, and when she resigned from the Goldman board in 2010, her shares were worth more than $4 million.) Simmons spoke enthusiastically about helping poor children get to Brown, and supporting them financially after they got there. But when I asked her whether the legacy system, which explicitly favors the children of alumni, should be abolished, the conversation turned personal. "No, I have a granddaughter. It's not time yet," she said with a laugh.

Marx understood the dangers of a capitalist Serrata—indeed he was counting on it. "The capitalist system carries within itself the seeds of its own destruction," he famously argued. Marx predicted that the rising capitalist class, like the shortsighted Venetian elite, would overreach itself and create a system that so effectively consolidated its supremacy that it would eventually choke off economic growth and become politically unsustainable.

The most astonishing political fact of the past two centuries is that that didn't happen. Unlike the Venetian elite, Western capitalists submitted themselves to creative destruction, to the competition of new entrants, and created ever more inclusive economic and political orders. The result is the most vigorous era of economic progress in human history.

Marx himself was one cause of that willingness of the elites to share— the fear of communist revolution was a powerful motivation for reform. It was better to give the working class an effective political voice, and a social safety net, than to risk having their Bolshevik vanguard seize power altogether.

Another reason the twentieth century was the century of inclusion was that the business elite, particularly the Americans, who were its unchallenged world leaders, understood that they could prosper only if the middle class prospered, too. The age of mass production required a mass market—as Henry Ford put it, he needed workers, including his own, to make enough money to buy his cars.

For the plutocrats, globalization may be reducing both this political incentive and this economic one to support inclusion. That's because in today's interconnected economy, Western democracies can import economic demand from the emerging markets, and the emerging markets can import democracy from the West. To put it another way, Western businesses are less dependent on a prosperous domestic middle class because they can now sell to the rising middle class of the emerging markets. Henry Ford needed a domestic middle class with buying power; increasingly, his successors can look to the emerging markets to supply those mass consumers.

Meanwhile, the oligarchs who prosper in extractive emerging market regimes don't need to worry too much that repression at home is cutting them off from the innovation that democracies are better at nurturing. Communist Chinese princelings can import technology from the West; Russian oligarchs can invest directly in Silicon Valley's hottest start-ups. And all of them can buy second homes in Manhattan and Kensington and villas on the Côte d'Azur and send their children to British boarding schools and American Ivy League universities.

There's another way that globalization and its twin economic force, the technology revolution, are reducing the pressure on the plutocrats to make their societies more inclusive, or to keep them that way. That is what you might call the cultural Serrata, which is already separating the plutocrats from everyone else—even without formal political divisions like the Golden Book. As the economic gap between the plutocrats and everyone else becomes a chasm, they are coming to inhabit their own global gated community. Indeed, the gap is becoming so wide and so apparent that even the right, traditionally allergic to discussions of class, has started to take notice. Conservative sociologist Charles Murray's big new idea is that the 1 percent and the 99 percent live in different cultures; the big issue in the 2012 Republican primary was whether Mitt Romney's hundreds of millions put him at too far a remove from ordinary voters.

This cultural Serrata matters because it increases the political myopia of the plutocrats. Add to that ordinary greed and a society that has turned its capitalists into popular heroes and you have an economic elite primed to repeat the mistake of the Venetian merchants—to drink its own Kool-Aid (or maybe prosecco is the better metaphor) and to conflate its own self-interest with the interests of society as a whole. Low taxes, light-touch regulation, weak unions, and unlimited campaign donations are certainly in the best interests of the plutocrats, but that doesn't mean they are the right way to maintain the economic system that created today's super-elite.

Elites don't sabotage the system that created them on purpose. But even smart, farsighted plutocrats can be betrayed by their own short-term self-interest into undermining the foundations of their own society's prosperity. In 1343, La Serenissima petitioned the pope for permission to trade with the Muslim world. Here is how the city made its case: "Since, by the Grace of God, our city has grown and increased by the labors of merchants creating traffic and profits for us in diverse parts of the world by land and sea and this is our life and that of our sons, because we cannot live otherwise and know not how except by trade, therefore we must be vigilant in all our thoughts and endeavors, as our predecessors were, to make provision in every way lest so much wealth and treasure should disappear."

Intel founder Andy Grove, with his faith in the virtue of paranoia, could not have made a better argument for the importance of trade and traders to the city's continued prosperity. But it was this same elite who, a few decades earlier, had begun the process of economic exclusion that would eventually transform La Serenissima from a trading power to a museum. Gus Levy, who was the senior partner of Goldman Sachs between 1969 and 1976, a decade we are coming to look back on as that firm's golden era, said his philosophy was one of "long-term greed." If the plutocrats are smart, that's the philosophy they'll adopt today. But, as even Levy's successors at mighty Goldman Sachs are learning, that can be harder than it sounds.

ACKNOWLEDGMENTS

All the errors and oversights in this book are, of course, my own. But its virtues build on the work I've done over the past two decades as a journalist and the people who taught me while I did it. In particular, this book draws on my work for the *Financial Times* covering Russia, Ukraine, and Eastern Europe, and on *Sale of the Century*, my book about the rise of the oligarchs. Work I did for the *Financial Times* in the United States, particularly a profile of George Soros and an essay on Canadian banks, also inform this book. My *Atlantic* cover story on the global super-elite was my first public articulation of the ideas in this book; research I did for my *Atlantic* essay on Skolkovo, the Russian Silicon Valley, also proved useful. My weekly column for Reuters and the *International Herald Tribune* was a valuable space for working out my thinking, as were Reuters video interviews and the Reuters magazine.

I am grateful to many colleagues, editors, and sparring partners. Chief among them: Martin Wolf, Alison Wolf, John Lloyd, David Hoffman, John Gapper, Felix Salmon, Jim Impoco, Jim Ledbetter, Mike Williams, Stuart Karle, Alison Smale, Anatole Kaletsky, David Rohde, David Wighton, Gary Silverman, Francesco Guerrera, John Thornhill, Alan Beattie, Krishna Guha, Robert Thomson, Annalena McAfee, Andrew Gowers, Richard Lambert, Daniel Franklin, Sebastian Mallaby, Fareed Zakaria, David Frum, Arianna Huffington, Eliot Spitzer, Steve Brill, Anya Schiffrin, Steve Clemons, Susan Glasser, and Ali Velshi. Dennis Gartman and Joshua Brown, two business thinkers whose work I admire, generously allowed me to quote their writing at length. Steve Adler, my boss, has been uniquely and crucially supportive, providing vital intellectual guidance and emotional encouragement. I owe a special debt to Don Peck, who edited my 2011 *Atlantic* essay and read and improved a first draft of this book; James Bennett, who commissioned the piece; and to David Bradley.

This book draws on a vast body of academic research. Some scholars have become important sounding boards and advisers, too. They include Larry Summers, Daron Acemoglu, Emmanuel Saez, Jacob Hacker, Alan Krueger, Branko Milanovic, Daniel Kaufmann, Ian Bremmer, Peter Lindert, Michael Spence, Joe Stiglitz, Theda Skocpol, Anders Aslund, Roman Frydman, Rob Johnson, Sergei Guriev, Michael McFaul, Ernesto Zedillo, John Van Reenen, Raghuram Rajan, Shamus Khan, and the late Yegor Gaidar.

I sometimes describe my own political philosophy as being simply "Canadian," and my Maple Leaf community has been central to my thinking. Important friends and teachers are Roger Martin, Geoff Beattie, Mark Carney, Diana Carney, Paul Martin, Dominic Barton, Mark Wiseman, David Thomson, John Stackhouse, Anne McLellan, Annalise Acorn, Don Tapscott, and Morris Rosenberg.

Many plutocrats have helped me to understand their world and some have become friends (though that does not mean we always agree). They include: George Soros, Eric Schmidt, Victor Pinchuk, David and Mary Boies, Nikesh Arora, Jeff Immelt, Peter Weinberg, Mark Gallogly, Roger Altman, David Rubenstein, Bill Ford, Bob Rubin, Klaus Schwab, Aditya Mittal, Mikhail Fridman, Vladimir Gusinsky, and Igor Malashenko.

My editors, researchers, and agents have been amazingly committed. Above all, the wise and brilliant Ann Godoff has steered this book through many iterations and tolerated my efforts to appoint her my surrogate mother. Peter Rudegeair, my erudite and fastidious researcher, has done a huge amount of research and has been an essential intellectual sounding board. Ben Platt, Ann's assistant, will one day run Penguin. He has been terrifically supportive and together with Peter rescued the endnotes. From Olympus, Marjorie Scardino and John Makinson blessed this project early on.

My agents, first Pat Kavanagh and Zoë Pagnamenta and now Andrew Wylie, found an audience for me and encouraged me to keep going. Andrew, who never sleeps, read my drafts seemingly before they were written.

Several colleagues and friends went above and beyond the call of duty to help pin down elusive facts. I am especially grateful to my colleagues Amy Stevens and Nate Raymonds for their legal expertise and to Kieran Murray, Dave Graham, Cyntia Barrera, and Krista Hughes in Latin America. Mark MacKinnon, a colleague from the *Globe and Mail*, generously shared his China expertise. Boris Davidenko, of *Forbes Ukraine*, helped with facts about my second homeland. Four professional fact-checkers—Rachael Brown, Ellie Smith, Nicole Allen, and Esther Yi—combed through the book collaboratively, meticulously, and at very short notice.

My best friends have been unflagging cheerleaders and sources of great ideas. Thank you Alison Franklin, Roberta Brzezinski, Lucan Way, Annette Ryan, Karen Berman. The Ukrainian women of Nannies, Inc., particularly Nadiya Basaraba and Ira Andreychuk, have kept my kids alive during the gestation of this book, which has often seemed to be my fourth child.

Finally, I am more dependent on my extended family than anyone else I know. My aunts Natalka Chomiak, Maria Hopchin, and Chrystia Chomiak, and my mother-in-law, Barbara Bowley, have been mothers and intellectual supporters throughout this project. My father, Don Freeland, and my sister Natalka Freeland have been critical intellectual and moral influences. My sister Anne Freeland and my cousin-sisters Katrusia Ensslen and Eva Himka have taken care of me and my brood. Above all, whatever is good about this book is thanks to my husband and writing comrade, Graham Bowley, and the three most important people in our lives—Natalka Bowley, Halyna Bowley, and Ivan Bowley.

NOTES

INTRODUCTION

ix **"The poor enjoy what the rich"** Andrew Carnegie, "Wealth," *North American Review* 148:391 (June 1889).

ix **"I was once told"** Branko Milanovic, *The Haves and the Have-Nots: A Brief and Idiosyncratic History of Global Inequality* (Basic Books, 2011), p. 84.

x **"I didn't attack them for their success"** Bill Clinton, *Back to Work: Why We Need Smart Government for a Strong Economy* (Knopf, 2011), p. 93.

x **"often the word 'rich'"** Graeme Wood, "Secret Fears of the Super-Rich," *The Atlantic*, April 2011.

xi **"If one looks closely"** Alexis de Tocqueville, *Memoir on Pauperism: Does Public Charity Produce an Idle and Dependent Class of Society?* 1835.

xii **"Americans grew together"** Claudia Goldin and Lawrence F. Katz, *The Race Between Education and Technology* (Belknap Press, 2008), p. 87.

xii **Ariely showed people** Michael I. Norton and Dan Ariely, "Building a Better America—One Wealth Quintile at a Time," *Perspectives on Psychological Science* 6 (2011).

xiii **"for the first time since the Great Depression"** For a more developed take on this, see Lawrence Summers, "The fierce urgency of fixing economic inequality," Reuters, November 21, 2011.

xiii **Look more closely at the data** Emmanuel Saez, "Striking It Richer: The Evolution of Top Incomes in the United States (Updated with 2009 and 2010 Estimates)," March 2, 2012. http://elsa.berkely.edu/~saez/saez-UStopincomes-2010.pdf

xv **"This association of poverty with progress"** Henry George, *Progress and Poverty: An Inquiry in the Cause of Industrial Depressions and of Increase of Want with Increase of Wealth; The Remedy* (Cambridge University Press, reprint, 2009), p. 8.

CHAPTER 1: HISTORY AND WHY IT MATTERS

2 **USA *Today* advised its readers** Deirdre Donahue, "Able, Entertaining *The Manny* Does Triple Duty," *USA Today*, June 18, 2007.

2 **"There's so much money"** Several CF interviews with Holly Peterson, 2009–2010.

3 **In 2005, Bill Gates was worth** Robert Reich, *Supercapitalism: The Transformation of Business, Democracy, and Everyday Life* (Knopf, 2007), p. 113.

3 **A 2011 OECD report showed** "Divided We Stand: Why Inequality Keeps Rising," OECD report, December 2011.

4 **"I've never understood in my life"** CF interview with Naguib Sawiris, November 18, 2011.

5 **"the World is dividing into two blocs"** Ajay Kapur, Niall Macleod, and Narendra Singh,

"Plutonomy: Buying Luxury, Explaining Global Imbalances," Citigroup Global Markets Equity Strategy report, October 16, 2005.

5 **"The U.S. stock markets and the U.S. economy"** James Freeman, "The Bullish Case for the U.S. Economy," *Wall Street Journal*, June 4, 2011.

5 **"very distorted"** Alan Greenspan, interview on NBC's *Meet the Press*, August 1, 2010.

6 **"consumer hourglass theory"** Ellen Byron, "As Middle Class Shrinks, P&G Aims High and Low," *Wall Street Journal*, September 12, 2011.

6 **On February 10, 1897, seven hundred members** Sven Beckert provides an excellent description of the Bradley Martin ball in *The Monied Metropolis* (Cambridge University Press, 2001) in his smart and highly readable account of New York City and the consolidation of the American bourgeoisie, pp. 1–2.

8 **"British history is two thousand years old"** Walter L. Arnstein, "Queen Victoria's Diamond Jubilee," *American Scholar*, September 22, 1997.

9 **"It is here; we cannot evade it"** All Andrew Carnegie quotations come from "Wealth," *North American Review* 148:391 (June 1889).

11 **"We have no paupers"** Thomas Jefferson, letter to Dr. Thomas Cooper, September 10, 1814. http://www.yamaguchy.com/library/jefferson/cooper.html.

12 **"nothing struck me more"** Alexis de Tocqueville, *Democracy in America* (Penguin Classics, 2003), p. 11.

12 **Data painstakingly assembled by economic historians** Peter Lindert and Jeffrey Williamson. "American Incomes Before and After the Revolution" (NBER Working Paper No. 17211, July 2011).

13 **"In America nearly every man"** Mark Twain and Charles Dudley Warner, "Author's Preface to the London Edition," *The Gilded Age: A Tale of Today* (Chatto & Windus, 1897).

14 **In 1980, the average U.S. CEO** "CEO Pay and the 99%," AFL-CIO Executive PayWatch report, April 19, 2012.

16 **Milanovic, the World Bank economist** Branko Milanovic, "Global Inequality: From Class to Location, from Proletarians to Migrants" (World Bank Development Research Group Policy Research Working Paper 5820, September 2011).

16 **"Britain's classic industrial revolution"** Chrystia Freeland, "The Rise of the New Global Elite," *The Atlantic*, January/February 2011.

16 **"The rate of technological change"** CF interview with Joel Mokyr, August 19, 2010.

17 **"The Treaty of Detroit" to the "Washington Consensus"** Frank Levy and Peter Temin, "Inequality and Institutions in 20th-Century America," MIT Economics Department Working Paper No. 07-17, June 2007.

18 **"The bottom line: we may not be able"** Conversation with author at Yale conference on the budget and inequality, April 30, 2012.

20 **"It is structurally much more extreme"** Chrystia Freeland, "Some See Two New Gilded Ages, Raising Global Tensions," *International Herald Tribune*, January 23, 2012.

21 **"We are seeing much more rapid growth in developing countries"** Ibid.

22 **A survey of nearly ten thousand** Michael E. Porter and Jan W. Rivkin, "Prosperity at Risk: Findings of Harvard Business School's Survey on U.S. Competitiveness," Harvard Business School, January 2012.

23 **"When a company is stressed and has issues"** CF interview with Michael Porter, January 17, 2012.

23 **"Although the overall pie is getting bigger"** CF interview with John Van Reenen, January 13, 2012.

23 **"Conservatively, it explains one-quarter"** David Autor, David Dorn, and Gordon Hanson,"The China Syndrome: Local Labor Market Effects of Import Competition in the United States," MIT working paper, May 2012.

24 **"lousy and lovely" jobs** Maarten Goos and Alan Manning, "Lousy and Lovely Jobs: The

Rising Polarization of Work in Britain," *Review of Economics and Statistics* 89:1 (February 2007).

24   **A recent investigation of the direct employment impact of the iPod** Greg Linden, Jason Dedrick, and Kenneth L. Kraemer, "Innovation and Job Creation in a Global Economy: The Case of Apple's iPod," *Journal of International Commerce and Economics* 3:1 (May 2011).

26   **Even though the devices are made in China** Greg Linden, Jason Dedrick, and Kenneth L. Kraemer, "Who Captures Value in a Global Innovation System? The Case of Apple's iPod," *Communications of the ACM* 52:3 (2007).

26   **Consider, for example, the argument Caterpillar** See James R. Hagerty and Kate Linebaugh, "In U.S., a Cheaper Labor Pool," *Wall Street Journal*, January 6, 2012.

26   **"Under the law of competition"** Carnegie, "The Gospel of Wealth."

27   **"The economic theory is very clear"** CF interview with Joe Stiglitz, January 26, 2012.

27   **"Well, first off, as a citizen of the world"** CF interview with Steve Miller, January 26, 2012.

28   **"These things have been going on for a couple of decades"** Freeland, "Some See Two New Gilded Ages."

28   **"India's gilded age is going to be a combination"** CF interview with Ashutosh Varshney, November 13, 2011.

28   **The two gilded ages can also get in each other's way** See Mark Landler, "Chinese Savings Helped Inflate American Bubble," *New York Times*, December 25, 2008.

29   **"In the long run, we are in good shape"** CF interview with John Van Reenen, January 13, 2012.

29   **"This is an exciting story"** Jim O'Neill, *The Growth Map: Economic Opportunity in the BRICs and Beyond* (Penguin, 2011), pp. 251–52.

30   **"Wealth will be created but also spent"** Reader feedback on "The Second Economy," McKinsey Quarterly Facebook post, November 1, 2011. http://www.facebook.com/note.php?note_id=10150536805679908.

30   **"I only hope you are right"** Ibid.

31   **Until a few years ago, the reigning theory** Richard A. Easterlin, "Does Economic Growth Improve the Human Lot? Some Empirical Evidence," in *Nations and Households in Economic Growth: Essays in Honor of Moses Abramowitz*, eds. Paul A. David and Melvin W. Reder (Academic Press, 1974).

31   **"Surprisingly, at any given level of income"** Angus Deaton, "Income, Health, and Well-Being Around the World: Evidence from the Gallup World Poll," *Journal of Economic Perspectives* 22:2 (Spring 2008).

31   **Two separate studies of China** See John Knight and Ramani Gunatilaka, "Great Expectations? The Subjective Well-Being of Rural-Urban Migrants in China," Oxford University Economics Department Working Paper 332, April 2007; and Martin K. Whyte and Chunping Han, "Distributive Justice Issues and the Prospects for Unrest in China," paper prepared for conference on "Reassessing Unrest in China," Washington, D.C, December 11–12, 2003.

32   **Betsey Stevenson and Justin Wolfers have found** Betsey Stevenson and Justin Wolfers, "Economic Growth and Subjective Well-Being: Reassessing the Easterlin Paradox" (Brookings Papers on Economic Activity, Spring 2008).

32   **I caught a glimpse of it at a World Bank panel** "Global Development Debate: Jobs and Opportunities for All," World Bank Institute conference, Washington, D.C., September 22, 2011.

33   **"If you join the union"** Ariel Levy. "Drug Test: Can One Self-Made Woman Reform Health Care for India, and the World?," *The New Yorker*, January 2, 2012.

34   **Families in the top 0.01 percent** Saez's complete data set available at http://elsa.berkeley.edu/~saez/TabFig2010.xls.

34 **"A recent academic study of the *Forbes* list"** Wojciech Kopczuk and Emmanuel Saez, "Top Wealth Shares in the United States, 1916–2000: Evidence from Estate Tax Returns," *National Tax Journal*, vol. 57, no. 2, part 2, June 2004, 482.

35 **"Although comparable data on the past are sparse"** "Global Wealth Report 2011," Credit Suisse Research Institute, October 2011.

35 **93 percent of the gains** Saez, "Striking It Richer."

36 **"Probably if you had looked at the situation"** CF interview with Emmanuel Saez, February 24, 2011.

CHAPTER 2: CULTURE OF THE PLUTOCRATS

38 **"Somebody ought to sit down"** Scott Turow, *Pleading Guilty* (Grand Central Publishing, 1994), p. 174.

39 **"men like Henry George"** Albert Einstein, letter to Anna George de Mille, 1934. http://www.cooperativeindividualism.org/einstein-albert_letters-to-anna-george-demille-1934.html.

39 **"the battle cry for all"** Joanne Reitano, *The Restless City: A Short History of New York from Colonial Times to the Present* (Taylor & Francis, 2006), p. 101.

39 **"Not even Lincoln had a more glorious death"** "Expressions of Regret: The Comments of Many Prominent Persons in New York Upon the Death of Henry George," *New York Times*, October 30, 1987.

40 **"I stopped a man"** Henry George, Jr., *The Life of Henry George* (Doubleday and McClure Company, 1900), p. 149.

40 **"Why should there be"** Ibid., pp. 468–69.

40 **"The present century has been marked"** Henry George, *Progress and Poverty* (D. Appleton and Co., 1886), pp. 3–4.

41 **"We are coming into collision"** Ibid., p. 5.

41 **"Some get an infinitely better"** Ibid., p. 7.

42 **"show that their sympathies"** Edward Robb Ellis, *The Epic of New York City: A Narrative History* (Carroll & Graf, 2005), p. 382.

43 **"born rich"** F. Scott Fitzgerald, "The Rich Boy," in *The Short Stories of F. Scott Fitzgerald*, ed. Matthew J. Bruccoli (Charles Scribner's & Sons, 1989), p. 317.

43 **"The ordinary progress of a society which increases in wealth"** John Stuart Mill, *Principles of Political Economy with Some of Their Applications to Social Philosophy* (Longmans, Green and Co., 1848), Book V, Chapter 2, Section 5.

43 **"Fat cats who owe it to their grandfathers"** Freeland, "The Rise of the New Global Elite."

43 **"As a consequence, top executives"** Thomas Piketty and Emmanuel Saez, "The Evolution of Top Incomes: A Historical and International Perspective," *American Economic Review* 96:2 (May 2006), p. 204.

43 **Speaking at a Columbia University conference** Paul Sullivan, "Scrutinizing the Elite, Whether They Like It or Not," *New York Times*, October 15, 2010.

44 **"Capital income excluding capital gains"** "Trends in the Distribution of Household Income Between 1979 and 2007," Congressional Budget Office study, October 2011, Section XI, p. 17.

44 **This is true even at the very, very top** Jon Bakija, Adam Cole, and Bradley T. Heim, "Jobs and Income Growth of Top Earners and the Causes of Changing Income Inequality: Evidence from U.S. Tax Return Data," working paper, April 2012, p. 4, footnote 3.

45 **"While I have been richly rewarded"** Leon G. Cooperman, "An Open Letter to the President of the United States of America," November 28, 2011. http://www.thestreet.com/tsc/common/images/pdf/Omega%20Advisor1.pdf.

45 **"We are fighting the caste system with capitalism"** Lydia Polgreen, "Scaling Caste Walls with Capitalism's Ladders in India," *New York Times*, December 21, 2011.

46 **"We have witnessed substantial changes"** Oliver H. Holiet, "Torsten Müller-Ötvös, CEO of Rolls-Royce," *Luxos* (Germany), Fall/Winter 2011–2012, p. 46.

47 **"During that 80-year period"** Goldin and Katz, *Race Between Education and Technology*, p. 4.

47 **In one example, the wage premium** Ibid., p. 50.

47 **Getting a college degree** Anthony P. Carnevale, Stephen J. Rose, and Ban Cheah, "The College Payoff: Education, Occupations, Lifetime Earnings," Georgetown University Center on Education and the Workforce, August 5, 2011.

48 **wage premium for a college education** Thomas Philippon and Ariell Reshef, "Wages and Human Capital in the U.S. Finance Industry: 1909–2006," National Bureau of Economic Research, working paper no. 14644, March 2011.

48 **"Most of the increase in wage inequality"** Thomas Lemieux, "Postsecondary Education and Increasing Wage Inequality," *American Economic Review* 96:2 (May 2006), pp. 195–99.

48 **That contest has prompted absurdities like the story of Jack Grubman** "The Wall Street Fix," PBS *Frontline*, May 8, 2003.

48 **"With those numbers in mind"** John Quiggin, "Cutthroat Admissions and Rising Inequality: A Vicious Duo," *Chronicle of Higher Education*, September 11, 2011.

49 **"There's a kid. You know"** CF interview with Larry Summers, November 22, 2011.

49 **"have the courage to follow your heart and intuition"** Steve Jobs, Stanford University commencement address, June 12, 2005.

50 **"Don't park ten blocks away"** Drew Gilpin Faust, "Living an Unscripted Life," 2010 baccalaureate speech, Memorial Church, Harvard University, Cambridge, Massachusetts, May 25, 2010.

50 **But the winner-take-all economy turns out** "The New Wave of Affluence," *Ad Age* Insights white paper, May 23, 2011.

50 **"of 55 American laureates, 34 worked"** Robert K. Merton, "The Matthew Effect in Science," *Science* 159:3810 (January 5, 1968), pp. 56–63.

50 **"The conditions of industry change so fast"** Alfred Marshall, *Principles of Economics*, Book VI, Chapter XII, Section 10.

50 **"A lot of professional writers apply here"** David Streitfeld, "Funny or Die: Groupon's Fate Hinges on Words," *New York Times*, May 28, 2011.

51 **This volatility makes us unhappy** See Carol Graham, *Happiness Around the World: The Paradox of Happy Peasants and Miserable Millionaires* (Oxford University Press, 2010).

51 **Carlos Slim, who bought his first** David Luhnow, "The Secrets of the World's Richest Man," *Wall Street Journal*, August 4, 2007.

52 **"flying class"** Scott Turow, *Pleading Guilty* (Grand Central, 1994), p. 304.

53 **When the European sovereign debt crisis** Eric Dash, "In Euro Era, Opening Bell Is a 2:30 A.M. Alarm," *New York Times*, December 10, 2011.

53 **"We are Wall Street"** Stacy-Marie Ishmael, "We Are Wall Street . . ." Alphaville blog, *Financial Times*, April 30, 2010.

53 **"The average tenure of a Fortune 500 CEO"** A. G. Lafley, "The Art and Science of Finding the Right CEO," *Harvard Business Review*, October 2011.

54 **"If you push towards an Apple world, a Google world"** CF interview with Eike Batista, September 23, 2011.

54 **The famous Whitehall study** The first Whitehall Study, begun in 1967 with a sample of 18,000 male civil servants, found higher mortality rates and prevalence of cardiorespiratory disease among those with lower employment grades.

55 **"and the law of competition between"** Andrew Carnegie, "Wealth," *North American Review* 148:391 (June 1889).

56 **"It's not possible in tech to frame your ambitions"** CF interview with Eric Schmidt, February 23, 2011.

56 **"Those of you who practice"** Pitch Johnson, lecture of venture entrepreneurship at Moscow's Polytechnic Museum, October 2010.

57 **"Britain now has a Wimbledon economy"** Harry Mount, "England, Their England: Foreign Money Now Dominates at the Most Traditional of Summer Fixtures," *The Spectator*, June 18, 2011.

58 **"There's an interaction between the global elite"** CF interview with Eric Schmidt. February 23, 2011.

58 **"The base of the wealth pyramid"** Global Wealth Report, Credit Suisse Research Institute, October 2011, pp. 16–17.

59 **"A person in Africa"** Chrystia Freeland, "The Rise of the New Global Elite," *The Atlantic*, January/February 2011.

59 **"I think, in a sad sense, these cities are so similar now"** CF interview with Aditya Mittal, November 11, 2010.

60 **"There are more and more global CEO meetings"** CF interview with Dominic Barton, November 30, 2011.

60 **"There is an emergent power in people"** CF interview with Eric Schmidt, February 23, 2011.

60 **"This is the new wave, the new trend"** Chrystia Freeland, "Global Seagulls and the New Reality of Immigration," *International Herald Tribune*, October 6, 2011.

62 **"Four out of every five Chinese entrepreneurs today"** GroupM Knowledge–Hurun Wealth Report 2011, p. 19.

63 **nearly 60 percent** Tim Adams, "Who Owns Our Green and Pleasant Land?" *The Observer*, August 6, 2011.

63 **a study of British and American CEOs** Elisabeth Marx, *Route to the Top: A Transatlantic Comparison of Top Business Leaders* (Heidrick & Struggles, 2007). http://www.heidrick.com/PublicationsReports/PublicationsReports/RoutetotheTop.pdf

63 **"I came to GE in 1982"** Chrystia Freeland, "Accepting the Rise of China," *International Herald Tribune*, January 20, 2011.

64 **"is not going to be the engine"** Chrystia Freeland, "U.S. Needs to Think Globally About Business," *International Herald Tribune*, October 20, 2011.

64 **"This year, almost 90 percent of our sales"** Freeland, "The Rise of the New Global Elite."

64 **"they don't think of themselves as American anymore"** Conversation with author at Council on Foreign Relations, New York, April 5, 2012.

65 **"I have three passports"** Freeland, "The Rise of the New Global Elite."

66 **"The largest metals group in the world is Indian"** Stephen Jennings, "Opportunities of a Lifetime: Lessons for New Zealand from New, High-Growth Economics," Sir Ronald Trotter Lecture, April 7, 2009.

66 **"They know how to provide mobile phones"** Chrystia Freeland, "Globalization 2.0: Emerging-Market Cross-Pollination," *The Globe and Mail*, October 1, 2010.

67 **"The proprietor of land is necessarily a citizen"** Adam Smith, *The Wealth of Nations*, Book V, Chapter II, Section 91.

67 **"We don't have castles and noble titles"** Benjamin Wallace, "Those Fabulous Confabs," *New York*, February 26, 2012.

68 **and where, in lieu of noble titles, an elaborate hierarchy of conference badges** Nick Paumgarten, "Magic Mountain: What Happens at Davos?" *The New Yorker*, March 5, 2012.

68 **"Combined, our contacts reach"** "Chris Anderson on TED's Nonprofit Transition." TED. February 2002. http://www.ted.com/talks/chris_anderson_shares_his_vision_for_ted.html.

70 **"Name one action"** Ginia Bellafante, "With Vows Exchanged, Break Out the Slides," *New York Times*, December 16, 2011.

71 **"The new philanthropists believe"** Matthew Bishop and Michael Green, *Philanthrocapitalism: How Giving Can Save the World* (Bloomsbury, 2008), pp. 2–3.

71 **"What they are doing is much more"** CF interview with Matthew Bishop, November 2011.

74 **"If we can apply the entrepreneurial"** Jamie Doward, "Can This 'Venture Philanthropist' Save Our Schools?" *The Observer*, May 29, 2005.

75 **"We have to figure out what makes"** Bill Gates, prepared remarks at the 2010 Annual Policy Forum of the Council of Chief State School Officers. http://www.gatesfoundation.org/speeches-commentary/pages/bill-gates-2010-ccsso.aspx.

75 **"Our foundation tends to fund more"** Jeff Guo, "In Interview, Gates Describes Philanthropic Journey," *The Tech*, April 23, 2010.

76 **"They can also do dangerous things"** Charles Piller and Doug Smith, "Unintended Victims," *Los Angeles Times*, December 16, 2007.

78 **whose members included two millionaires** Ibid.

78 **"was not Democracy"** Jeffrey A. Winters, *Oligarchy* (Cambridge University Press, 2011), p. 227. Subsequent statistics come from *Oligarchy* pp. 227–31.

79 **"income defense industry"** Ibid., p. xii.

79 **"There's class warfare, all right"** Ben Stein, "In Class Warfare, Guess Which Class Is Winning?" *New York Times*, November 26, 2006.

80 **"I think people making $5 million"** CF interview with Holly Peterson.

81 **Peering inside the top 1 percent** Brian Bell and John Van Reenen, "Bankers' Pay and Extreme Wage Inequality in the UK," CEP Special Report, April 2010. http://eprints.lse.ac.uk/28780/1/cepsp21.pdf.

81 **"There were about 150,000 Americans"** Jeffrey A. Winters, *Oligarchy*, (Cambridge University Press, 2011), p. 214.

82 **compiled a data set chronicling** Claudia Goldin and Lawrence F. Katz, "Transitions: Career and Family Life Cycles of the Educational Elite," *American Economic Review: Papers & Proceedings* 2008, 98:2, 363–69.

82 **"very poor and destitute respondents"** Carol Graham, *Happiness Around the World: The Paradox of Happy Peasants and Miserable Millionaires*, (Oxford University Press, 2010), p. 151.

82 **"the gains around them"** Chrystia Freeland, "For Dictators, Protests Offer 3 Lessons." *International Herald Tribune*, December 15, 2011.

83 **there were just 412 billionaires** *Oligarchy*, p. 215.

84 **For 47,745 of the 47,763 runners who competed** Dave Ungrady, "As Miles Add Up, So Do the Unforgettable Moments," *New York Times*, November 1, 2011.

86 **By 2007, the number of women** Daniel J. Hemel, "'07 Men Make More," *The Harvard Crimson*, June 6, 2007.

86 **women outnumbered men** Catherine Rampell, "Women Now a Majority in American Workplaces," *New York Times*, February 6, 2010.

86 **In 2010, about four in ten** Sarah Jane Glynn, "The New Breadwinners: 2010 Update," Center for American Progress, April 2012. http://www.americanprogress.org/issues/2012/04/pdf/breadwinners.pdf.

87 **In 1979, nearly 8 percent** "Jobs and Income Growth of the Top Earners and the Causes of Changing Income Inequality: Evidence from U.S. Tax Return Data," working paper, April 2012, p. 19. http://web.williams.edu/Economics/wp/BakijaColeHeimJobsIncomeGrowthTopEarners.pdf.

CHAPTER 3: SUPERSTARS

88 **"A society in which knowledge workers dominate"** Peter Drucker, "The Age of Social Transformation," *The Atlantic*, November 1994, p. 67.

88 **"It is probably a misfortune that"** Friedrich A. Hayek, *Law, Legislation, and Liberty, Volume 2: The Mirage of Social Justice* (The University of Chicago Press, 1976), p. 74.

88 **"It is possible that intelligent tadpoles"** R. H. Tawney, *Equality* (Capricorn Books, 1961), p. 108.

89 **samizdat manuscript** György Konrád and Iván Szelényi, *The Intellectuals on the Road to Class Power* (Harcourt Brace Jovanovich, 1979).

91 **The consensus, advanced most powerfully** David Autor, "The Polarization of Job Oppor-

tunities in the U.S. Labor Market," Center for American Progress and The Hamilton Project, April 2010.

91 **In a January 2012 speech about income inequality** Alan B. Krueger, "The Rise and Consequences of Inequality in the United States," remarks prepared for an event at the Center for American Progress, January 12, 2012.

93 **But the best explanation** See Noam Scheiber, "The Audacity of Data: Barack Obama's Surprisingly Non-Ideological Policy Shop," *The New Republic*, March 12, 2008.

93 **"Above all, Obama's form of pragmatism"** Cass Sunstein, "The Empiricist Strikes Back: Obama's Pragmatism Explained," *The New Republic*, September 10, 2008.

93 **Word crunchers found that the president's 2009 inaugural address** Justin Wolfers, "The Empiricist-in-Chief," *Freakonomics* blog, February 26, 2009.

94 **Elizabeth Billington was a diva** See Elizabeth Billington's entry in Philip H. Highfill, Kalman A. Burnim, and Edward A. Langhans, *A Biographical Dictionary of Actors, Actresses, Musicians, Dancers, Managers and Other Stage Personnel in London, 1660–1800* (SIU Press, 1993), pp. 122–29.

95 **"The relative fall in the incomes to be earned"** Marshall, *Principles of Economics*, Book VI, Chapter XII, Section 11.

96 **China's Ming Dynasty, which ruled the Middle Kingdom** Patricia Buckley Ebrey, *The Cambridge Illustrated History of China* (Cambridge University Press, 2010), p. 201.

96 **"A striking instance is that of writing"** Marshall, *Principles of Economics*, Book VI, Chapter XII, Section 9.

97 **"The number of persons who can be reached"** Ibid., Section 11.

97 **"Even adjusted for 1981 prices"** Sherwin Rosen, "The Economics of Superstars," *American Economic Review* 71:5 (December 1981), p. 857.

98 **In 1900, nearly all spectator entertainment** Gerben Bakker, "Time and Productivity Growth in Services: How Motion Pictures Industrialized Entertainment," LSE working paper 119/09, March 2009, p. 7 and table B1. http://eprints.lse.ac.uk/27866/1/WP119.pdf.

99 **$670,000 to produce** Ted Okuda and David Maska, *Charlie Chaplin at Keystone and Essanay: Dawn of the Tramp* (iUniverse, 2005).

99 **In 1859, Anthony Trollope** Francis Evans Baily, *Six Great Victorian Novelists* (Kennikat Press, 1969).

100 **"an entirely new economic model"** Chris Anderson, "The Long Tail," *Wired*, October 2004.

104 **"I'm a pilot, so I understand airplane economics"** CF interview with Eric Schmidt, February 23, 2011.

105 **median salary for American lawyers** William D. Henderson, "Three Generations of U.S. Lawyers: Generalists, Specialists, Project Managers," *Maryland Law Review*, vol. 70, no. 1, 2011.

105 **In 2011, a year when top partner paydays** See Nathan Koppel and Vanessa O'Connell, "Pay Gap Widens at Big Law Firms as Partners Chase Star Attorneys," *Wall Street Journal*, February 8, 2011; and Vanessa O'Connell, "Big Law's $1,000-Plus an Hour Club," *Wall Street Journal*, February 23, 2011.

105 **David Boies's hourly rate** Vanessa O'Connell, "With Oracle and Dodgers Waiting, Boies Not Ready to Retire," *Wall Street Journal*, August 1, 2011.

105 **average starting salary for a law school graduate** See the National Association of Law Placement's Employment Report and Salary Survey for the Class of 2010. http://www.nalp.org/uploads/Classof2010SelectedFindings.pdf.

105 **average lawyer earned** May 2011 National Occupational Employment and Wage Estimates, Bureau of Labor Statistics. http://www.bls.gov/oes/current/oes231011.htm.

106 **The most advanced example of this trend is e-discovery** See John Markoff, "Armies of Expensive Lawyers, Replaced by Cheaper Software," *New York Times*, March 4, 2011.

106 **(Meanwhile, DLA Piper, one of the law firms)** See Nathan Koppel and Vanessa

O'Connell. "Pay Gap Widens at Big Law Firms as Partners Chase Star Attorneys," *Wall Street Journal*, February 8, 2011.

107 **In the age of the global super-elite, even dentists** Joan Juliet Buck, "Drill, Bébé, Drill," *New York Times T Magazine*, August 10, 2011.

108 **Her 2011 single "Born This Way"** Dorothy Pomerantz, "Lady Gaga Tops Celebrity 100 List," *Forbes*, May 18, 2011; "The Celebrity 100," *Forbes*, June 6, 2011.

108 **Between May 2010 and May 2011** According to the Census Bureau, real median household income was $49,445 in 2010.

108 **Mrs. Billington's fabulous £10,000 income** CF e-mail correspondence with Peter Lindert, June 25, 2012.

108 **Mickey Mantle, the New York Yankees star hitter** Baseball Almanac, www.baseball-almanac.com/players/player.php?p=mantlmi01.

108 **Compare that with Alex Rodriguez** USA Today Salaries database, http://content.usatoday.com/sportsdata/baseball/mlb/salaries/player/alex-rodriguez.

108 **Adjusted for inflation, Rodriguez's earnings** According to the Major League Baseball Players Association, the average salary for a Major Leaguer was $3,095,183 in 2011.

110 **In a study of concert ticket prices** Alan B. Krueger, "The Economics of Real Superstars: The Market for Rock Concerts in the Material World," *Journal of Labor Economics* 23:1 (2005).

111 **"very, very lucrative"** Chrystia Freeland, "The Rise of Private News," *Columbia Journalism Review*, July/August 2010.

115 **As late as 1920** Mary Schenck Woolman, *Clothing—Choice, Care, Cost* (Lippincott, 1922).

117 **"For much of the twentieth century, labor and capital"** Roger L. Martin and Mihnea C. Moldoveanu, "Capital Versus Talent: The Battle That's Reshaping Business," *Harvard Business Review*, July 2003.

118 **"In the knowledge society the employees"** Drucker, "The Age of Social Transformation."

120 **Wall Street investors, such as hedge fund managers** Steven N. Kaplan and Joshua Rauh, "Wall Street and Main Street: What Contributes to the Rise in the Highest Incomes?," *Review of Financial Studies* 23:3 (March 2010). pp. 1004–50.

121 **"When I graduated from college"** CF interview with David Rubenstein, April 27, 2011.

121 **But the real mass revolution sparked by the rise of entrepreneurial finance** Christine Harper, "Goldman CEO Blankfein Gets $67.9 Million Bonus, New Pay Record," Bloomberg News, December 24, 2007; David Segal, "$100 Million Payday Poses Problem for Pay Czar," *New York Times*, August 1, 2009.

121 **We got a glimpse of that way of thinking when federal agents** Suzanna Andrews, "How Rajat Gupta Came Undone," *Bloomberg Businessweek*, May 23, 2011.

123 **twenty thousand people competed** Michael Klein and Michael D. Schaffer, "City Slivers Seen on Philly 'Idol,'" *Philadelphia Inquirer*, January 17, 2008. Just 0.1% of Philadelphia contestants made it to the next round of *American Idol* auditions; in contrast, 7.1% of applicants to Harvard were admitted that year.

123 **Merton found that scientists who published frequently** Merton, "The Matthew Effect," pp. 56–63.

126 **You can see the same power of accidental celebrity at work** Alan T. Sorensen, "Bestseller Lists and Product Variety," *The Journal of Industrial Economics* 55:4 (December 2007), pp. 715–38.

126 **Matthew Salganik and Duncan Watts tested** Matthew Salganik and Duncan Watts, "Leading the Heard Astray: An Experimental Study of Self-Fulfilling Prophecies in an Artificial Cultural Market," *Social Psychology Quarterly*, vol. 71, no. 4, 2008, pp. 338–355.

127 **sent a memo** Jeffrey Katzenberg, "The World Is Changing: Some Thoughts on Our Business," Walt Disney Company memorandum, January 11, 1991. http://www.lettersofnote.com/2011/11/some-thoughts-on-our-business.html.

130 **The ideas Katzenberg laid out in his 1991 memo** Eduardo Porter and Geraldine Fabrikant, "A Big Star May Not a Profitable Movie Make," *New York Times*, August 28, 2006.

130 The terms of the deal were undisclosed Bernard Weinraub, "Disney Settles Bitter Suit with Former Studio Chief," *New York Times*, July 8, 1999. *Dick Tracy* cost Disney $47 million to produce. See James B. Stewart, *DisneyWar* (Simon & Schuster, 2005), p. 111.

131 "the stewards of a rich man" Smith, *Wealth of Nations*, Book V, Chapter I, Section 107.

131 a seminal paper published in 1931 Gardiner C. Means, "The Separation of Ownership and Control in American Industry," *The Quarterly Journal of Economics,*1931.

132 "the princes of industry" Adolf Augustus Berle and Gardiner Coit Means, *The Modern Corporation and Private Property* (Transaction Publishers, 1932), p. 4.

132 "different from and often radically opposed to" Ibid., p. 114.

132 Berle and Means were leading architects of the New Deal Glenn Fowler, "Gardiner C. Means, 91, Is Dead; Pricing Theory Aided U.S. Policy," *New York Times*, February 18, 1988.

133–34 "The average salary plus bonus for top-quartile CEOs" Michael C. Jensen and Kevin J. Murphy, "Performance Pay and Top-Management Incentives," *Journal of Political Economy* 98:2 (April 1990), pp. 225–64.

134 The companies under their stewardship Roger Martin, "The Age of Customer Capitalism," *Harvard Business Review*, January 2010. Figures on America's GDP from 1932 to 1976 come from Angus Maddison.

135 By one measure, the academic advocates of pay for performance Carola Frydman and Dirk Jenter, "CEO Compensation," *Annual Review of Financial Economics* 2 (December 2010), pp. 75–102.

135 Between 1993 and 2003 the top five executives Lucian Bebchuk and Yaniv Grinstein, "The Growth of Executive Pay," *Oxford Review of Economic Policy* 21:2 (2005), p. 283.

135 These were, of course, the decades when the 1 percent Marianne Bertrand, "CEOs," *Annual Review of Economics* 1:1 (2009), p. 130.

135 Until the early 1980s, the chief executive earned Kaplan and Rauh, "Wall Street and Main Street," pp. 1004–50.

136 "A 10 percent increase" Brian Bell and John Van Reenen, "Firm Performance and Wages: Evidence from Across the Corporate Hierarchy," CEP Discussion Paper No. 1088, May 2012. http://cep.lse.ac.uk/pubs/download/dp1088.pdf.

137 The surge in CEO salaries Kevin J. Murphy and Jan Zabojnik, "Managerial Capital and the Market for CEOs," (Queen's Economics Department Working Paper No. 10, October 2006. p. 1).

137 "The six-fold increase of U.S. CEO pay" Xavier Gabaix and Augustin Landier, "Why Has CEO Pay Increased So Much?," *Quarterly Journal of Economics* 123:1 (2008), pp. 49–100.

138 "In the U.S., you can more or less do" Chrystia Freeland, "Capitalism Without the Capitalists," *International Herald Tribune*, December 22, 2011.

138 A decade ago, two young economists Marianne Bertrand and Sendhil Mullainathan, "Are CEOs Rewarded for Luck? The Ones without Principals Are," *Quarterly Journal of Economics* 116:3 (August 2001), pp. 901–32.

139 "We cannot continue to see chief executives' pay" Julia Werdigier, "British Government Looks to Rein in Executive Pay," *New York Times*, January 23, 2012.

140 "The Lin story has broken out into the general culture" David Carr, "Media Hype for Lin Stumbles on Race," *New York Times*, February 19, 2012.

CHAPTER 4: RESPONDING TO REVOLUTION

141 "A lesson from the technology industry" Reid Hoffman and Ben Casnocha, *The Start-Up of You: Adapt to the Future, Invest in Yourself, and Transform Your Career* (Crown Business, 2012), p. 71.

141 Eight days later, George Soros hosted twenty Chrystia Freeland, "The Credit Crunch According to Soros," *Financial Times*, January 30, 2009. Unless otherwise specified, all quotes in this section originally appeared in this piece.

142 **an average of 31 percent** Charles Morris. *The Sages*. p. 3.

142 **According to a study by LCH Investments** Rick Sopher, "Great Money Managers," self-published by LCH Investments, November 2011. After retiring in 2010, Soros was overtaken the following year by Bridgewater's Ray Dalio.

143 **"I converted my hedge fund into a less aggressively managed vehicle"** George Soros. *The Crash of 2008 and What It Means*. p. 122.

144 **only one of them had foreseen** Justin Lahart, "Bears Top List of Economic Forecasters," *Wall Street Journal*, February 13, 2009. The fifty-one did even less well on unemployment—none came close to predicting it would rise to 6.9 percent by the end of 2008.

144 **"No one realized the extent and magnitude of these problems"** Statement of Richard S. Fuld, Jr., before the United States House of Representatives Committee on Oversight and Government Reform, October 6, 2008.

144 **"I made a mistake"** Transcript of House of Representatives Committee on Oversight and Government Reform Hearing on the Role of Federal Regulators, October 23, 2008.

144 **"we always assume regime stability"** McFaul e-mail to CF, February 22, 2011.

145 **"active inertia"** Donald Sull, "Why Good Companies Go Bad," *Financial Times*, October 3, 2005.

145 **"These failed firms"** Clayton Christensen, *The Innovator's Dilemma: When New Technologies Cause Great Firms to Fail* (Harvard Business School Press, 1997), p. xv.

146 **"vast, silent, connected"** W. Brian Arthur, "The Second Economy," *McKinsey Quarterly*, October 2011.

147 **Facebook's Mark Zuckerberg** Zuckerberg attended Ardsley High School for two years before transferring to Phillips Exeter Academy.

147 **"Dopamine, a pleasure-inducing"** Ajay Kapur, Niall Macleod, and Narendra Singh, "Plutonomy: Buying Luxury, Explaining Global Imbalances," Citigroup Global Markets Equity Strategy report, October 16, 2005.

153 **"I recognize that sometimes survival requires a positive effort"** CF interviews with George Soros, May 2009 and December 2008.

153 **"My theory of bubbles was a translation"** CF interview with George Soros, May 2009.

153 **"That experience has allowed him to see through artifice"** CF interview with Jonathan Soros, July 14, 2009.

153 **"Whenever I read about people not seeing it coming"** CF interview with Keith Anderson, June 26, 2009.

154 **"They have their own style and their own exposure"** CF interview with George Soros, May 2009.

154 **Soros "didn't interfere in the running of their accounts"** Ibid.

154 **"Basically, it involved a large amount of hedging"** Ibid.

154 **Soros was not only unfamiliar with fancy new derivatives** Ibid.

154 **"In a time like this, where the uncertainty is so big"** CF interview with George Soros, December 16, 2008.

154 **"That's what makes this macro investing"** CF interview with Keith Anderson, June 26, 2009.

155 **"I was very lucky"** CF interview with Azim Premji, January 25, 2012.

155 **"India is growing at 8 percent"** CF interview with Ashutosh Varshney, November 13, 2011.

156 **"You could start a business"** Kaitlin Shung, "Chinese 'Fugitive' Lai Changxing Faces Deportation in Canada," *China Briefing*, July 13, 2011.

156 **"Well, the U.S., like I said"** CF interview with David Neeleman, September 14, 2010.

157 **"The next ten years"** Chrystia Freeland, "Working Wealthy Predominate the New Global Elite," *International Herald Tribune*, January 25, 2011.

158 **Following the model of Nucor, which revolutionized** Ibid. pp. 101–8.

160 **"Yes, you need to be bold and extremely committed"** Jennings, "Opportunities of a Lifetime."

161 **"Slow or hesitant business leaders"** CF interview with Aditya Mittal, November 11, 2010.

162 **"If Lai Changxing were executed"** Mark Mackinnon, "Lai's sentencing marks the end of China's Great Gatsby," *The Globe and Mail*, May 18, 2012.

163 **He calls that period his "lost years"** Parmy Olson, "The Billionaire Who Friended the Web," *Forbes*, March 28, 2011.

165 **"There was a period of time"** Miguel Helft, "The Class That Built Apps, and Fortunes," *New York Times*, May 7, 2011.

165 **"I felt, having been late"** John Seabrook, "Streaming Dreams," *New Yorker*, January 16, 2012.

165 **published a 143-page report** "Big data: The next frontier for innovation, competition, and productivity," McKinsey Global Institute, May 2011. http://www.mckinsey.com/insights/mgi/research/technology_and_innovation/big_data_the_next_frontier_for_innovation.

166 **"People have always asked me"** CF interview with Larry Fink, October 20, 2010.

168 **"Firestone's historical excellence"** Donald Sull, "The Dynamics of Standing Still: Firestone Tire & Rubber and the Radial Revolution," *The Business History Review*, vol. 73, no. 3 (Autumn 1999), pp. 430–64.

168 **"An ossified success formula"** Donald Sull, "Ingrained success breeds failure," *Financial Times*, October 2, 2005.

168 **"Basically, we are living in a world"** Stephen Jennings, "Opportunities of a Lifetime: Lessons for New Zealand from New, High-Growth Economics," Sir Ronald Trotter Lecture, April 7, 2009.

169 **"A disruptive event now needs"** Michiyo Nakamoto and David Wighton, "Citigroup chief stays bullish on buy-outs," *Financial Times*, July 9, 2007.

170 **"I've been through probably six crises"** CF interview with Peter Weinberg, June 25, 2009.

171 **the ability to "pivot"** Caroline O'Connor and Perry Klebahn, "The Strategic Pivot: Rules for Entrepreneurs and Other Innovators," *Harvard Business Review* blog network, February 28, 2011.

172 **Flickr's genesis was in 2002** See Jessica Livingston, *Founders at Work: Stories of Startups' Early Days* (Apress, 2007), pp. 257–264.

172 **"One thing that I've both wrestled with"** Chrystia Freeland, "The Credit Crunch According to Soros," *Financial Times*, January 30, 2009.

172 **"My conceptual framework, which basically emphasizes"** CF interview with George Soros, December 16, 2008.

173 **"It's an almost aggressive pessimism about his own ideas"** CF interview with Jonathan Soros, July 14, 2009.

173 **"The businesses and institutions underpinning"** Jennings, "Opportunities of a Lifetime."

173 **"The group of winners is churning at an increasing and rapid rate"** "Measuring the Forces of Long-Term Change: The 2009 shift index", Deloitte Center for the Edge, December 2009, p. 115.

174 **"There are a lot of young entrepreneurs"** Sam Grobart and Evelyn M. Rusli, "For Flip Video Camera, Four Years from Hot Start-Up to Obsolete," *New York Times*, April 12, 2011.

175 **"If you want to get a reputation"** Warren Buffett, Berkshire Hathaway Inc. 2006 Annual Report, February 28, 2007.

175 **"Almost to a man, they lay great emphasis"** Merton, "The Matthew Effect," pp. 56–63.

175 **The power of choosing the right work is equally pronounced** Graeme Wood, "Secret Fears of the Super-Rich," *The Atlantic*, April 2011.

176 **"sudden wealth syndrome"** "Rich Man's Burden," *The Economist*, June 14, 2001.

176 **"I had one friend"** CF interview with Viktor Vekselberg, September 7, 2010.

177 U.S. political scientists in 1999 Stephen E. Lucas and Martin J. Medhurst, "American Public Address: The Top 100 Speeches of the Twentieth Century," National Communication Association, Seattle, Washington, November 8–12, 2000.

177 "It was the middle" Franklin Delano Roosevelt campaign address on progressive government at the Commonwealth Club in San Francisco, California, September 23, 1932.

179 "In Russia, all the property" Chrystia Freeland, "The Next Russian Revolution," *The Atlantic*, October 2011.

180 "to buy an apartment" Ibid.

181 "When I graduated" Richard Cree, "Profile: Reid Hoffman," *Director*, July/August 2009.

182 "I was focused on my CV" CF interview with Reid Hoffman, February 17, 2012.

183 "After the eBay/PayPal deal" Hoffman and Casnocha, *The Start-Up of You*, p. 169.

184 "Once-great companies" Ibid., p. 18.

184 "You were born an entrepreneur" Ibid., p. 3.

184 "the mind-sets and skill sets" Ibid., p. 4.

185 "Over the last ten years" "The Mobile Revolution: Driving the Next Wave of Productivity and Growth," Council on Foreign Relations meeting, March 30, 2011. http://www.cfr.org/information-and-communication/mobile-revolution-driving-next-wave-productivity-growth/p24545.

186 U.S. workers take an average 30 percent pay cut Till von Wachter, Jae Song, and Joyce Manchester, "Long-Term Earnings Losses due to Mass Layoffs During the 1982 Recession: An Analysis Using U.S. Administrative Data from 1974 to 2004," Columbia University Economics Department Discussion Paper Series DP0910-07, April 2009.

187 "Your education isn't fungible" CF interview with Michael Spence, April 15, 2011.

187 "For the last sixty or so years" Hoffman and Casnocha, *The Start-Up of You*, p. 5.

187 "Remember: If you don't find risk, risk will find you" Hoffman, *The Start-Up of You*, p. 188.

187 "In the past, when you thought" Ibid., p. 187.

CHAPTER 5: RENT-SEEKING

188 "They steal and steal and steal" From Chrystia Freeland, *Sale of the Century: Russia's Wild Ride from Communism to Capitalism* (Crown Business, 2000), pp. 67–68.

188 "Eating increases the appetite" Ibid., p. 233.

189 risked becoming "an unequal oligarchy, or worse" Raghuram Rajan, "Is There a Threat of Oligarchy in India?" Speech to the Bombay Chamber of Commerce on its Founders Day Celebration, September 10, 2008.

189 "quiet coup" Simon Johnson, "The Quiet Coup," *The Atlantic*, May 2009.

190 "lower the amount of government spending" Paul Ryan, "Saving the American Idea," Remarks to the Heritage Foundation, October 26, 2011. http://blog.heritage.org/2011/10/26/video-rep-paul-ryan-on-saving-the-american-idea/.

191 "Once more, I am reminding you" "Ukraine: Country's Largest Steel Mill Sold at Auction," *Radio Free Europe/Radio Liberty*, October 24, 2005.

192 "It was like a football game!" *The Economist*, October 27, 2005.

192 "hate me—they don't understand" See Chrystia Freeland, "Tea with the FT: Yulia Tymoshenko," *Financial Times*, August 16, 2008.

193 number of billionaires relative to the size Ruchir Sharma.,"The billionaires list," *Washington Post's Wonkblog*, June 24, 2012.

193 economic historians have found that Russia's oligarchs Steven Nafziger and Peter Lindert, "Russian Inequality on the Eve of the Revolution" (working paper, March 13, 2011).

194 according to calculations by Branko Milanovic Branko Milanovic, *The Haves and the Have Nots: A Brief and Idiosyncratic History of Global Inequality* (Basic Books, 2011), pp. 41–45.

194 **"A person must be rich or poor"** Smith, *Wealth of Nations*, Book I, Chapter V, Section 1.

196 **the only place in Mexico** Luhnow, "The Secrets of the World's Richest Man."

196 **Slim was a vocal supporter of his friend's reform effort** Slim continued to advocate privatization in subsequent decades. He was the cover boy of the 2012 *Forbes* billionaire issue, which named him the richest man on the planet. In the accompanying story, *Forbes* asked Slim for his "plan to reboot the economy" of the world. Among Slim's recommendations: "Let's talk about Spain. It has a lot of highways and they are all free. They should charge users and sell [the highways] to the private sector."

197 **a study by Mexican and American political scientists** Isabel Guerrero, Luis-Felipe López-Calva, and Michael Walton, "The Inequality Trap and Its Links to Low Growth in Mexico," in *No Growth Without Equity: Inequality, Interests, and Competition in Mexico*, ed. Santiago Levy and Michael Walton (World Bank, 2009).

200 **"When it came to spectrum"** "All Lines Are Busy," *Outlook*, November 29, 2010.

200 **"India has been overwhelmed"** CF interview with Kiran Bedi, November 11, 2011.

201 **"Corruption is endemic"** CF interview with Rajiv Lall, November 13, 2011.

201 **"The Gini coefficient"** CF interview with Arun Maira, November 13, 2011.

201 **"The tendency is that people"** CF interview with Kris Gopalakrishnan, November 12, 2011.

204 **According to Hurun, the seventy richest members of the NPC** "China's Billionaire People's Congress Makes U.S. Peers Look Like Paupers," Bloomberg News, February 27, 2012.

205 **"There are skeletons"** Chris Hogg, "What Brought Down China's Huang Guangyu?," BBC, May 18, 2010.

205 **China's billionaires understand that notoriety is dangerous** Russell Flannery, "China Leads the World in Billionaire Flame-Outs," *Forbes*, March 9, 2012.

205 **the party's official policy of pursuing "harmonious growth"** Liu Jie, Kong Xiaohan, and Tian Ye, "Premier Wen Targets Causes of Instability, Stresses Fair Treatment of Disadvantaged Groups," Xinhua, February 27, 2011.

206 **"original sins"** Philip P. Pan, *Out of Mao's Shadow: The Struggle for the Soul of a New China* (Simon & Schuster, 2008), p. 156.

206 **over the past three decades, China's average per capita income** International Monetary Fund, World Economic Outlook database, April 2012; National Bureau of Statistics of China; Jeremy Page, Bob Davis, James T. Areddy, "China Turns Predominantly Urban," *Wall Street Journal*, January 18, 2012; "Income of Urban and Rural Residents in 2011," January 30, 2012.

207 **"What moves this structure is not a market economy"** Carl E. Walter and Fraser J. T. Howie, *Red Capitalism: The Fragile Financial Foundation of China's Extraordinary Rise* (John Wiley & Sons, 2011), pp. 22–23.

207 **Unlike their Russian comrades, China's red oligarchs** Laurie Burkitt, "Landed Ladies Top List of China's Richest Women," *China Real-Time Report* blog, *Wall Street Journal*, September 29, 2011.

208 **"What would the chairman of China's largest bank do"** Walter and Howie, *Red Capitalism*, p. 187.

208 **The subtle hand of the Chinese government** Shu-Ching Jean Chen, "China's Power Queen," *Forbes*, January 3, 2008; "Li Xiaopeng Appointed Vice Governor of Shanxi Province," *People's Daily Online*, June 12, 2008.

208 **Another sign of the political nature of wealth in China** Audra Ang, "Chinese Tycoon Gets 18 Years in Fraud Case," Associated Press, July 15, 2003.

209 **"If they wanted to, China's authorities could probably find"** "Face Value: Scandal in Shanghai," *The Economist*, August 14, 2003.

209 **"If only a few people are rich, then we'll slide into capitalism"** "China's Bo Signals Wealth Gap Breached Unrest Trigger Point," Bloomberg News, March 9, 2012.

209 **But at the same time, Bo was a princeling** Jeremy Page, "Children of the Revolution," *Wall Street Journal*, November 26, 2011.

209 **(Guagua denies driving the Ferrari)** Andrew Jacobs and Edward Wong, "Disgraced Chinese Official's Son Tries to Defuse Sports Car Scandal," *New York Times*, April 25, 2012.

209 **Guagua was educated at Harrow** Jeremy Page, Brian Spegele, and Steve Eder, "'Jackie Kennedy of China' at Center of Political Drama," *Wall Street Journal*, April 9, 2012.

209 **Since Bo Xilai's fall from grace** "Bo Xilai Clan Links Included Citigroup Hiring of Elder Son," Bloomberg News, April 23, 2012.

209 **Bo was one of China's rising leaders** Jamil Anderlini, "Bo Xilai's Wife Arrested in Murder Probe," *Financial Times*, April 10, 2012.

210 **"The emphasis once again is shifting much more"** CF interview with Stephen Roach, April 10, 2012.

210 **"Our banks earn profit too easily"** Dinny McMahon, Lingling Wei, and Andrew Galbraith, "Chinese Premier Blasts Banks," *Wall Street Journal*, April 4, 2012.

211 **"this would be devastating for both our city and nation"** Charles E. Schumer and Michael R. Bloomberg, "To Save New York from London," *Wall Street Journal*, November 1, 2006.

211 **"When asked to compare New York and London"** "Sustaining New York's and the US' Global Financial Services Leadership," McKinsey report, January 22, 2007.

213 **The arguments in the report are so wrong that it is easy to mock** Aaron Lucchetti, "Moving the Market: Why Spitzer Is Backing Study That Endorses Less Regulation—Restrictive Climate Said to Draw Business Away from New York," *Wall Street Journal*, January 23, 2007.

213 **Two days before Bloomberg and Schumer took to the op-ed pages** R. Glenn Hubbard and John L. Thornton, "Is the U.S. Losing Ground?" *Wall Street Journal*, October 30, 2006.

213 **"Our society seems to have an increased tendency"** Remarks by Secretary Henry Paulson to the Economic Club of New York, as released by the Department of the Treasury, November 20, 2006.

213 **A final U.S. contribution from the department of irony** John A. Thain, "New York Faces Challenges to Its Market Dominance," letter to the editor, *Wall Street Journal*, November 25, 2006.

214 **"Gordon Brown patrolled the conference corridors"** Howard Davies, "Balls Must Save Us from U.S. Regulatory Creep," *The Independent*, January, 27, 2007.

215 **he resigned as director of the LSE** "LSE Director Sir Howard Davies Resigns over Libya Links," BBC, March 4, 2011.

216 **"I totally understand why Dick Fuld couldn't do it"** CF interview with John Thain, September 16, 2008.

216 **"The perspective of government"** All attributed quotes from this section originally appeared in Chrystia Freeland, "What Toronto Can Teach New York and London," *Financial Times*, January 29, 2010.

218 **"The highest earnings by occupation"** Claudia Goldin and Lawrence F. Katz, "Transitions: Career and Family Life Cycles of the Educational Elite," *American Economic Review: Papers & Proceedings 2008*, 98:2, 363–69.

219 **One of the most comprehensive analyses** Bakija, Cole, and Heim, "Jobs and Income Growth," p. 55, table 7; see also the explanation on p. 24.

219 **The numbers in the UK, where the ascendancy of finance** Brian Bell and John Van Reenen, "Bankers' Pay and Extreme Wage Inequality in the UK," CEP Special Report, April 2010.

220 **"From 1909 to 1933 the financial sector"** Thomas Philippon and Ariell Reshef, "Wages and Human Capital in the U.S. Financial Industry: 1909–2006," NBER Working Paper, March 2011.

222 **"In the financial industry, the United States"** CF interview with Christopher Meyer, February 21, 2012.

222–23 laws increasing regulation of the finance and real estate sectors Deniz Igan, Prachi Mishra, and Thierry Tressel, "A Fistful of Dollars: Lobbying and the Financial Crisis," IMF Working Paper 09/287, December 2009.

223 "Well, of course, I wrote" Freeland, *Sale of the Century*, p. 176.

223 Washington had occupied Wall Street Sarah Palin, "How Congress Occupied Wall Street," *Wall Street Journal*, November 18, 2011.

226 One study of the SEC "Revolving Regulators: SEC Faces Ethics Challenges with Revolving Door," Project on Government Oversight report, May 13, 2011.

226 It is easy to understand the appeal of switching Philippon and Reshef, "Wages and Human Capital," p. 21.

CHAPTER 6: PLUTOCRATS AND THE REST OF US

229 "If you really wanted to examine" Richard D. Lyons, "Fears of H.E.W. Cuts Spur Protests at Inflation Parley," *New York Times*, September 19, 1974.

229 "He was remembering now" Robert Harris, *The Fear Index* (Knopf, 2012).

229 "A stranger to human nature" Adam Smith, *The Theory of Moral Sentiments* (Cambridge University Press), 2004, p. 63.

230 If you ever have to work at a call center Unless otherwise specified, all quotes and descriptions from this section are drawn from the author's August 2010 visit to Zappos headquarters.

231 "free from boring work environments" This quote appears on the jobs section of Zappos .com.

235 "the palace of the millionaire" Carnegie, "Wealth."

236 "the marginal return for extra dollars does drop off" Jeff Guo and Rob McQueen, "Gates Asks Students to Tackle the World's Problems," *The Tech*, April 23, 2010.

236 "you can drive your Rolls-Royce around" CF interview with Eric Schmidt, February 23, 2011.

236 "If a man is not an oligarch" Chrystia Freeland, *Sale of the Century: Russia's Wild Ride from Communism to Capitalism* (Crown Business, 2000), p. 320.

237 "treated business exclusively" "Prison Exchange: Mikhail Khodorkovsky Looks Back on His Choices," *Radio Free Europe/Radio Liberty*, September 21, 2009.

237 "That this talent for organization" Carnegie, "Wealth."

237 "We ended up making twenty-four times our money" Bloomberg TV interview with Steve Schwarzman, November 30, 2011.

238 "We live in a bubble" Brad Stone. "It's Always Sunny in Silicon Valley," *Bloomberg Businessweek*, December 26, 2011.

238 "I recently talked to an IT engineer" Matt Rosoff, "Eric Schmidt: We Don't Talk about Occupy Wall Street in the Valley Because We Don't Have Those Problems," *Business Insider*, December 23, 2011.

239 "Is society's nobility" Paul Piff, Daniel M. Stancato, Stephane Cote, Rodolfo Mendoza-Denton, and Dacher Keltner, "High social class predicts increased unethical behavior," *Proceedings of the National Academy of Sciences*, 109 (2012), 4086–91.

241 "You know, historically" CF interview with B. N. Kalyani, November 13, 2011.

241 "meet somewhere in the middle" CF interview with Kris Gopalakrishnan, November 12, 2011.

242 "So long as our leaders tell us that we must trust them" Daniel S. Loeb, "Third Point LLC Second Quarter 2010 Investor Letter," August 27, 2010.

243 "like when Hitler invaded Poland in 1939" Jonathan Alter, "A 'Fat Cat' Strikes Back," *Newsweek*, August 15, 2010.

244 "Since fair is fair, tax loopholes in the financial industry" Mike Bloomberg, "How the Super Committee Can Balance the Federal Budget," remarks prepared for Center for American Progress/American Action Forum event, November 8, 2011.

244 **"The top 1 percent of New Yorkers pay over 40 percent"** Shira Ovide, "Billionaire Tells Occupy Wall Street to Get Off His Lawn," Deal Journal blog, *Wall Street Journal*, October 11, 2011.

245 **"Acting like everyone who's been successful is bad"** Max Abelson, "Bankers Join Billionaires to Debunk 'Imbecile' Attack on Top 1%," Bloomberg News, December 20, 2011.

245 **"not a question"** CF interview with Jeff Immelt, October 17, 2011.

245 **"Capitalists are not the scourge that they are too often made out to be"** Leon G. Cooperman, "An Open Letter to the President of the United States of America," November 28, 2011.

246 **"People don't realize how wealthy people self-tax"** CF interview with Foster Friess, February 9, 2012.

247 **"I think [the ultrawealthy] actually"** Melissa Harris "Billionaire Opens Up on Politics," *Chicago Tribune*, March 11, 2012.

248 **"We celebrate income disparity and we applaud the growing margins"** Neil Hume, "God Bless Income Disparity," Alphaville blog, *Financial Times,* November 17, 2011.

249 **"wealth is fleeing the country"** From a February 22, 2012, e-mail, sent out by Lindsay Rafayko of Empower Public Relations.

250 **"We may need an escape plan"** Yardeni Research Daily E-mail Briefing, December 8, 2011.

250 **a few modern-day plutocrats are actually trying to build** Jonathan Miles, "The Billionaire King of Techtopia," *Details*, September 2011.

250 **"I have yet to talk to anybody who doesn't say"** "Governance Blueprints from Global Leaders," signature lecture panel, Centre for International Governance Innovation's "An Unfinished House: Filling the Gaps in Global Governance" conference, Waterloo, Canada, October 28, 2011.

251 **"For successful people to say the nasty end of the income distribution"** CF interview with Mohamed El-Erian, June 15, 2010.

251 **"No nation can tolerate for long excessive shifts in income"** CF e-mail correspondence with Mohamed El-Erian, October 10, 2011.

252 **Mark Carney is not most people's idea of a radical** See the following articles in *The Globe and Mail*: Andrew Willis, Tavia Grant, and Heather Scoffield, "Playing a New Game, in a New Arena," October 5, 2007; Heather Scoffield, "Mark Carney Takes Up His Mission," January 25, 2008; Jeremy Torobin, "Mark Carney: A Common Touch, an Uncommon Task," January 13, 2012.

253 **"I have called it anti-American"** Rachelle Younglai and Philipp Halstrick, "JPMorgan's Dimon's Aggressive Style May Hurt Bank Cause," Reuters, September 29, 2011.

253 **Another participant remembered Dimon's remarks** Tom Braithwaite and Patrick Jenkins, "JPMorgan Chief Says Bank Rules 'Anti-US,'" *Financial Times*, September 12, 2011.

253 **JPMorgan, which earns around a quarter** According to the bank's 2011 annual report, total net revenue was $97 billion and managed revenue from outside North America was $25 billion.

254 **After the meeting Blankfein sent Carney** Tom Braithwaite, "Dimon in Attack on Canada's Bank Chief," *Financial Times*, September 26, 2011.

254 **Dimon, who stands by the substance** This account was drawn from background conversations with Wall Street bankers, as well as Kevin Carmichael, Tara Perkins, and Grant Robinson's "Bankers, Regulators Square Off amid Turmoil," *The Globe and Mail,* September 26, 2011. See also "JPMorgan's Dimon's Aggressive Style May Hurt Bank Cause,"

254 **"He's my governor and I'm very proud of that fact"** Kevin Carmichael, "Carney, Waugh Spar over New Banking Rules," *The Globe and Mail*, September 25, 2011.

255 **"It is hard to see how backsliding would help"** Mark Carney, "Some Current Issues in Financial Reform," remarks to the Institute of International Finance, Washington, D.C., September 25, 2011.

256 **between 2003 and 2011, at least fourteen Chinese** Emma Dong, "China Executes 14 Billionaires in 8 Years, Culture News Reports," *Bloomberg News*, July 22, 2011.

256 **"In the 1990s, of course, free enterprise, capitalism, and so forth"** Howard Fineman, "Jed S. Rakoff: Federal District Judge of New York's Southern District (The Inspirationals)," *Huffington Post*, December 27, 2011.

256 **"I placed too much confidence"** David J. Lynch, "Dimon-Bernanke Faceoff Shows Frustration over Regulation amid Kohn Regrets," Bloomberg News, July 7, 2011.

257 **"The Fed listens to Wall Street and believes what it hears"** Willem H. Buiter, "Central Banks and Financial Crises," Federal Reserve Bank of Kansas City's Maintaining Stability in a Changing Financial System symposium, Jackson Hole, Wyoming, August 23, 2008.

258 **Dimon even left his own star-studded fifty-second** Kate Kelly, "Inside the Fall of Bear Stearns," *Wall Street Journal*, May 9, 2009.

258 **President Obama's favorite banker** Jackie Calmes and Louise Story, "In Washington, One Bank Chief Still Holds Sway," *New York Times*, July 18, 2009.

258 **"Most of the bad actors are gone"** "What Dimon Told Bernanke," *New York Times Dealbook*, June 8, 2011.

259 **"My daughter called me from school one day"** Sewell Chan, "Voices That Dominate Wall Street Take a Meeker Tone on Capitol Hill," *New York Times*, January 13, 2010.

259 **the attitude they betrayed as "jaded"** Mark Carney, "The Economic Consequences of the Reforms," remarks to the Bundesbank, September 14, 2010.

259 **more than 100 to 1** Jamie Dimon's 2011 pay package totaled $23 million, compared to Ben Bernanke's $199,700 salary in 2011.

259 **CFTC officials took the Megabus** Ben Protess. "U.S. Regulators Face Budget Pinch as Mandates Widen," *New York Times Dealbook*, May 3, 2011.

260 **"New and better rules"** "Some Current Issues in Financial Reform"

260 **"The argument that financial institutions"** Dave Clarke, "JPMorgan's Dimon Loses Clout as Reform Critic," Reuters, May 11, 2012.

261 **"CEOs have duties to their shareholders"** Harris, "Billionaire Opens Up on Politics."

262 **"True capitalism lacks a strong lobby"** Luigi Zingales, "Capitalism After the Crisis," *National Affairs* 1 (Fall 2009).

262 **"no car with my name"** Lee Iacocca, *Iacocca: An Autobiography* (Bantam, 1984), p. 108.

262 **"The Foundation exists and thrives"** Text of Ford's letter to Alexander Heard as published in *Foundation News*, March/April 1977.

263 **"He has a right"** Heather Mac Donald, "The Billions of Dollars That Made Things Worse," *City Journal*, Autumn 1996.

263 **Ford was the second-highest-paid** "Who Gets The Most Pay?" and "The Dimensions of American Business: A Roster of the U.S.'s Biggest Corporations," *Forbes*, May 15, 1977.

263 **Ford's letter crystallized a fear** An example of this anxiety is the 1971 letter Lewis Powell, then a corporate lawyer and a future Supreme Court justice, wrote to Eugene Sydnor, Jr., the director of the U.S. Chamber of Commerce. In it, Powell argued, "The overriding first need is for businessmen to recognize that the ultimate issue may be survival—survival of what we call the free enterprise system, and all that this means for the strength and prosperity of America and the freedom of our people."

264 **"the academic and business communities"** Irving Kristol, "On Corporate Philanthropy," *Wall Street Journal*, March 21, 1977.

264 **"programs and policies, such as social security"** Mac Donald, "The Billions of Dollars That Made Things Worse."

265 **the five largest papers** Clifford Marks, "In Media Coverage, Deficit Eclipses Unemployment," *National Journal*, May 16, 2011.

267 **"It just doesn't make sense for people"** David Burt, "Grad School Scrutinized," *Yale Daily News*, September 21, 2011.

267 **"as bank robber Willie Sutton"** Drew Gilpin Faust, "Baccalaureate Address to the Class of 2008," Cambridge, MA, June 3, 2008.

268 **"we love Greg Mankiw"** Allison Gofman, "Walking Out on Results," *Harvard Political Review*, November 6, 2011.

268 **"My first reaction was nostalgia"** N. Gregory Mankiw, "Know What You're Protesting," *New York Times*, December 3, 2011.

268 **The only four fields** Professor salary figures come from the Chronicle of Higher Education's *2011 Almanac of Higher Education,* August 21, 2011.

268 **Even as they cash their speaking fees** Emily Flitter, Kristina Cooke, and Pedro da Costa, "Special Report: For Some Professors, Disclosure Is Academic," Reuters, December 20, 2010.

269 **Winner-Take-All Politics** A big hat tip here to Jacob Hacker!

269 **an increasing number of politicians are members** Eric Lichtblau, "Economic Downturn Took a Detour at Capitol Hill," *New York Times*, December 26, 2011.

269 **One academic study has suggested that serving in Washington** Alan J. Ziobrowski, James W. Boyd, Ping Cheng, and Brigitte J. Ziobrowski, "Abnormal Returns from the Common Stock Investments of Members of the U.S. House of Representatives," *Business and Politics* 13:1 (2011).

269 **But a different study by LSE and MIT researchers challenged** Andrew Eggers and Jens Hainmueller, "Capitol Losses: The Mediocre Performance of Congressional Stock Portfolios, 2004–2008," MIT Political Science Department Research Paper No. 2011-5, December 2, 2011.

270 **Between 2000 and 2007 the Clintons earned $111 million** Kenneth P. Vogel, "Tax Returns Show How Clintons Got Rich Quick," *Politico*, April 4, 2008.

270 **Tom Daschle, the former Democratic Senate majority leader** David D. Kirkpatrick, "In Daschle's Tax Woes, a Peek into Washington," *New York Times*, February 1, 2009.

270 **senators were 50 percent** Larry Bartels, "Economic Inequality and Political Representation," in *The Unsustainable American State*, eds. Lawrence Jacobs and Desmond Kin (Oxford University Press, 2009), pp. 167–96.

271 **You could see the power of these networks** Richard Teitelbaum, "How Paulson Gave Hedge Funds Advance Word of Fannie Mae Rescue," Bloomberg News, November 29, 2011.

272 **"The proportion of people with training and experience in finance"** Zingales, "Capitalism After the Crisis."

273 **"It turns out that if I pay"** CF interviews with Dan Ariely, December 2010 and January 2011.

274 **"We are deeply social animals"** "Working Wealthy Predominate the New Global Elite," *International Herald Tribune*, January 25, 2011.

274 **"'Yes, he would give them'"** Jane Austen, *Sense and Sensibility* (Dover, 1995), p. 3.

CONCLUSION

277 **"We may have democracy"** *Mr. Justice Brandeis, Great American,* ed. Irving Dilliard (Modern View Press, 1941), p. 42

277 **"The society that puts equality"** Milton Friedman, "Free to Choose," PBS, 1980.

279 **The story of Venice's rise and fall** Daron Acemoglu and James A. Robinson, *Why Nations Fail* (Crown, 2012), pp. 152–56.

280 **"There's a lot of anger in society because of what the government did"** CF interview with Eric Schmidt, February 23, 2011.

281 **"It's probably true that some activities are truly creative"** CF interview with Emmanuel Saez, February 24, 2011.

282 **"A truly great business"** Warren Buffett, Berkshire Hathaway Inc. 2007 Annual Report, February 29, 2008.

283 **Great Gatsby Curve** "The Rise and Consequences of Inequality in the United States."

283 **statistics have shown** See Thomas B. Edsall, "The Reproduction of Privilege," *New York Times "Campaign Stops"* blog, March 12, 2012.

284 **worth more than $4 million** See Felix Salmon, "Simmons Leaves Goldman's Board," Reuters, February 13, 2010.

284 **whether the legacy system** For a good exploration of this topic, see Elyse Ashburn, "At Elite Colleges, Legacy Status May Count More Than Was Previously Thought," *Chronicle of Higher Education*, January 5, 2011.

286 **"Since, by the Grace of God"** Roger Crowley, *City of Fortune: How Venice Ruled the Seas* (Random House, 2012), p. xxviii.

BIBLIOGRAPHY

Acemoglu, Daron, and David Autor. "Skills, Tasks and Technologies: Implications for Employment and Earnings." In *Handbook of Labor Economics Volume 4*. Orley Ashenfelter and David E. Card, eds. Elsevier, 2010.

Acemoglu, Daron, and James A. Robinson. *Why Nations Fail: The Origins of Power, Prosperity, and Poverty*. Crown Business, 2012.

Ariely, Dan. *Predictably Irrational: The Hidden Forces That Shape Our Decisions*. Harper, 2009.

Atkinson, Anthony, Thomas Piketty, and Emmanuel Saez. "Top Incomes in the Long Run of History." *Journal of Economic Literature* 49:1 (2011). pp. 3–71.

Autor, David. "The Polarization of Job Opportunities in the U.S. Labor Market." Center for American Progress and The Hamilton Project. April 2010.

Autor, David, and David Dorn. "The Growth of Low-Skill Service Jobs and the Polarization of the U.S. Labor Market." MIT working paper. April 2012.

Autor, David, David Dorn, and Gordon Hanson. "The China Syndrome: Local Labor Market Effects of Import Competition in the United States." MIT working paper. August 2011.

Bajpai, Nirupam, Jeffrey D. Sachs, and Ashutosh Varshney (eds.). *India in the Era of Economic Reforms*. Oxford University Press, 2000.

Bakija, Jon, Adam Cole, and Bradley T. Heim. "Jobs and Income Growth of the Top Earners and the Causes of Changing Income Inequality: Evidence from U.S. Tax Return Data." Working paper. April 2012.

Bartels, Larry M. *Unequal Democracy: The Political Economy of the New Gilded Age*. Princeton University Press, 2008.

Bebchuk, Lucian A., Alma Cohen, and Holger Spamann. "The Wages of Failure: Executive Compensation at Bear Stearns and Lehman 2000–2008." *Yale Journal on Regulation* 27 (2010). pp. 257–82.

Bebchuk, Lucian A., and Yaniv Grinstein. "The Growth of Executive Pay." *Oxford Review of Economic Policy* 21:2 (2005). pp. 283–303.

Beckert, Sven. *The Monied Metropolis: New York City and the Consolidation of the American Bourgeoisie, 1850–1896*. Cambridge University Press, 2001.

Berle, Adolf A., and Gardiner C. Means. *The Modern Corporation and Private Property*. Transaction Publishers, 1932.

Bertrand, Marianne, "CEOs." *Annual Review of Economics* 1:1 (2009). pp. 121–50.

Bertrand, Marianne, and Sendhil Mullainathan. "Are CEOs Rewarded for Luck? The Ones Without Principals Are." *Quarterly Journal of Economics* 116:3 (August 2001). pp. 901–32.

Bishop, Matthew, and Michael Green. *Philanthrocapitalism: How Giving Can Save the World*. Bloomsbury, 2008.

Bremmer, Ian. *The End of the Free Market: Who Wins the War Between States and Corporations?* Portfolio, 2010.

Christensen, Clayton M. *The Innovator's Dilemma: When New Technologies Cause Great Firms to Fail.* Harvard Business School Press, 1997.

Cohan, William D. *Money and Power: How Goldman Sachs Came to Rule the World.* Doubleday, 2011.

Collins, Jim. *Good to Great: Why Some Companies Make the Leap . . . and Others Don't.* Harper-Business, 2001.

Congressional Budget Office. "Trends in the Distribution of Household Income Between 1979 and 2007." October 2011.

Cost, Jay. *Spoiled Rotten: How the Politics of Patronage Corrupted the Once Noble Democratic Party and Now Threatens the American Republic.* Broadside Books, 2012.

Cowen, Tyler. *The Great Stagnation: How America Ate All the Low-Hanging Fruit of Modern History, Got Sick, and Will (Eventually) Feel Better.* Dutton, 2011.

Crowley, Roger. *City of Fortune: How Venice Ruled the Seas.* Random House, 2012.

Diamond, Peter, and Emmanuel Saez. "The Case for a Progressive Tax: From Basic Research to Policy Recommendations." *Journal of Economic Perspectives* 25:4 (Fall 2011). pp. 165–90.

Djilas, Milovan. *The New Class: An Analysis of the Communist System.* Mariner Books, 1983.

Drucker, Peter F. *Landmarks of Tomorrow.* Harper, 1959.

Edsall, Thomas Byrne. *The Age of Austerity: How Scarcity Will Remake American Politics.* Doubleday, 2012.

Ford, Martin. *The Lights in the Tunnel: Automation, Accelerating Technology and the Economy of the Future.* CreateSpace, 2009.

Frank, Robert H. *The Darwin Economy: Liberty, Competition, and the Common Good.* Princeton University Press, 2011.

Frank, Robert H., and Philip J. Cook. *The Winner-Take-All Society: Why the Few at the Top Get So Much More Than the Rest of Us.* Penguin, 1996.

Freeland, Chrystia. "The Rise of the New Global Elite." *The Atlantic.* January/February 2011.

———. *Sale of the Century: Russia's Wild Ride from Communism to Capitalism.* Crown Business, 2000.

Friedman, Thomas L. *The World Is Flat: A Brief History of the Twenty-First Century.* Farrar, Straus and Giroux, 2005.

Frydman, Carola, and Dirk Jenter. "CEO Compensation." *Annual Review of Financial Economics* 2 (December 2010). pp. 75–102.

Frydman, Roman, and Michael D. Goldberg. *Beyond Mechanical Markets: Asset Price Swings, Risk, and the Role of the State.* Princeton University Press, 2011.

Fukuyama, Francis. *The End of History and the Last Man.* Free Press, 1992.

———. "The Future of History: Can Liberal Democracy Survive the Decline of the Middle Class?" *Foreign Affairs.* January/February 2012.

Gabaix, Xavier, and Augustin Landier. "Why Has CEO Pay Increased So Much?" *Quarterly Journal of Economics* 123:1 (2008). pp. 49–100.

Galbraith, John Kenneth. *The Affluent Society.* Houghton Mifflin, 1958.

———. *The Great Crash, 1929.* Houghton Mifflin, 1954.

Gilligan, James. *Why Some Politicians Are More Dangerous Than Others.* Polity, 2011.

Goldin, Claudia, and Lawrence F. Katz. *The Race between Education and Technology.* Belknap Press, 2008.

Goos, Maarten, and Alan Manning. "Lousy and Lovely Jobs: The Rising Polarization of Work in Britain." *Review of Economics and Statistics* 89:1 (February 2007).

Graham, Carol. *Happiness Around the World: The Paradox of Happy Peasants and Miserable Millionaires.* Oxford University Press, 2010.

Greenspan, Alan. *The Age of Turbulence: Adventures in a New World.* Penguin Press, 2007.

Greenwald, Bruce C. N., and Judd Kahn. *Globalization: The Irrational Fear That Someone in China Will Take Your Job*. John Wiley & Sons, 2008.

Grove, Andrew S. *Only the Paranoid Survive: How to Exploit the Crisis Points That Challenge Every Company*. Crown Business, 1999.

Hacker, Jacob S., and Paul Pierson. *Winner-Take-All Politics: How Washington Made the Rich Richer—And Turned Its Back on the Middle Class*. Simon & Schuster, 2010.

Hayek, Friedrich A. *Law, Legislation, and Liberty, Volume 2: The Mirage of Social Justice*. University of Chicago Press, 1978.

Henriques, Diana B. *The Wizard of Lies: Bernie Madoff and the Death of Trust*. Times Books, 2011.

Hoffman, David E. *The Oligarchs: Wealth and Power in the New Russia*. Public Affairs, 2002.

Hoffman, Reid. *The Start-Up of You: Adapt to the Future, Invest in Yourself, and Transform Your Career*. Crown Business, 2012.

Hsieh, Tony. *Delivering Happiness: A Path to Profits, Passion, and Purpose*. Business Plus, 2010.

Jensen, Michael C., and Kevin J. Murphy. "Performance Pay and Top-Management Incentives." *Journal of Political Economy* 98:2 (April 1990). pp. 225–64.

Johnson, Simon, and James Kwak. *13 Bankers: The Wall Street Takeover and the Next Financial Meltdown*. Pantheon, 2010.

Johnston, David Cay. *Free Lunch: How the Wealthiest Americans Enrich Themselves at Government Expense (and Stick You with the Bill)*. Portfolio, 2007.

———. *Perfectly Legal: The Covert Campaign to Rig Our Tax System to Benefit the Super-Rich—and Cheat Everybody Else*. Portfolio, 2003.

Judt, Tony. *Ill Fares the Land*. Penguin Press, 2010.

Kaletsky, Anatole. *Capitalism 4.0: The Birth of a New Economy in the Aftermath of Crisis*. Public Affairs, 2010.

Kaplan, Steven N., and Joshua Rauh. "Wall Street and Main Street: What Contributes to the Rise in the Highest Incomes?" *Review of Financial Studies* 23:3 (March 2010). pp. 1004–50.

Khan, Shamus Rahman. *Privilege: The Making of an Adolescent Elite at St. Paul's School*. Princeton University Press, 2010.

Kindleberger, Charles P. *Manias, Panics, and Crashes: A History of Financial Crises*, fifth edition. John Wiley & Sons, 2005.

Konrád, George, and Ivan Szelényi. *Road of the Intellectuals to Class Power: Sociological Study of the Role of the Intelligentsia in Socialism*. Branch Line, 1979.

Krueger, Alan B. "The Economics of Real Superstars: The Market for Rock Concerts in the Material World." *Journal of Labor Economics* 23:1 (2005).

Lemann, Nicholas. *The Big Test: The Secret History of the American Meritocracy*. Farrar, Straus and Giroux, 1999.

Levy, Santiago, and Michael Walton (eds.). *No Growth Without Equity?: Inequality, Interests, and Competition in Mexico*. World Bank Publications, 2009.

Lindert, Peter, and Jeffrey Williamson. "American Incomes Before and After the Revolution." NBER Working Paper No. 17211. July 2011.

Maddison, Angus. *Contours of the World Economy 1–2030 AD: Essays in Macro-Economic History*. Oxford University Press, 2007.

Mallaby, Sebastian. *More Money Than God: Hedge Funds and the Making of a New Elite*. Penguin Press, 2010.

Marshall, Alfred. *Principles of Economics*. Nabu Press, 2010.

Martin, Roger L. *Fixing the Game: Bubbles, Crashes, and What Capitalism Can Learn from the NFL*. Harvard Business Review Press, 2011.

Martin, Roger L., and Mihnea C. Moldoveanu. "Capital Versus Talent: The Battle That's Reshaping Business." *Harvard Business Review*. July 2003.

Merton, Robert K. "The Matthew Effect in Science." *Science* 159:3810 (January 5, 1968). pp. 56–63.

Meyer, Christopher. *Standing on the Sun: How the Explosion of Capitalism Abroad Will Change Business Everywhere*. Harvard Business Review Press, 2012.

Milanovic, Branko. *The Haves and the Have-Nots: A Brief and Idiosyncratic History of Global Inequality*. Basic Books, 2011.

Mills, C. Wright. *The Power Elite*. Oxford University Press, 2000.

Mokyr, Joel. *The Lever of Riches: Technological Creativity and Economic Progress*. Oxford University Press, 1990.

Murphy, Kevin J. "Top Executives Are Worth Every Nickel They Get." *Harvard Business Review*. March 1986.

Murphy, Kevin J., and Jan Zabojnik. "Managerial Capital and the Market for CEOs." Queen's Economics Department Working Paper No. 10. October 2006.

Murray, Charles. *Falling Behind: The State of White America, 1960–2010*. Crown Forum, 2012.

Nasar, Sylvia. *Grand Pursuit: The Story of Economic Genius*. Simon & Schuster, 2011.

Noah, Timothy. *The Great Divergence: America's Growing Inequality Crisis and What We Can Do About It*. Bloomsbury, 2012.

O'Neill, Jim. *The Growth Map: Economic Opportunity in the BRICs and Beyond*. Portfolio, 2011.

Pan, Philip P. *Out of Mao's Shadow: The Struggle for the Soul of a New China*. Simon & Schuster, 2008.

Pettis, Michael. *The Volatility Machine: Emerging Economics and the Threat of Financial Collapse*. Oxford University Press, 2001.

Philippon, Thomas, and Ariell Reshef. "Wages and Human Capital in the U.S. Finance Industry: 1909–2006." Working paper. March 2011.

Phillips, Kevin. *Wealth and Democracy: A Political History of the American Rich*. Broadway, 2002.

Pickett, Kate, and Richard Wilkinson. *The Spirit Level: Why Greater Equality Makes Societies Stronger*. Bloomsbury, 2009.

Piketty, Thomas, and Emmanuel Saez. "The Evolution of Top Incomes: A Historical and International Perspective." *American Economic Review: Papers and Proceedings* 96:2 (May 2006). pp. 200–205.

———. "Income Inequality in the United States, 1913–1998." *Quarterly Journal of Economics* 118:1 (2003). pp. 1–39.

Porter, Eduardo. *The Price of Everything: Solving the Mystery of Why We Pay What We Do*. Portfolio, 2011.

Rajan, Raghuram G. *Fault Lines: How Hidden Fractures Still Threaten the World Economy*. Princeton University Press, 2010.

Rajan, Raghuram G., and Luigi Zingales. *Saving Capitalism from the Capitalists: Unleashing the Power of Financial Markets to Create Wealth and Spread Opportunity*. Princeton University Press, 2004.

Rand, Ayn. *Atlas Shrugged*. Random House, 1957.

Ratigan, Dylan. *Greedy Bastards: How We Can Stop Corporate Communists, Banksters, and Other Vampires from Sucking America Dry*. Simon & Schuster, 2012.

Rosen, Sherwin. "The Economics of Superstars." *American Economic Review* 71:5 (December 1981).

Rothkopf, David. *Power, Inc.: The Epic Rivalry Between Big Business and Government—and the Reckoning That Lies Ahead*. Farrar, Straus and Giroux, 2012.

———. *Superclass: The Global Power Elite and the World They Are Making*. Farrar, Straus and Giroux, 2008.

Saez, Emmanuel. "Striking It Richer: The Evolution of Top Incomes in the United States." http://elsa.berkeley.edu./~saez/saez-UStopincomes-2010.pdf. March 2, 2012.

Skocpol, Theda. *Diminished Democracy: From Membership to Management in American Civic Life*. University of Oklahoma Press, 2003.

Sloan, Alfred P., Jr. *My Years with General Motors*. Doubleday, 1964.

Smith, Adam. *The Wealth of Nations*. Bantam Classics, 2003.

Sorkin, Andrew Ross. *Too Big to Fail: The Inside Story of How Wall Street and Washington Fought to Save the Financial System—and Themselves*. Viking, 2009.

Soros, George. *The Crisis of Global Capitalism: Open Society Endangered*. Public Affairs, 1998.

Spence, A. Michael. "The Impact of Globalization on Income and Employment: The Downside of Integrating Markets." *Foreign Affairs*. July/August 2011.

———. *The Next Convergence: The Future of Economic Growth in a Multispeed World*. Farrar, Straus and Giroux, 2011.

Spence, A. Michael, and Sandile Hlatshwayo. "The Evolving Structure of the American Economy and the Employment Challenge." Maurice R. Greenberg Center for Geoeconomic Studies working paper. Council on Foreign Relations Press, March 2011.

Sull, Donald. *Why Good Companies Go Bad and How Great Managers Remake Them*. Harvard Business Review Press, 2005.

Taleb, Nassim Nicholas. *The Black Swan: The Impact of the Highly Improbable*. Random House, 2007.

Walter, Carl E., and Fraser J. T. Howie. *Red Capitalism: The Fragile Financial Foundation of China's Extraordinary Rise*. John Wiley & Sons, 2011.

Winters, Jeffrey A. *Oligarchy*. Cambridge University Press, 2011.

Wolf, Martin. *Why Globalization Works*. Yale University Press, 2004.

Yergin, Daniel. *The Prize: The Epic Quest for Oil, Money, and Power*. Simon & Schuster, 1991.

———. *The Quest: Energy, Security, and the Remaking of the Modern World*. Penguin Press, 2011.

Zakaria, Fareed. *The Post-American World*. W. W. Norton, 2008.

INDEX